Self Po

Anneke Wills

HIRST

Anneke Wills: Self Portrait

First Published September 2007
by Hirst Books Ltd

Hirst Books Ltd, Suite 285 Andover House, George Yard, Andover, Hants, SP10 1PB

ISBN 978-0-9557149-0-0

A CIP catalogue record for this book is available from the British Library.

Design by Tim Hirst. Cover photo restored by Larry Dyde.

Printed and bound by ASAP UK Ltd, Global House, Rumbridge St, Totton, Southampton, Hampshire, SO40 9DT
www.asapuk.net

Paper stock used is natural, recyclable and made from wood grown in sustainable forests. The manufacturing processes conform to environmental regulations.

www.hirstbooks.com
www.annekewills.com

Credits

All photographs, drawings and paintings are from the author's personal collection, unless detailed below. The paintings and drawings are all by Anneke Wills, with the exception of Sir Richard Grenville.

All images relating to The Alberts are from Tony Gray's personal collection.

Page 10 – Sir Richard Grenville after an unknown artist, © National Portrait Gallery, London
Page 30 – The Riley, from the personal collection of Robert Malpas
Page 82 – Radio Times cover reproduced courtesy of BBC Radio Times Magazine © BBC Worldwide.
Page 113 – The Troubadour, reproduced courtesy of The Troubadour
Page 116 – The Strange World of Gurney Slade, kindly donated from the personal collection of Paul Goodhead
Page 118 – 'Brickman and Newberg', photographer unknown
Page 136 – Peter and Wendy Cook, from the personal collection of Wendy Cook
Page 146 – At Windsor Castle, kindly donated from the personal collection of Angela Douglas
Page 205 – Kenneth More and Angela Douglas, from the personal collection of Angela Douglas
Page 212 – Kine Magazine, from the personal collection of Julian Knott
Pages 225 –229 – Doctor Who Images © BBC Worldwide
Page 232 – Doctor Who Artwork, by Ian F. Burgess © 2007 CiNEFFIGY
Page 229 – Anthony Newley, photographer unknown
Page 288 – Mai and David Zetterling press photo, origins unknown
Page 290 – Jasper, Lucy and Daisy Cook, from Wendy Cook's personal collection

Songs are quoted throughout as part of the story, to evoke the times. All lyrics and song titles remain the property of the artistes, writers and composers concerned. No copyright infringement is intended.

Every attempt has been made to contact the copyright holders of materials and images used in this book; if any have been overlooked, the Publishers would be pleased to hear from them directly.

Foreword

By Angela Douglas

On the door of my fridge I have a picture of Anneke picking vegetables, for her lunch perhaps, from the glorious garden in front of her cottage in deepest Devon. Tranquil. Dreamlike. Roses round the door. But her life hasn't always been as soft - had it been, she wouldn't have this story to tell.

This image is a far cry from Anneke in the city and the story you are about to read. As a close friend, who like many close friends, fade in and out of each other's lives, I believe that the links in the chain of such friendship always remain.

Meeting her for the first time is as vivid for me as if it were yesterday. Both 14 years of age. Both teenage actresses. She - blonde, long legged and big brown eyed. Me - blonde, long legged and big blue eyed – what separated us was her obvious confidence – her air of self-belief. It was at an audition. We were up for the same role. Sitting on the edge of a table her legs swinging to and fro, and showing off her perfect smile, I thought,

'They're bound to cast her … she's so pretty' Where were her nerves? Mine were trickling all over me.

Now let's fast forward to the 60s. They say that if you can remember the 60s you weren't really there! Well, Anneke thankfully can, and she most certainly was there, up and running with the best of the 'in-crowd'! She draws for us the landscape of the time - bright and strong, and writes lovingly of her mother and her brother Robin.

She doesn't claim to be the perfect mother to her two cherished children - Polly and Jasper – but the sense of deep love is reflected in her written words. At times her story has seemed to be like a skater on ever thinning ice. 'Survivor' must be her middle name!

We eventually met properly in 1962. We were both asked to screen-test for a film called *Some People*. Much to my relief, when we met at the studio, I was told that this time, we were up for different roles! We shared the next very happy and exciting 3 months filming in and around Bristol. We became closer than close - sharing our dreams of the lives we hoped were before us. I was with her as she struggled through a long labour - rubbing her back and singing -

♫ *Love, love me do …* ♫

- as beautiful little Polly came into the world. Longing for a baby of my own, I found it impossible to suppress my tears.

This is a memory book, rather than one of rigid fact and formal statistics. A flow of memories of a long time ago, of hurts and disappointments. She recalls, in some instances, exhilaration of happiness – in others, her deep sense of loss. Between one life and another, Anneke has been on an enlightened journey.

Angela Douglas
London, 2007

Introduction and Thanks

There is an old Tibetan teaching that says we should all write our life stories. Three times. I imagine that the first time you tell all the stories, the second time you've pared down to the essentials and the third might be - I was born, I breathed, I died. But since this is my first time, I am telling all the stories!

When I read the acknowledgements in books, I'm struck by the author's heartfelt gratitude for the support, tolerance and patience shown by those around them. Now I understand why...

In September 2006 at Regenerations - the Doctor Who convention – Tim Hirst suggested that I write my story. I was reluctant at first, and offered a barrage of objections – each of which, Tim knocked down – so in the moment, I said 'Yes' and lit up with the excitement, and kept all my friends awake till 5am, telling stories!

From that moment I have hardly been able to sleep. Sometimes it's been great – I've got a story to tell! – sometimes, it's panic. Who do I think I am, to put pen to paper?

Writing an autobiography is like putting your head on the block!

I have gone back into my past - this time with a forgiving eye - and relived so much, some of it amazing, some of it deeply painful. At the start of the story, I found myself using my childhood voice, having accessed that place where nothing is forgotten. I have avoided 'hindsight analysis' – telling it only from the understanding I had at the time.

Such extraordinary people I've known and loved. The shining lights of the sixties. Together, we were experiencing a renaissance; a flowering of new thought and understanding. We were consciously breaking through the restrictions into which we were born. Revolution was in the air and the arts world flourished like never before.

I was there. And this is my story.

I wrote it all by hand and Tim Hirst, Jenny Leslie and Brenda Mossman transcribed; it was their enthusiasm that really encouraged me.

My thanks go first to all the fans who have given me the encouragement and support to make this possible. Over the years I have been truly overwhelmed by the affection shown to me by fans of my work; I would not have had the confidence to write this book without that love.

Thanks to Ian Burgess, for all the cleaning up of my few precious old photos, and for providing a brand new piece of art especially for this book.

Also, to Stefan Sundin, for all the research and for being such a good listener and a dear friend. Thanks to Jaz Wiseman for his help with the *Strange Report* chapter.

Immense gratitude to all my friends and family who have understood my need to be an utter hermit; I apologise for never returning your calls.

Thanks to Tim who has held my hand all the way. I left the commercial side to him while I focussed on the writing process. He has been everything from public relations manager to designer. His dedication to the project has been extraordinary, and thanks also for my extra silver highlights!

And of course, to Jasper Gough – my son – a big hug!

Finally, I am deeply indebted to the beautiful, unique and sometimes flawed people who helped to make me who I am; without these people, there would be no story to tell.

for my mother

Sir Richard Grenville after an unknown artist,
Oil on canvas, 17th Century

Chapter 1

At Flores in the Azores

One of my ancestors was an Elizabethan pirate, Sir Richard Grenville. He served Queen Elizabeth 1. Sir Richard's father, Roger Grenville, was the captain of Henry VIII's favourite warship - The Mary Rose, which tragically sank in 1545, during a skirmish with the French in Portsmouth Harbour. Roger Grenville and five hundred of his crew were drowned.

Sir Richard, in his position as Sheriff of Devon and Cornwall, was in charge of defending West Country against the arrival of the Spanish Armada.

He was the first person on British soil to smoke tobacco. His cousin Sir Walter Raleigh had brought it back from America. Legend has it that these two Elizabethan gentlemen were having their smoke, in their doublets and hose, when an over-zealous servant rushed up and drenched them with a bucket of water, thinking they were on fire.

Sir Richard achieved immortality when he sailed his little ship 'The Revenge' straight into a fleet of 53 Spanish ships of war. The Spanish battleships were like castles on the seas but his passion was so great he fought madly on. The Spaniards were amazed at his bravery - they gave him an honoured sea burial and he entered history as one of the great Elizabethan heroes.

Alfred Lord Tennyson wrote a poem, *The Revenge*, which young boys for generations, learned word for word -

'At Flores in the Azores, Sir Richard Grenville lay … '

The 'Revenge'

My grandfather, himself a renowned and decorated First World War hero, called his son Alaric, after the Visigoth King who brought Rome to its knees in ancient times - (no pressure there then!) My father was sent to Harrow, one of the finest schools in England, where, like many of the young elite, he was taught Latin and the classics, and was bullied, buggered and starved. One of his strongest memories was, in desperation, having to eat his toothpaste.

As a young man he was very handsome and charming, and loved to drive his Lagonda to the south of France; to frequent the casinos and woo the women; to paint and draw, and to fly small planes (he gave my mother a white leather flying helmet when they met). He loved antiques and fine things …

My mother - Anna - was born of a large Dutch family living in Rotterdam – with the surname 'Arts'. My grandfather, Johanes Arts, a respected painter of fine art, came from a long line of Dutch painters, going back to the 16th century when Dutch painting was at its peak. My grandmother must have been quite a woman to marry a difficult, volatile alcoholic artist in the 1900s and have four children. My Uncle Hans became a fine painter in California after the war.

In her teens, my mother appeared in a school drama production of *The School for Scandal* in which she played Lady Teazel. One of the teachers at the Sarah Bernhardt School saw her, and Sarah

Bernhardt herself came to a performance to see this 'exceptional talent'. My mother remembers her coming down the street in her Braugham. This wonderful carriage. She invited my mother to go to her school. She remembers the discussions with her parents,

'The child is talented! She could become a great actress!'

'No, it's not possible.' (it seems that painting is OK but acting isn't - interesting Dutch morality!) So of course, as soon as I'm born a girl, I'm destined to fulfil her thwarted ambition …

She lived in Rotterdam in the late 1920s, and became a beautician for Elizabeth Arden but left - sneaking out of the back door, never to return - because she used a depilatory instead of a dye on a particular client, so the lady's hair was going to fall out in clumps!

She was very pretty and very bright, spoke five languages, did some modelling and had posh boyfriends; one of whom was a Russian Prince. She went to Paris, and then on to the south of France, where she met my father. It was love at first sight. They both dropped their current beaus and off they went to England to get married. They rented a little house in Chelsea, and filled it with antiques. They had their honeymoon in Paris where, one morning, having their breakfast in a lovely French hotel, he was hidden behind his newspaper. So, with her elegant little silver and enamel lighter, she set light to the bottom of it.

'You didn't marry me to sit and read The Times!'

You can just see them, can't you? This beautiful bohemian couple. She had a swan's down bed jacket, their luggage was calf skin, covered in labels of French hotels…Hotel de Paris…

She had a Springer spaniel called Jock who followed her around the dance floor; as they danced in evening clothes in nightclubs in Knightsbridge.

My mother was taken to the baronial home in Evesham to meet my father's parents. The house was very large and very cold, with only small electric fires. They were served cider and thinly sliced beef. My father proudly showed her the Plantagenet fireplace.

'It would be much nicer with a fire in it,' she sniffed, 'and haven't they got any *wine*?' They were not impressed – who is this mad, outspoken foreigner? They refused to call her Anna – too foreign - so instead, they called her Anne. And, they cut him off.

On Friday 13th January 1936, my brother Robin Richard Hans

Willys was born. His initials are the same as his grandfather's. They wanted to go to France to lead their dream life, he would paint, she would write, but the war was approaching and he didn't want to be a part of it … he chose to be a conscientious objector. My mother told Robin and I about the day when he opened a letter from his family, and how shocked he was when a white feather fell out. They offered to pay off all his gambling debts if he would uphold the family honour and join up, so reluctantly he accepted. He was posted in the north of England training, and training others, for most of the war. He came home when he could get leave.

The bombing in London had become so ghastly that my mother rented a tiny house in Walton-on-Thames. Meanwhile, Holland had surrendered to the Nazis so she was separated from her family, who were living in horrendous conditions in Rotterdam - communication was very difficult - and she was pregnant with me.

Chapter 2

War Years

On October 20th 1941 I am born, just after lunch. I am called Anna Katarina - Anneke for short - although I am never christened. Fulmer Chase is a private nursing home for officers' wives. My mother is starving hungry after I am born and when she asks for something to eat she is told that lunch is finished, to which she retorts,

'Typical English!'

Lady Churchill comes to inspect and encourage the mothers and babies and confides in her,

'They all look like my husband at this age.'

Fulmer Chase is a few miles from Pinewood Studios where 27 years later I will have my own suite of dressing rooms while starring in a TV series …

She is alone with two young children in the middle of the war, in what, for her, is a foreign country. She decides to get out of London and looking in the ads of *The Lady* magazine she applies for a job as companion to lovely, old, blind Lady Pinney, in Dorset, who lives in a Tudor house with a walled garden – full of fruit and vegetables. When I am crawling, she will put me in the middle of the lawn and it will take me about half an hour to crawl to the edge. It gives her about half an hour to 'get on'. One time, she is late, and I am in the flower bed, eating the flowers … Lady Pinney says,

'Now Anna, don't let the children eat too many strawberries …'

'No, no, Lady Pinney', she replies, while motioning for us to stuff our faces. This walled garden will become deeply embedded in my psyche as my blueprint for happiness. As well as the bliss of my pram. *My Pram!* With its little flap and hood and so cosy inside when it rained. How devastated I am when they tell me I am too big for it.

Robin is six and he needs to go to school. So the next job she applies for is as a gardener at the Sunrising Boarding School in North Dorset. My mother has never gardened in her life – so far her life has been one of an intellectual beauty, but this is wartime and she needs to find a place of work where she can have Robin and me with her. She is a fiercely loyal and loving mother and very brave, just like her mother. So when the two lesbians who run the boarding school take her around the extensive vegetable gardens she is busy, making it up as she goes along,

'Ah cabbages, ah yes, well um, we do it differently in Holland!' The two ladies aren't fooled but they find her very attractive (!) and they take her on. She's five foot six, slender, with auburn hair that she will later henna, usually at home. She has an open, intelligent face with a high forehead and beautiful eyes, brown and almond shaped and utterly captivating when she's telling a funny story. She speaks with a strong Dutch accent.

The next day she is up early and across the hedge, because she's seen an old man digging in the next garden, so she hops over and pleads with him,

'For God's sake, help me, I need this job and I know nothing about gardening.' And so he shows her how to dig and how to sow and after a while she has licked those acres into shape, producing plenty of food for us all and learning to be a gardener which nourishes her spiritually all her life.

My father's family give her no support at all. They have a large home in Evesham. This is wartime; have they no pity on her, alone with two young children, and her family starving in Holland? I never have any communication with them at all. Robin gets Christmas and birthday presents. Was it because he was the son and heir and I was the daughter of that foreigner? And called Anneke!

Later, Robin forms a very touching relationship with his grandfather. They lunch in the Army and Navy Club off Piccadilly. Robin calls him 'the old man', and it is he who tells Robin all about our ancestry. Robin tries to tell me but by the time I am old enough to listen, I'm not that interested. I know that they have hurt my mother deeply.

We have moved to Kings Road, Windsor. It is 1944 and the worst winter for fifty years. Windsor's famous Long Walk is deep in snow, with the milkman coming in a sled. I've got a little velvet quilted cap with flowery lining and a new camel coat. Sometimes we have meals in the British restaurant in Eton High Street and a three course lunch costs 2/3d. Our drawing room is on the first floor, there is a small garden in the front, and a yellow front door. I play with my dolls outside on the step in the early morning sunshine. Robin goes to Caldecot Prep School in Farnham Common. He's eight years old and bicycles five miles to school every day. We have to share bath water. I do 'biggies' in the bath and he's disgusted. My mother allows me to do her hair.

'Would you like more pins?' she says.

'No, you need more hair!' My mother has a sun lamp and we have to wear goggles and sit bare-chested in front of this buzzing blue lamp on a stand.

My father is six foot five, so to me, he lives at the top of these very long legs and he is always cross with me because I can't keep up with him when he strides along. I'm sitting at the dining table, and I don't want to drink my milk, so he pulls my head back by my hair and tries to force it down. Now I am coughing and choking and he's hitting me. I go to a children's party, in a luxurious house with thick cream carpets. My father is late picking me up. All the other children and their parents have gone home, and so I'm sitting alone in the hall. A delicious perfumed lady in a soft satin dress assures me he'll soon come. I don't care! I hope he never comes! I want to live here with her.

My mother is having a rest one afternoon when she suddenly wakes up in a panic - she's had a dream in which I am running across the road and the next moment I'm lying on the ground - I've been run over.

'Where are the children?!' she calls out to the mothers help.

'They are down by the stream catching tadpoles.' My mother runs to the front door to see us walking back from The Long Walk carrying our jam jars and homemade fishing poles and she calls out.

'Anneke come quickly!' I see her and waving happily I charge across the road. She is not quick enough to stop me and the milkman's cart is upon me. Suddenly I'm lying in the road. Luckily I only have bruises. Later there is a big murder story - a man called Christie. There is a picture in the papers of a group of people - my mother points one of them out.

'He did it!' Later she would be proved right.

The psychic ability is passed down the female genes.

A year later, May 8th 1945, and the war is over. We have a party - where strangely, the grown ups don't seem to mind that we are squidging the jelly between our fingers and being wild. We all have photos taken in the back garden with a Brownie 127. My mother is only 29, but she looks twice that. There are terrible rows behind closed doors, my mother and father shouting at each other.

One morning on my bedside table I find four half-crowns. No note. Robin says,

'Daddy's left us.' My mother cries and cries. Much later in our lives she will tell us the truth, that she had so proudly saved all the money he had sent her during the war years as well as her own savings.

'Good', he had said, 'give me the money and I'll go to France and find that lovely home we have always wanted.' And so he had taken all the money and left for South Africa with an Austrian woman he had just met. He broke my mother's heart; she loved him to the end of her life.

I find his love letters amongst her papers when she dies. One starts, 'Darling, do you remember the Lagonda?'

This is the only photo I have of my father, taken in his 70s.

My mother will learn that her mother and her sister have both died of starvation. Her younger sister is also starving in a P.O.W camp on the Belgian border.

We take a train to St. Maw's in Cornwall. On the train we meet a dashing squadron leader with watery blue eyes and a handlebar moustache.

Tim Craxton enters our lives …

We have rented a little furnished cottage on top of the hill overlooking the harbour. We have a Spaniel called Jasper. Robin and I play in the early summer countryside, making houses in the wheat, the freedom of running in the sunshine, riding on top of a hayrick … I slide off the back as we go round the gate post and I have to have a stitch or two in my forehead. But I love the horses and I want to go again. There is a huge sun on the bottle of malt, we drink very concentrated orange juice and we have to take radio-stoleum, which is fish oil, so it is good for us all – but I hate it. My grandfather comes to visit from Holland. He has a white goatee beard, a beret and smokes Dutch cigars. He doesn't stay with us long but I love forever the smell of cigars. He makes me sit for a portrait but I can't sit still and I fidget too much and he flies into a rage and destroys the canvas.

One day Robin and I are playing with Jasper in the garden.

'Just popping to the post box', says my mother.

'Can we come, can we come?' we ask.

'Well alright, but I must be quick, I've left the lunch on.' When we turn to walk back up the hill the flames are emerging from the kitchen window. She's left the chip pan burning. Robin and I are thrilled with the fireman leaping over our beds with huge hose pipes.

We have to stay the night with a friend of my mother's who has a house on stilts on the beach. In the early summer, with the moon just as it is, there is a very high tide and in the morning the little house is filled with two feet of water. We drive through the night in Tim's Riley car to Farnham Common.

The only photos of my mother, Robin and me and Uncle Hans and his wife.

Chapter 3

Farnham Common

It's very late and very dark when we arrive so we're bundled off to bed. At dawn the next day I get up and step out of the French doors. Across a big veranda and down the steps and out across the landscaped garden, the large, dew-covered lawn, the wood pigeons are calling to each other. The bungalow is in the middle of Burnham Beeches. The early morning sunshine sends shafts of light through the trees. The morning is soft. I see a path leading down through the blossoming rhododendrons. I follow it, unafraid, to a little stream that is flowing all along the bottom of our garden. I kneel down beside it on a mossy bank and I feel so happy and at peace. *A sense of belonging.* I will play alone for hours, dreaming of building a little hut, making a fire, cooking my food and all the time the sounds of the woods, the pigeons, the smell of the leaves and the moss.

We have neighbours. Through a thick dark path is another garden, a big house, 10 acres, the Garnham family. He is a professor at the Tropical Disease Hospital in London. Carolyn and Jasper are the youngest children in this large family. They are Robin's age so they form a gang with me, the pesky hanger-on. Jasper has a gun and shoots rabbits for lunch. Mrs Garnham calls,

'Lunch is ready!"

'What's for lunch?'

'Bunny!'

The Garnham children know these woods very well. Burnham Beeches is 540 acres of ancient Woodland. The pollarded beech trees go back 500 years, and the trunks are so split that we can climb inside. These hiding places lend themselves perfectly to gun games. Robin and Jasper have got these pellet guns. They are actually quite dangerous - so there is an element of fear when we play. I can hear the pellets twanging off the bark of the tree right where I'm hiding. There are awful tests that have to be taken – climb up that branch, swing across to there, and then drop five feet … It's always

Carolyn, the Garnham's house, and Jasper, with his 12-bore and bunny

frightening and quite often I'm left stuck in a tree, crying.

One time I am in the Garnham's kitchen, it is getting dark and being the youngest I have to go home. It is past my bedtime, so very reluctantly I set off down the narrow dark path which seems even spookier with just my little torch. When suddenly – Woo-hooo! - What's that I see? A white shape in the trees! I hurry on, my heart pounding but here they are again - ghosts - now they are moaning - in white sheets - flashing - Victorian fish knives! I run home, screaming hysterically. Robin's punishment is to watch over me until I fall asleep. For a week.

I stay awake for as long as I can -

'I'm not asleep yet!

I have some light relief from the intense gun games. There is a little family of gypsies who live in a tumble-down encampment at the edge of the wood. I love helping to brush their ponies and wash their babies. My mother says,

'You mustn't play with them, they're gypsies.'

'But they are my friends!' I protest.

I am sent to Miss Porter's, a school on the crossroads of Farnham Common. I learn to say my prayers on my knees, to sew, to read and write and do my tables. I love the smell of the sharpened pencils. I like to sit close to my red-haired friend Archie at lunchtime because I can play with his willy under the tablecloth. Here I have my first boyfriends, Simon and Andy Langton; their father is David Langton, the actor. I will go to their house and we will look at comics, and kiss.

Jasper and the gang are growing bolder. One hot summer day they make me lie spread-eagled on the lawn - they hammer the metal croquet hoops over my wrists and ankles and then they are off to Burnham Beeches swimming pool. There has been a big scare, an outbreak of I.P. (infantile paralysis) and the papers are full of images of crippled children and it frightens me, and the swimming pool is a dangerous place to go because that's where you catch it. I'm sobbing and I'm very traumatised. When the grown-ups eventually find me I have sunstroke. Robin, Jasper and Carolyn are given a very severe talking to and are grounded for a week.

The most naughty thing Carolyn and I do is to get hold of a Dr. Barnardos box and go around the village collecting money … in the end we have five pounds. I tell my mother because I think we've been so clever. Mrs Garnham grounds Carolyn for a week. My mother says,

'Let's have a feast!'

I am given a red plastic handbag for Christmas. I love it and carry it everywhere.

Tim Craxton is a continuing presence. He comes from a famous musical family. He is very gentle, and he laughs and sings Schubert love songs. He has won a DFC (Distinguished Flying Cross) for his bravery. He had flown back into enemy territory in his Spitfire to rescue his men. He brings us maple sugar from Canada. *SUGAR!*

My mother persuades him to say he's engaged to her sister Tilly so that she can be rescued from her war camp. Tilly's story is very sad. At the beginning of the occupation of Holland she meets, falls in love with, and gets pregnant by a German officer. She tries to follow him in war-torn Europe, has a miscarriage by the side of the road and is then placed in a P.O.W camp until the end of the war. She never finds her officer. My mother sends her a photo of the man she must say she's engaged to, a British RAF squadron leader.

Tim flies to the camp and they meet on either side of the wire fence, declaring lost love, and are married there and then. She becomes Tilly Craxton. He flies her back to England and she returns to us in Farnham Common. When I see her, although I'm told she is my aunt, she frightens me, because instead of fingernails she has bloody stumps – four years of malnutrition.

Another war victim is Stanley Parker, a gentleman and a cousin of film actor Cecil Parker, and physically very similar. He sits a lot in a garden chair wrapped in tartan blankets and smiles and smokes his pipe.

Tim and my mother sing together -

♫ *I wooed her in the summer time and in the winter too-oo*
And the only thing that I ever did wrong
Was to save her from the foggy foggy dew' ♫

My mother's heart-throb is Lesley Howard. She is heartbroken when the plane he is in is shot down by the Germans - they thought that Churchill was on board.

My mother has given me a lovely little book about a girl called Anneke, who wears red strappy shoes. One day she loses one in the stream and she runs after it, and her adventures begin. It's all in Dutch, so my mother translates it for me.

We are taken to see Windsor Castle. Tim lifts me up on the parapet of the round tower. On purpose I shake off my little red strappy shoe, because I want to see if my adventures will begin. I love watching it fall hundreds of feet down below and land on the steep grass hill. What a fuss! They have to get a castle worker to climb the hill to retrieve it. We go to St. Georges Chapel where our Grandfather has a special seat as a Knight of the Garter – a big privilege. Everyone is whispering in awe of this honour - and I'm wriggling because I need a wee-wee and I don't want to do it on the floor of this Church.

Meanwhile, I'm in trouble again. I've done a portrait (which is rather good) of Miss Porter, who has a black dress, a hooked nose, her hair in a bun and a large wart with a black whisker sprouting out of it.

Miss Porter haunts me now as I tweak my own whiskers!

My mother says,

'Everyone, for you, was a friend. When the war was over we all went to church to celebrate and when everyone stood on their feet and sang, you joined in with your favourite song,

'Mrs Brown went to town, with her knickers hanging down …'

We make our first journey to Holland after the war. A steam train to Paddington; so many people – the deep carpets of a plush hotel; trays of teas and comfort and relatives hugging us and rides in taxis; sleeping on trains and boats, the excitement of arriving at the Hook of Holland. At the customs, to my horror, they rip off the head of my smiling open-mouthed doll because she's rattling. I have been stuffing those awful radio-stoleum pills inside her instead of inside me! This is the start of a lifelong distrust for officials.

Arriving in Rotterdam we see mostly piles of black brick, like in London, and gaping buildings and chaos. But out in the countryside there are windmills and people wearing clogs and loads of bicycles. We go to see some people in an old dwelling. There's a pump in the floor and cows lined up again along a wall and a sort of balcony with beds on. This image is emblazoned in my heart. This interior I know and love and will paint later, from memory.

We go to see Tante Toste, my mother's aunt. She lives in a big house in an even bigger garden in Blaricum with huge old trees and wide streets. A large round lamp hangs over the dining table with many blue and white check lampshades. They say Grace. Robin and I get uncontrollable giggles. They are plying us with food and when we finish our plates, they bring us more, so we're stuffed, and all the time they speak in Dutch about the war - and the Germans - and hug Robin and me. The milkman comes in a cart with a pony who I make friends with.

Me, cousin Jan, and Robin in Blaricum

Rotterdam is flattened; they have all suffered so much. Later my uncle Hans tells me stories as we sit in his home in Oakland, California, of how they had survived.

He tells me how he met a woman in the street who was so worried because she couldn't feed her cat.

'I'll give it a good home' said Uncle Hans. That night the family cooked and ate it, and smoked dust from beneath the floorboards rolled up in newspaper. It was their humour that saved them.

Looking back on how brave they were, I'm humbled.

Back to England, my mother, white faced and determined. We carry a large picture that Opa – my grandfather - has painted in an ornate gold frame. It is of my mother in 1915 in a high-chair, and her mother in a high-collared white dress, an oil lamp over the table. I love this painting, and we carry it with us until eventually she sells it in need of funds. I'm very sad about this loss. Eventually, when she's very broke, she sells the family silver and all the fine china and a few sticks of antique furniture we'd hung onto, but I'm mostly sad about the painting.

January 1947, it starts to snow. It snows and freezes until March; it is the worst winter for years. Even Big Ben freezes! The country grinds to a halt. We have log fires and candles, and once again the milkman comes on a sled. There are forty foot drifts and even the sea is frozen over in places. We are used to dressing in bed because it is so cold that the inside of the windows are covered in ice, and we have paraffin stoves that smell and the flickering flame makes lovely patterns on the ceiling as we fall asleep.

School is closed and we toboggan everywhere. Robin wears a balaclava. When the snow melts the Thames bursts its banks and Eton High Street is full of rowing boats. We think it is very exciting. We love snuggling up in a warm bed and listening to my mother tell stories of how naughty she was when she was growing up. She would have to bring the weekly bucket of eels home to cook but one day, she forgets to put the lid on, and eels are slithering around the kitchen floor - she will always love to eat smoked eels and roll mops. She gave her teacher a little packet of dropjes - little liquorice sweets, except they were goat's droppings. Playing truant and being hidden in a basket full of furs on a delivery bicycle. My mother described that wonderful old city of Rotterdam, the diamond quarter with the old Hassidic Jews with pigtails, the cafes and lights all along the Maas, ships and little boats and sailors from all over the world. And we would ask for more.

'Tell us stories of the olden times.' This wonderful old city, that she told Robin and me so many stories about, totally obliterated, there was hardly anything left. All the streets where she had grown up and played, and later dined and danced in the restaurants and bars, all gone.

Moe, now that I have your eyes I can see it all.

Tim Craxton wants to marry my mother but his family are not keen – she's a Dutch divorcee with two children, not what they have in mind for their eldest son.

Robin and I steal the Christmas decorations from Woolworths in Windsor. We're very pleased with ourselves. We simply fill up our basket and walk out.

The owners of the bungalow have returned from India, so we have to move again. My mother has found us a thatched cottage near Windsor with diamond-paned windows and a 'morning room' with a little twinkling gas fire. The house agent who has showed us around has a black moustache and a lecherous look in his eyes. She's making eyes at him. His name is Roy.

There is a huge storm and Robin makes me stand in the middle of the lawn and feel the thunder and the lightning. I am standing on the kitchen table, and Tilly's measuring and pinning me into a marigold costume. My first part in a school play. My mother always has total faith in my becoming an actress. In spite of all our moving, Robin and I stay at our respective schools, about the only stable thing in our lives. The 441 bus featured hugely in our choice of homes.

My mother manages to save up enough for us to have a week-long summer holiday. Tim will take us in his Riley. We are coming down a steep hill on the way to the South Coast he teaches us to shout,

'Get ready, get set, drop your bombs!' as we reach the bottom. RAF chat … he calls me his honey. He really loves me and sings me *You are my Sunshine*. We stay in Walnut Tree Cottage, West Wittering, it's a walk to the beach. There are maddening, cheerful grown ups making me take more risks in the cold, grey waves than I like. Wedged into a break-water out of the wind, my mother and Tilly in large white sunglasses and 1940s knitted wool swimsuits, rubbing us with wet sandy towels and plying us with sandy sandwiches, and we love every minute of it.

A Riley Nine Gamecock

Back in the boarding house we play Chinese Chequers and eat burnt toast. The lady who owns Walnut Tree Cottage embroiders and I'm fascinated; she shows me how to make flowers out of all the beautiful coloured silks. We work on a tablecloth she's making with trellises and Hollyhocks and ladies in crinolines. I will collect embroidery forever. I have a collection to this day. Little country tablecloths with lovely light patterns embroidered by our Mothers and our Grandmothers.

Tim takes me to Bosham; he's mad about sailing. Nobody tells me that the little sailing boat is *supposed* to keel over to its side as we're crashing through the waves, so I just think that we are sinking, and hang on in panic to the sides,

'Oooohhh … make it stop!' but they just laugh, and tell me everything is alright …

On the way home my mother and Tim are on a pub crawl, stopping at lovely old pubs. This was before they were all taken over by the big breweries. We are happily left outside with our lemonade and crisps with the little blue salt packets inside, watching the little sports cars coming and going.

'Can we have fiss 'n' bits in Gobbleming?' – this becomes a family story (Fish & Chips in Godalming).

One year we go to the Isle of Wight. Robin and me are paddling in a creek in Shanklin and running down a purple heathered slope towards the setting sun. Robin is ahead of me calling out -

'Watch out for the adders!'

I go back there in 2000 in search of a memory.

Chapter 4

Perrimans

It's 1950 and Roy the estate agent has found us another house. It is called 'Perrimans', it's very ugly - built in the 1930s on the Bath Road in Slough. He is now living with us. Robin and I hate him. He loves to taunt her about her poshness; about her brats – that's me and Robin. His mother lives in a council house. He puts on a posh voice but when he's drunk, it falls off. He wears a navy blue blazer with brass buttons, suede shoes, and a paisley cravat.

My mother has started her own business, a domestic agency. She's getting young girls out of Holland and placing them with families in England. Tim Craxton is still around, on the edges of our lives. He picks the Dutch girls up at Liverpool Street Station and puts them onto other trains to their destinations. Over the years that follow, this will become an ongoing drama. These young teenagers have just come out of war-torn Holland so of course, they start getting into trouble - stealing, running away, or flirting with the husbands or sons. Some are just utterly miserable and homesick. Wherever we live from now on, there will always be some young Dutch people around us, laughing, crying and smoking. Robin and I both learn to speak and understand Dutch. Nothing formal, just enough to be able to eavesdrop on the juicy gossip. My mother is always on their side, fiercely loyal to her extended family.

From now on she will always have an office wherever we live, spending many hours typing away on her Underwood. Whenever she has an important letter to send she seals it with sealing wax and imprints the Willys coat of arms with her gold signet ring.

Perrimans has a large garden and we employ a gardener to grow the vegetables. He usually comes on Saturday afternoon after he's been to the pub, so when the peas and beans grow up they are all in wobbly rows. My mother won't get rid of him, even though he's an old drunk. Robin has to mow the lawn. One day I am delighted to see he has mown his initials, RW.

My mother is hopelessly tone deaf but it does not stop her doing awful renditions of Marlene Dietrich who she loves. *Falling in love again* ... It's so excruciatingly awful that Robin and I will start bashing the sofa pillows or each other,

'No stop! Please stop, we can't stand it!'

Every evening Robin and I listen to *Dick Barton – Special Agent.* It is really exciting. He's given a little steam engine machine which I am not allowed to play with. He reads *Beano* and *Hotspur* and *The Eagle.*

We get a new fangled thing called a 'pressure cooker' but my mother doesn't understand how it works. It explodes and we have dripping cabbage all over the kitchen walls. Roy and she begin to have terrible rows. At one point she's throwing all his clothes out of the top window. We see his underpants and shirts fluttering onto the front lawn. We are hopeful that he may leave us but no, it's worse - she's pregnant.

I've begun to paint and I do a still life of a blue and white Chinese vase. Like most mothers after the war, she is very strict about us eating everything on our plates. I sit miserably staring at a pile of broad beans going stony cold. When everyone has left the table I stuff them into a plant pot. I'm found out when they begin to sprout.

Roy wants to put 'the price of his car' on a horse called Nicklecoin, who is in the Grand National. My mother is dead against it. They have terrible arguments about it and in the end, he doesn't put the bet on and the horse wins. He gets very drunk and beats her up.

We are embarrassed by a rude painting of her, which my father had painted when they first met. She is lying naked on a blue sofa. Roy is very derisive. She buys me a blue and white cotton dress with a white collar. It's my first new dress and I hang it right by my bed so that I can see it even when I fall asleep.

My mother has a cockney communist friend who promises he can stop her smoking by hypnotising her. She's hooked on Wills Woodbines. He dangles a medallion in front of her nose and repeats,

'It's an 'orrible 'abit! It's an orrible 'abit!' but it makes her laugh so much she can't concentrate. Nothing will stop her smoking, right to the end.

Robin has joined the Cubs and I think I might join the Brownies, but only because I like the uniform.

The new baby is nearly here. The big laundry basket is like a wicker trunk and is sent to the laundry once a week. We've now painted it yellow and put a mattress in and this will be 'the baby's cot'. I have to stay with my friend Jean who lives in the local council houses. Every day we will pass the house on our way to school. If a girl is born, a white rose will be placed in the window. If a boy, a red rose. One morning, there it is, a red rose. I go to school and in morning prayers I'm transported, I feel one with Jesus. I'm having to keep my growing interest in religion under wraps because my mother is an atheist. She pooh-poohs religion as hypocritical rubbish,

'A man in the clouds with a white beard! Grow up! All those Dutch people pray on Sunday and steal your bike on Monday!' But in this house there is a picture of Jesus on the wall in my bedroom and I have secretly started to talk to him,

'Thank you for this lovely baby.'

It's July 1st 1950. He is named Nicholas and I love him utterly. He has lovely brown eyes and thick dark lashes, he rolls around on the bed in his little vest with baby powder on his little bottom. I will protect him and care for him for years. Later we walk in the bog gardens in Virginia Water – he is in a pushchair in his romper suit.

Meanwhile, Roy and my mother's fighting has become very violent. He gets drunk and beats her up every Saturday night. I'm afraid to bring my friends home but one weekend my friend Jenny comes to stay and, *Oh crikey*, the shouting and screaming has begun. We decide to get help for my mother. It's very late at night and snowing so we put on Wellingtons and overcoats over our nighties and run up to the main road where we wave to passing cars.

'Please stop!' One does, it's a police car. We're babbling our story. He drives us back to Perrimans, up the drive to the front door. Roy opens the door, all smiles. He calls the policeman 'old boy'.

'Thank you for returning the girls. We were worried. Wife's upset, old boy, you understand.' *Horror!* This is not what we had expected. The police car drives off; he slams the door and is grinning at us.

'Now you little bitches … ' We run upstairs and lock the door.

Luckily he doesn't pursue us. I will never have another friend to stay and I will never forget this.

At the end of Robin's last term at Caldecot we go to see him in his school play - it is *French Without Tears* by Terrence Rattigan. Robin plays the French teacher - he's now fluent in French so he's very funny and my mother and I clap hard when he takes his bow.

I go to see the film *Kim* which is based on Rudyard Kipling's story of a little boy in India. It stars Errol Flynn as his friend. I am thrilled … I feel as though I *know* this land and these colours …

I've written a play which I perform on the front steps. It's about a woman who can't pay her bills - my mother's communist friend says,

'It's very realistic!'

Roy has got Robin's pellet gun and is teasing me and holding it against my bottom.

'Stop it, you'll hurt her' pleads my mother.

'Don't be silly it's not real!' He pulls the trigger and the pellet lodges itself well into the surface of my skin.

I *hate, hate, hate* this man.

Chapter 5

The Millstream

My mother has managed to save some money and she sees an advertisement for a houseboat for sale for £100. We leave beastly Perrimans and are very excited to move into the boat which is moored at Bray. It is a converted motor torpedo boat which went to Dunkirk and has recently been converted into a home. It's called 'The Millstream'. It is seventy two feet long and eighteen feet wide. My mother - and Roy - have the large cabin in the bows where there is a tin bath in a cupboard. There is a tiny kitchen with a gas stove and a sink, and then a room for Nicholas's cot just beside. Steps lead up to the deck, a large salon with red and white checked curtains, a dining table and a little anthracite stove. Robin's cabin, then my tiny cabin and my mother's office. The toilet is an 'Elsan' and has to be emptied - mostly by me - every few days. At the back there is a wooden walkway with a small dinghy tied to it. There is a gangplank which takes us up onto the mooring - a wild field of about half an acre – full of willow trees. To get to the road we have to go through another field owned by Mr. Vaslet, who has a gaggle of geese who chase us and honk and try to bite our legs as we bicycle through, squealing. I have to go to a new school, Braywick Village School. My mother and I go to meet the head teacher, Miss Burgess. She likes me and I will be happy here.

My mother gets Robin a scholarship to Pangbourne Nautical College. He hates it and spends the next few years running away. The first time he runs away he turns up on the boat in the middle of the night. He has hitch-hiked home. My mother's expecting him because the school has telephoned so she's ready with her rage and recriminations. They drive him back. Another time they drive him back and I stow away in the boot, which is open at this time, so I am under a blanket behind the back seat, popping up when they stop at a pub. Robin appreciates the gesture; Roy and my mother are angry because they want to have a pub crawl on the way home. They do it anyway, and I sit in the back and wait for them. The hours of waiting outside pubs …

Poor Robin. He tells me horror stories of life at Pangbourne. The morning runs in shorts in the middle of winter, the cold showers, the beds having to be made four inches exactly, no lumps or otherwise there are ghastly forfeits. He teaches me how to do knots - a reef , and not a granny.

What he feels is *bugger Sir Richard Grenville*; this is not the life for him; he is reading Tennyson and Keats and he wants to be a romantic poet and have lots of girlfriends.

I get my first pair of new American trousers called 'jeans'. I am not allowed to wear them at school. They have a particular smell which I love. I bike to school through Bray and along a wooded causeway. Nicholas is growing up and has a maddening little mouth organ which he blows tunelessly as he waddles around the deck. Often there will be a sudden a silence, then a splash.

'Nicholas is in the water!' Someone will jump in to rescue him. Not my mother though, she can't swim. She also never learns to drive a car.

'I'd be hopeless. I'd be looking at all the flowers.'

One of Nicholas' other tricks … he loves to stand behind the dining table, beside the open window so you can't reach him, and pop the silver into the river. The Willys family silver still sits at the bottom of the Thames in Bray. One time he throws my mother's purse in and one of Robin's handsome friends dives in and rescues it. What a hero, in my nine year old eyes.

We have a television now, a little Bush upright which has a screen full of very wobbly waves. Sometimes we have to fiddle with the aerial for hours, often holding it out of the window of the boat (or sometimes in a cup of tea works!), so we can watch favourites like *Muffin the Mule*.

Roy continues to get drunk and frighten us all to bits. One night in the deep winter there is a big storm - my mother and I are sitting all cosy by the fire watching Richard Hearne as *Mr. Pastry* - when we hear him coming across the fields singing and cursing. Suddenly we are plunged into darkness – he has cut the tow ropes. The boat lurches into the fast flowing main stream and as we struggle to climb up on the deck, we are heading - quite fast in the winter current - towards the weir. It's very frightening. He's on the bank laughing, my mother is screaming.

'Help us! Help!' We eventually crunch to a halt on the edge of the weir and are rescued later by neighbouring boat owners.

I am now the main carer for Nicholas. As Roy and my mother are always fighting and arguing, I make him porridge, get him dressed and off to his nursery before I go to school. I act, write and direct my first play at school. It's called *Evil Eye the Witch.* Miss Burgess invites the press so I get notices in the Maidenhead paper. I'm called a 'talented pupil'. My mother is very proud, as is Robin. He says,

'It's in the genes.' I don't see what my American trousers have to do with it!

Miss Burgess takes us on nature walks. We collect wild flowers and write the names in columns. Pages and pages. Cowslips, oxlips, cuckoo flowers, corn crowfoot, poppies, cornflowers, great burnet, dog daisies, self heal, yellow rattle, knapweed, spotted orchids, harebells. We compete to see whose list is longest. So many wild flowers are now lost.

There is a corner of the playground with high walls and fig trees. We will play 'House' under the trees, with elaborate rituals of sweeping and cooking. One of my friends already has breasts - I'm fascinated and she shows them to me. I want some of those! Nothing yet. So I can still play bare-chested. We are taken in a bus to Maidenhead swimming pool to learn to swim. I'm hopeless, I hate having my head under water, but I love the tomato sandwiches.

Robin comes to meet me from school. He is wearing his Pangbourne uniform. I am so proud of him in front of my school friends. Our finances are always very precarious and whenever we've reached rock bottom, my mother will declare a 'feast on tick'. We will have an account at the local shop which has everything we need: vegetables, stationery, paraffin, biscuits in glass fronted cabinets all along the counter, baskets of wool, packets of cereals, and tins of corned beef, stamps and string. They'll cut you a slice of fruit cake or cheese, but for us a feast means baked beans and chocolate cup cakes and Wills Woodbines for her. We have been on rationing since the war, but we are not deprived.

The boat is painted pale green. Every holiday my mother nags us all to paint and scrape. We seem to do this year-round!

We love the river life. The Dutch girls and my mother will sit on the deck smothered in sun oil, smoking and gossiping and calling out cheeky remarks to the passing cabin cruisers. The Maid Lines cabin cruisers are painted green with names like Maid Marion, Maid Magdelene, Maid Molly. There are punts with awnings, so couples can moor up, and let the canvas sides down, and sleep in privacy. There are skiffs and big steamers full of passengers. And the dinghy is mine. In the summer holidays I love to get up at dawn. The river is like a glass pond. The reflections of the willows on Monkey Island are perfectly still. I row along the banks. The families of ducks are my friends. The swans can be unnerving when they chase each other but I love the brown teenage swans. It's my own world of water and light, secret moorings and overhung trees, little beaches to pull up on. And when the river is busy with boats, it is fun, to row close to their wake and feel the boat rocking.

One dark winter's night my mother is nagging me to empty the Elsan. Now, this involves me lugging the heavy can up the gangplank and, somewhere on the edge of the wild field, digging a fair sized hole and emptying it all in and filling the hole over with clods and stamping in it; not something I want to be doing on a cold night.

'I'm doing it!' I say, and tip the beastly thing over the back of the boat into the pitch dark river. *Hah!* Who would know? During the winter months, my dinghy is often full of rain water which I have to bail out. The next morning we wake up to a frost. The dinghy is brim-full of frozen turds. My mother roars with laughter,

'It serves you right!' She loves to tell this story. Dutch humour loves anything to do with poop and pots and bottoms.

I am bicycling around Bray in my little shorts and no top. I notice, with alarm, that I've got two bumps on my chest and I realise the tomboy game is up. I'm becoming a girl. Drat it!

My mother has a slipped disc and the people at the hospital have put a plaster cast around her middle. It's driving her mad and she decides to 'get the bugger off' so she sits in the tin bath, in the bows of the boat, and I have to pour hot water from the kettle over it till finally it begins to melt. It's horribly messy. We pull away strips of plaster and canvas. She's had a few and she's chuckling. I feel exasperated with her.

It's my tenth birthday and Robin gives me a copy of *The Rubaiyat of Omar Khayyam*. In it he writes,

'For Anneke, Hoping she's in a better mood when she receives this than the one she was in last night when I came to borrow a pen to write this with.'

Madeline Rose is a friend of mine and she's very pretty. She lives in Maidenhead on the banks of the river. She has a huge jar of farthings. At the beginning of summer holidays we divide it up and start playing Pontoon. By the end of the summer I owe her 2,500 farthings.

My comics are full of schoolgirl dramas, cheering the heroine on. *Come on Jennifer!* She's winning the running cup. The 1950's films are full of Doris Day in ballerina length dresses, pinched waists and frilly aprons.

I have a friend who goes for riding lessons. It's not cheap but my mother sees how keen I am so off I go to the Holyport Riding School. I have jodhpurs and boots and a yellow aertex shirt and a tie with horseshoes and whips on it. I'm mucking out stables and grooming the ponies and cleaning the tack, in lieu of lessons. My friend has a pony called Amber who lives in a field and we ride him as often as we can, cantering around the countryside with the wind in our faces; taking it in turns; one on the bike. We get *Horse and Hound* magazine and read *Moreland Mousey* and learn all the points, the withers, the hocks, and about the bits, the martingales and the curb chains. Robin teases me and calls me 'horse-mad'.

Every night my mother ties my hair up in four little white strips of cloth, just as her mother had done for her and her sisters. I dampen the washing for her and as soon as I'm old enough I clean - the Dutch are famous for their cleanliness - she even has a little jug and cloth by the lavatory 'in case it's taking too long you can wipe the walls a bit while you're there'. Polishing her collection of horse brasses and copper lamps is also my job. This is how she was taught as a child - my grandmother, a strong and disciplined woman, had trained all three daughters in the tasks of the family, in Holland in the 1920s.

Tim Craxton's current love is Sam Arnold-Foster. Robin and I have been invited to the Arnold-Foster ancestral home in Wootton Basset in Wiltshire. It's a grand 18th century house, four stories high, made in mellow Bath stone, standing in large grounds. We have a room each. Mine has a four poster bed and looks out over a high walled vegetable garden. We have our own little sitting room where we play Monopoly in front of a coal fire … it's very luxurious and we love it. Next morning, breakfast is served in the dining room with tall French windows opening out onto the lawns. Scrambled eggs and kippers are under large silver 'hats' on the sideboard. We sit at a long table, I'm feeling very shy and I'm still hungry but I daren't help myself ... so I'm scraping my plate hopefully. A smiling Mrs Arnold-Foster asks,

'Would you like some more, Anneke?'

'No no,' I reply, nonchalantly. 'I wasn't doing that so I could have *more* …'

Robin is play-fighting on the croquet lawn, with a girl called Ros who is his age. They are laughing and I am feeling left out. 'Anyway, he can't like her 'cos she's got lumpy navy blue knickers!'

Sam comes and takes me to the stables and I ride a lovely strawberry Roan called Mrs. Starling, who is quiet and gentle, has a wide back and a lovely trot. We are off through the summer lanes … into my 'happiness blue print'.

My mother takes us to see a Christmas play at the Theatre Royal, Windsor. Mary Kerridge runs the theatre and Robin and I are friends with her daughters. The play is called *The Land Where the Rainbow Ends*. It is total magic and I want to be one of those children on stage. I love the theatre, the gold proscenium and red plush seats, the orchestra and the moment when it all goes quiet and the curtain rises. I love it still, that magic moment.

Roy and my mother are fighting again. He is being so cruel to her, I can't bear it. I want to hurt him back. The only thing I can find is a pair of nail scissors. I run from the boat crying and feeling so angry and helpless. I go to his little red car parked by the gate and find his big winter coat on the seat. I try to cut it but it's very thick so I start sawing away at the pocket with the little scissors.

Now, he has seen me from the boat windows and he's storming along the path towards me, shouting and swearing. I panic. I drop the coat and try to run back along the towpath but he's following me, and he's faster. I turn then and put up my hands in front of me and say,

'Catch me, then', like it's some terrible game. He hauls me, protesting, into the boat, shoves my mother into the kitchen and locks the door. He's got the broom in his hand.

She is shrieking,

'Don't hurt her Roy! Don't hurt her!' He locks the other door, bashes the broom end off the handle and with a ghastly satisfaction he throws me over his knee and beats me senseless.

I come to, throwing up, with my mother and a neighbour bathing my bruises and whispering in shocked tones. I lie on my stomach and sleep off the pills they have given me. It is a week before I can return to school, and normal life.

And a lifetime to get over it.

I have to sit on pillows as the bruises turn from yellow to black. My mother tells Roy not to return. Everyone is shocked. We don't tell Robin, it is already hard enough on him being so miserable at Pangbourne. He knows that Roy is violent and that there are scenes, but we are too ashamed to tell him how severe it has got. And, of course, she takes him back. She is hooked to this man, and to this drama.

Was this a place where she could work out all her rage and pain of her terrible losses during the war? To lose a mother, and a sister, and a husband, all in such a short space of time, holding it all together for us, with no support at all. She'd come through but she, like many others, was damaged by those experiences. Now she was acting it out.

Roy tries to get her committed. He taunts Robin and me with,

'Yeah, your mother's mad, you know that? She's going to be locked up, and then what will happen to you?' sniggering, knocking back more beer.

She did, in fact, have electrical shock treatment. WHAT?! Delayed shock, and extreme grief, and who was taking care of her?

The doctors simply didn't understand. Many of my friends' mothers were fairly bananas in those days, how were they supposed to settle into normal lives, just like that? They didn't. Many took to the bottle; she was acting it all out in this relationship. And we were the victims.

I plot Roy's murder. I run it through my mind at night.

'I'll hit him over the head with a saucepan but I don't want to kill him 'cos I don't want to go to prison, I just want to knock him out for a few years.'

How can I get out of this nightmare?

Chapter 6

Child's Play

1952 is a year of huge changes. In February I have to have a tooth out so my mother and I go to London where as a treat we go to the theatre to see Ibsen's *The Wild Duck*. Michael Gough is in it. She says.

'That man is one of our best actors ...'

Next day we go to Harley Street, it's raining and cold and the doorman opens the door and greets us with,

'Good morning, the King's died.'

They give me gas, I hate passing out, when I regain consciousness I feel nauseous and all the way home I'm being sick and bleeding. The one place my tongue wants to explore is that gaping hole.

Our mooring has become very overgrown. Next door there is a neat house and garden owned by an American family. They complain to my mother about Nicholas running about our mooring naked. My mother goes over, and tears them off a strip as Robin and I cheer her on from behind the brambles,

'There's nothing wrong with a naked child except in your minds!'

At school we all have to learn the new Queen's speech…

'I declare before you all that my whole life, whether it be long or short, shall be devoted to your service and to the service of our great imperial family to which we all belong…'

The young Queen touches us girls. We all watch the Coronation on the television. After the war and the rationing it's all symbolically comforting us, the Queen in robes with a crown on her head. All is well.

♫ *Fairytales can come true it can happen to you …* ♫
- Frank Sinatra

Tim Craxton has a friend called Hugh Falkus whose friend, Margaret Thompson, is looking for a group of children to be in the film she is making. He puts me up for a part. I go along to an audition. I have no idea what an audition is but I want to be in this film. Margaret Thompson is very nice.

'Do you have an audition piece?'

'Um … no … but I can do the Queen's speech!' I say brightly - 'Turn your back, close your eyes'. And in the Queen's high, thin voice, I begin,

'I declare, before you all …' When I finish she turns with a big smile. Everyone is smiling. I've got the part. I can't wait to tell my mother. I know this will make her happy.

I have missed my 11 Plus exam and must do the papers alone in Miss Burgess's sweet little sitting room next to the schoolroom. But what is this?

'If one *squiggle* is to that *squiggle* then another *squiggle* is to another kind of *squiggle*,'

'WHAT??!!' I haven't been taught any of this rubbish! I've learnt the names of all the wild flowers, I've written a play. This is an insult to my intelligence!

I fail my 11 Plus.

Anyway, I am off to Southall Studios to start the filming of *Child's Play*. I am taken in a great big Daimler, the studio car. And while at wardrobe being measured, I meet the other children including Christopher Beeny, who is a young *star!* Peter Sallis, Mona Washbourne and Dorothy Allison are also in the cast. It will take eight weeks to shoot. There are stills to be taken and we begin to work on some of the interiors in the studio. I love the smell of new sets being made, the sound of the red light bell, the huge padded door closing, the sudden stillness and then,

'Shooting now … rollover ... speed … action!'

In *Child's Play*

The story is based in fact. A group of children, one of whom has a father who is a scientist, figure out a way to split the atom using a piece of Krakatoa rock, which is still active. Many adventures follow. I play the nurse in the gang. The main action is filmed in and around Hambledon in Hampshire. The first night we are on location and we children join the rest of the cast at a large table for dinner at the Catherine Wheel Hotel in Henley-on-Thames. I'm wearing one of my costume dresses as it's my best. It seems completely glamorous to me. We are served 'Duck a l'orange' and a chocolate soufflé. I can't wait to telephone my mother and tell her.

'Huh, lucky you,' she says, 'I've only got baked beans.' I don't feel guilty for long. The sun shines and it is early summer. They have even given me my own special shot with a pony and a riding jacket. I am allowed to keep the jacket. I receive £9 as my fee, which I am proud to give to my mother.

I've seen *Child's Play* recently; it is a gem (*Child's Play* should not be confused with the later horror film of the same title!). We had a wonderful team of people and it shows a time before cars and TV aerials and wires and signs ruined our lovely villages and countryside. I will always love to work together in a team – the make-up and wardrobe and designers, the sparks and the camera crews who are all so focussed on creating this piece of drama. When the film comes out I get a notice in the Maidenhead paper …

'… and Anneke Willys, who is pretty enough to remind one of a very young Pier Angeli …' My mother is proud of me – I don't know who Pier Angeli is – I want to go riding on Amber, and I want to go to the school that Christopher Beeny goes to.

Following this acting debut my mother starts pestering the local education authorities to try to get me into the Cone Ripman Stage School, later to become the Arts Educational.

When she puts her mind to something, no-one and nothing will stand in her way. She is immensely articulate and daunting so before long I have an appointment at the education offices in Aylesbury. We go up together by train. A large room, a long table, a row of grown-ups asking me questions.

'What are you reading?'

'Rudyard Kipling, The Rubaiyat of Omar Khayyam, Bambi?'

'Why do you want to act?' I tell them the story my mother loved to tell us of seeing Sarah Bernhardt on the stage; at the time my mother saw her, this famous actress was an old lady in a wheelchair. The lights on stage had been dimmed, and she was playing a young officer in the First World War, and you believed she *was* this young man, and it was very moving. That … is acting.

By the end of that summer we have a reply. I have got a grant but my scholarship can't come into force until spring. Another friend of Tim Craxton's steps forward - my fairy godmother - Lady Vane Jane Tempest Stewart, Marchioness of Londonderry. She offers to pay for my first term at the Cone Ripman and also says that I may stay with her in Londonderry House in Park Lane for a few weeks until other arrangements can be made.

♫ *Do not forsake me oh my darling* ♫
- from *High Noon*

I say goodbye to Miss Burgess, who has tears in her eyes, because she believed in me. Robin is pleased for me, Nicholas is sad, but learns to cook his own porridge. And my mother is happy and sad and proud and bossy and over the top as usual. I prepare for London and a new life; I'm thrilled and excited and nervous. In September I will leave for Londonderry House which is a huge mansion on the edge of Hyde Park. (Later it will be pulled down and The Hilton Hotel will be built on the site).

The school has sent us a huge uniform list. It includes summer and winter street clothes - not cheap, good quality. And lots of shoes – street, ballet, points, tap, character. Leotards, national skirt, Greek tunic, house coats, and on, and on. My mother says,

'Do they think I'm made of money? You'll have to make do for now.'

Travelling in London on my own is scary for me. The school is in Upper Berkeley Street, behind Marble Arch. Two huge houses five storeys high with massive rooms on the ground and first floors and two spiral staircases. It has been *the* London stage school for many years and has a great reputation for producing some of the best dancers in the Royal Ballet and the drama department is growing fast.

I'm given a grey housecoat, no belt, and told that scholarship girls can wear these. Well, I'm not having this, so slowly, during that first term I managed to *acquire* my entire uniform. The cloak rooms are in the basement, small, untidy and with a huge lost and found box. By the end of term I have a herringbone winter coat, flannel skirt, stripy blue shirt, royal blue sweater and blue webbing belt with the ornate metal clasp, as well as my dancing and practice gear. When my mother asks where I got these things, I'm vague,

'Oh, off a friend, second hand, someone too big for them.' So that was my uniform problem sorted.

That first day, I stand in assembly in this large ballroom with huge mirrors and ballet barres and parquet floors. After assembly we all scatter up the spiral staircases to the classrooms where for half a day we will learn English, arithmetic, history and art. After lunch, which is held in the basement dining room, we have a busy schedule of singing, ballet, voice coaching, modern dance, tap dance and much more. And, what a treat to find Carolyn Garnham is here! She's a year ahead of me, but happy to see me and very supportive. It's just like my favourite book *Ballet Shoes* by Noel Streatfield, and I'm living it. When we pass the principals in the passageway, these two wonderful old women with silver hair in buns and shawls around their shoulders, we must curtsy and say,

'Good morning Miss Cohen … Good afternoon Miss Ripman.'

I get the bus down Park Lane to Londonderry House. Upstairs in the elegant oak-panelled flat I'm given supper and go to bed in my beautiful room. In the morning the butler pulls the curtains and places a tray of delicious breakfast with grapes, which I have never eaten before, on the table by the window, and then pulls out a chair for me. Crumbs!

Lady Margaret and her husband, film director Hugh Falkus, are giving a dinner party. Niall McGuinnis, and Siobhan McKenna who are both renowned Irish actors are telling wonderful stories about the Irish theatre world. They are making a great fuss of me, and I love it. I want to help Rory, the butler, but he won't let me. Another night, Rory, who is now my friend, is whispering and winking. He takes me out of the flat and through another door, and we are on a balcony, high up in the domed ceiling of Londonderry House. Down below is the ballroom, all lit up. Music is playing, and people in evening dress are dancing, but I am only allowed a brief glimpse – I have homework to do.

Tim takes me to see Siobhan McKenna playing Saint Joan. Now I want to play that part when I'm older. He gives me the play and I learn the monologue that begins.

'My voices were right! They told me you were fools …'

At the school I'm put in the 'Checcetti' class which is a Russian form of ballet. My little body is stiff and bending and stretching these little muscles is painful. Everyone seems much better than me. As we change classes we get a glimpse of all the ballet students bustling by in their purple leg warmers and flushed faces. These are the ones who will go on to the Royal Ballet. But I am with the drama students. I have noticed the prettiest girl I have ever seen, with pale blonde hair and blue grey eyes. I discover that she is Julia (Toots) Lockwood and her mother is Margaret Lockwood, the famous film actress. By the end of that first term we are friends.

One of my inspirational teachers and allies is a gentle beauty called Miss Joyce. She teaches us literature. She opens the door for me into the worlds of Jane Austen, Chaucer, Shakespeare, and the great poets.

I meet the art teacher, feisty Mrs. Scott, and I love her at once. She's a very pretty blonde; she wears wonderful colours, turquoise and black, saffron and magenta. *I will love and wear these colours all my life; such is the influence of great and inspirational teachers.* At the beginning of our term with her, some mousey new pupils come whining up,

'Please Mrs. Scott, my mother says I don't have to do art 'cos I'm no good at it!'

'Rubbish!' she says, 'Everyone must do art!'

In one of our first classes, she blindfolds us and takes us through various sensory experiences – tasting, feeling, listening, and placing appropriate colours with our fingers on our papers. We will make sculptures and papier-mâché flying fishes and by the end of term I have painted that farmhouse in Holland with the cows and the pump in the floor. She loves it, and me. At the end of that first term, I win the Art Cup.

The acting teachers are Alexander Dore and Anthony Sharp, who lives in Windsor and I will see him on Slough station and hide because he's a bit daunting. In class they are brilliant and funny, and we are given 'scenes' to do. Miss Fisher is the school agent, and she becomes my ally. Over the next few years she gets me an astounding amount of work. We learn articulation, enunciation, and elocution - qualities I do believe have now become extinct! At the end of term we have to do our set pieces. I do a piece about Angelina Patti. There I am, back in the huge ballroom, in front of the whole school. *Very nervous.* I get through it and later I am awarded the Drama Cup. Two cups in the first term! I have won great friends and also some big enemies, whose noses are put out of joint by this precocious newcomer.

At lunchtime we eat lots of beetroot and beef and steamed puddings, spotted dick and chocolate semolina. The academic part of our schooling lacks inspiration. French is endless vocabulary, history is hopeless. I study the Tudors for four years. All from dictation, no time for questions, this teacher is going for high marks. She manages to make this fascinating subject *deadly dull!* I fail hopelessly.

I am improving at ballet, stretching and exercises at the barre. Our teacher wears tights and has her hair in a bun. She also carries a cane, which she sometimes whacks us with -

'And one - two – three – and …' When I am practicing my ballet in the field by the boat - Robin chases after me, teasing and imitating my moves - *Chassé, Chassé, Spring, Hop!* We will learn floaty Greek dances inspired by Isadora Duncan, and lots of character dancing in circles inspired by ancient country dance. Modern dance, - we like this - to the music of *Seven Brides for Seven Brothers.*

♫ *Oh, the barnyard is busy – in a regular tizzy …* ♫

We get good at tap-dancing.

'Step-ball-change, and step-ball-change!' - rows of us doing time steps. The boys do all this as well. We have a group of pianists, old ladies carrying their music in baskets, who bash away on the pianos and knit during the boring bits. Our singing teacher is Miss Simpson, an old alcoholic with a hideous old tarty wig which keeps slipping, and, she can't control us.

We go to Foyles and get our copies of plays by J.M. Barrie, Terence Rattigan and J.B. Priestley. We do scenes and we mime, improvise and do stage craft. How to sit elegantly on the stage. I love every minute of it, giving total attention. However, in the academic classes, I am a disrupter; our poor Geography teacher gives up on me totally. We stand as she enters the room,

'Good afternoon Lower 4B'

'Good afternoon Miss Maliphant'.

'Sit down. Anneke out. Now today we will … ' And I will stand out in the corridor, leaning over the balustrade, watching the heads of the people crossing the hall, five floors down. Sometimes I am sent to the 'Heads'. I have to sit in 'disgrace' on the red seat in the central hall of the school, so that my shame is apparent to everyone. They are not unpleasant meetings. I like these women – the Heads - they understand my creative spark, they admonish me, and encourage me to be more supportive of the teachers. Miss Fisher is more blunt,

'You may be disruptive but you are very good for the school's reputation at the BBC. Now I think they've got another job for you, would you like that?'

We have an art show. The paintings are displayed all through the main halls. One inspired student has painted Adam and Eve, their 'bits' painted more from imagination than knowledge. There is a furore, *Disgusting! Rude! Take them down at once*! *Shameful!* We cheer Mrs. Scott as she storms down five stone flights, getting redder and redder with a hammer in her hand. We hear

'Nothing shameful, all in your minds! I'll resign!' The paintings stay up and Mrs. Scott stays on.

The school becomes the Arts Educational and starts to move with the times.

One day, I too feel Mrs. Scott's wrath. I have done a painting of Hyde Park and the plane trees, and I've dribbled white paint all over it, to represent snow. Now, she is exploding.

'Facile! Facile! You're better than that! Work harder!'

Meanwhile, my two weeks of being waited on by the butler are up and I am to move in with Tim Craxton, who I now call my uncle. He has a flat in Maida Vale above a café, with his vintage car garage behind. The first day I get back and he's busy with a car but gives me the key and tells me to help myself. *To what?!* There's not much food in the cupboard but I don't like to grumble so next day I get the bus down the Edgeware Road with my tummy rumbling. The following evening I get back and he's not there at all. He's famously unpunctual, if he's invited to dinner - he may turn up next day and be amazed if you are put out. He will lose all sense of time when he is busy with his passion - his vintage cars. But now the cupboard is really bare. He must be shopping, I think, I've given him my ration card. By nine o'clock I'm afraid, and a fight has broken out in the street below. In his address book by the telephone is an entry, *Craxton - Essie and Harold.* Perhaps his mother will know where he is, and I dial – Hampstead 2965.

'Mrs Craxton, it's Anneke, I don't know where Tim is and there's no food and um … '

She interrupts with,

'My Dear, lock the door, pack your suitcase and wait for me. I shall knock three times.'

A while later she arrives and bundles me into the back of her vintage Rolls Royce and drives me up to Kidderpore Avenue, Hampstead, where I will live for the next six years.

Chapter 7

The Craxtons

I feel honoured to talk about this extraordinary family, of which I was blessed to be a part. Their influence on me has been nothing short of profound.

Essie Craxton is a truly remarkable woman. She is the matriarch of a talented and wonderful family. Her husband, Professor Harold Craxton, later OBE, is a composer and piano teacher of great renown. At this time he is teaching at the Royal Academy and is giving private lessons to some of the greatest pianists in the world, many of them coming out of post-war Poland and Hungary. They have six grown up children – Tim, my 'uncle' the squadron leader; Janet, leading oboist in the BBC Symphony Orchestra; John, the painter; Anthony, who works at the BBC and produces the broadcasts of all the Queen's speeches; and Robin and Michael, who become family men.

They had been living in Grove End Road but their house had been bombed and they have now moved to Kidderpore Avenue, a very large Arts and Crafts house in Hamsptead. The front steps lead up to a round hall with a tiled floor. There is a large letter rack because there are lots of people in this house. Later, my love letters from boyfriends will be placed in this rack. Doors into a very large inner hall; on the left, double doors into the study. On the right, door into the dining room. The staircase, passage, loo and stairs to the basement which is full of store rooms and workshops and the door to the kitchen and straight ahead, double doors with glass in the top so if you stand on the first step of the stairs you can see who's playing the piano in the studio. This wonderful room – oak panelled with a winding staircase up to a balcony, an open fire, three grand pianos and the whole of the back wall is windows looking out over the garden. As you enter the kitchen it has a pantry which has large wooden draining boards and double sinks. And the trolley! (more about The Trolley later). Janet will make glass cupboards to display her Greek BC pottery in the pantry and this leads into a large square kitchen which has a big table where we prepare the meals. There is a Rayburn, and washing hangs up high above it on a wooden rack. A door into a tiled pantry, which I am amazed to see has slate shelves full of pies and puddings, and pheasants and rabbits hanging, and enamel pots full of grains and baskets of onions and potatoes and racks of wine. I've never seen anything like it. Then there is a scullery with a washing machine for the clothes, more sinks and plate racks and the first fridge I have ever seen. Steps lead down into the garden. I will come home from school and sit at the kitchen table, driving the cook mad with my chatter. She will teach me to cook. I learn to make treacle tart and béchamel sauce and runny scrambled eggs and soup with sherry.

My bedroom is above the hall so it has a curved window. Janet's room is next to mine and I listen to her practice her oboe every night. What a gift - she will become the foremost female oboe player of her day. She also has a grand piano in this room so sometimes the Mozart Players rehearse in there. Janet's hobby is carpentry so one of the workshops in the basement is hers.

John's studio is on the other side of me. He is in Greece when I arrive.

The bathroom has a mural painted by John. Mr. and Mrs. Craxton's bedroom is at the back looking over the garden. I love sitting on the mahogany lavatory seat and looking at the patterns in the art nouveau tiles.

On the top floor, Doctor Margaret Rowbotham lives over Janet's room. Sylvia Faulkner, Mrs Craxton's sister, who was a ballet dancer and danced with the Russian Ballet in her youth, also lives here. She has a sitting room with yet another grand piano. She is so petite, with turned-out toes, a shawl and her silver hair plaited around her head and a twinkle in her eyes. And Stella the cook, a friend of John and Janet's, also lives up here. They have a kitchen, too, so they are self contained.

The entire home is filled with exquisite antique furniture which has all been bought on the cheap. Everything is Dutch or French,

18th century. I will learn all this later while spending time with John.

Aubusson carpets, the paintings, Dutch 16th century or works by Graham Sutherland, Lucien Freud or John Craxton. Both the dining room and study have jungles in their windows – large groups of plants are tangled up and growing into each other. Later in my life when I am designing interiors I will always include 'a jungle of plants.'

Then there is the eccentricity. Mrs. Craxton is a hoarder, having lived through two World Wars, so in countless armoires, chests of drawers and plastic bags, she keeps her collection of clothes. She is forever saying,

'Ah, now, I may have just the thing, a nice warm coat. Now let me see …' and she'll be shuffling away in some pile. Quite often it isn't what you want to be seen dead in, but she is insistent.

On my first day at school from Kidderpore Avenue, Mrs. Craxton insists that she will come and help me get the right bus. We stand at the stop and when it comes, Mrs Craxton says,

'*Conductah*, will you make sure that Anneke gets *orf* at George Street?' I can see the people in the top of the bus sniggering and I am so embarrassed.

Every day the secretary, Daisy, arrives to sit at the desk in the study and organise Mr. Craxton's appointments. The two cleaners also arrive and start working their way around the house. Lessons happen all over the house – music, music, music – people coming and going, it's always busy. I am in heaven and I never want to leave. Mr. and Mrs. Craxton are very kind people and they take me into their hearts. I will look in the appointment book and when one of my favourite pianists – Peter Katin or Denis Mathews - is coming for their master class with Mr. Craxton. I will climb up onto the balcony and snuggle secretly into the couch, and be transported by the music.

The Craxtons' dining room and study

Mrs. Craxton is a provider. She opens her door with,

'Have you eaten?' It doesn't matter if it's 1.30 in the morning, it's always,

'Have you eaten? I'm sure we have something.' And off she goes into the kitchen, adjusting the many pairs of specs she dangles down her front. She's sort of crumpled in the middle, and has flat feet that turn out as she walks. She returns with plates of delicious leftovers.

Which brings me to the Trolley. The Trolley is a feature of daily Craxton life. I can hear its sound now as it emerges from the kitchen, loaded up with steaming food, rattling across the parquet floors to the dining room. Quite often there are 10 to 14 people to feed. The table is laid with silver and cut glass. Mrs. Craxton, presiding.

'Now, Sir John, can I tempt you to a little game pie?'

Meanwhile Mr. Craxton goes around the table and pours you your glass of wine. He has such beautiful manners. He always sits on Mrs. Craxton's left and after dinner he relaxes in his armchair with his Du Maurier in a cigarette holder. All the offspring have complete respect for Mr. and Mrs. Craxton. Sometimes, Mrs Craxton will be disapproving of John, as he does have a tendency to be snobby, something which she abhorred. In her eyes, everyone was worthy of respect, no matter what. There is no class distinction in the Craxton household. Sir John Barbirolli, conductor of the Hallé Orchestra, will sit at the table with Fred and Pearl the bus conductors. Everyone is treated with the same respect. Once or twice a week Michael and Alice and their children will come; Robin and Enid; Tim and his amours; and later, John, and his. They get a television in the dining room and will pull it out to watch me in my plays, giving me kind and observant critiques.

Mr. Craxton has an extraordinary and dry wit and Janet and John are extremely bright and funny and nothing is sacred, so they laugh and joke about musical life, the ins and outs of orchestral musicians.

The conversations around the dinner table are amazing. Sometimes Mrs. Craxton will stop them if they are being too cruel. Anthony comes in for a lot of ribbing because of the Royal broadcasts – they love to make fun of that.

Sir Malcolm Sargent, conductor of the BBC orchestra, comes to dinner and Janet dresses as a maid and serves him. Great fun is had, as well as all the creative work going on in the house.

I never want to go to bed.

After every meal The Trolley is trundled back into the pantry and everyone will wash and dry and put away the dishes. Tea and coffee is made and we will sit in front of the studio fire and listen to a concert on the wireless.

Sometimes Janet is playing and Mrs. Craxton will ask me,

'Who is the composer? What's the name of the symphony? Which movement is it?' Everyone smiles at me indulgently and I squirm with embarrassment, hoping to get it right. I will be invited to join them at recitals at the Wigmore Hall.

Outside in the road is the collection of vintage cars which they are all mad about. The Austin Tourers, the Rileys, the Rolls Royce, all in varying states of disrepair, and being constantly overhauled by Janet and Tim. The lovely image of Mrs. Craxton driving Mr. Craxton to the Royal Academy, in the old Rolls Royce, she sits erect with specs on the end of her nose and he's small and squat with his bashed-up trilby and his cigarette in its holder.

Tim takes me in his Austin Tourer (circa 1929) to Duxford Airfield. I climb into a Tiger Moth and he flies me around the countryside. I'm frightened and I love it, it's the first time I have ever flown and my scarf is fluttering out of the window! On the way home we visit some of his friends in a large Elizabethan Manor at the end of an overgrown drive. There is a vast kitchen with a stone floor and chickens are clucking in and out. There are lots of children and we eat crumpets in front of a huge fire. Later Tim teaches me to drive the Riley in the driveway. I just *love* these adventures.

In October I have my twelfth birthday and Mrs. Craxton kindly gives me a party. I invite about fifteen children from school. Christopher Beeny is one, Toots Lockwood another. *My gang.* The table in the dining room is loaded with food. We all sit down and - fall into an embarrassed silence. I think they are overcome to be sitting in such splendour and I am being polite as Stella, Daisy and Mrs. Craxton fuss around us. But we soon drop the shyness and the party ends up with us all running wildly and shrieking around the house. Mrs. Craxton wastes nothing - we collect the bottle-tops, the string, the paper. She is the original recycler! Sometimes when she offers a slice of treacle tart to Mr. Craxton he will murmur politely,

'Hmm, what vintage?' Because of course, she will never waste a morsel of food. We never waste food. We always finish what's on our plates. I still do.

♫ *How much is that doggy in the window?* ♫
- Lita Rosa

That first Christmas, I have a part in *Alice in Wonderland* at the Q Theatre, Chiswick. I will understudy Toots, who plays Alice, and I also play a Tiger-Lily. We all go to Leichners to get our theatre make-up lessons and on to Berman's for our costumes. I love the smell of the make up and the dressing room lights and being on the stage. I don't like being shouted at by the drunken, bad-tempered director. Although I'm the understudy, the costume doesn't fit me and I've never rehearsed. During one performance, Toots has a bad cold and is on stage swaying and hanging onto the mushroom and I'm in the wings praying she doesn't faint. This will become my nightmare for life – I'm on stage, the costume doesn't fit and I don't know my lines.

Toots is our inspiration. She writes and directs us in all sorts of performances. She and I do a version of *We're A Couple of Swells*, dressed as tramps.

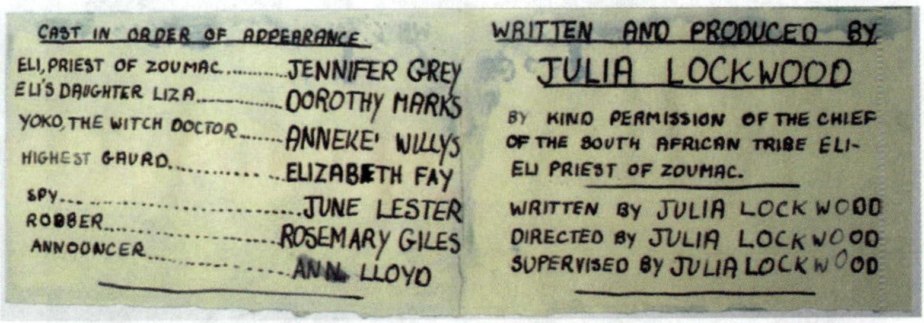
CAST IN ORDER OF APPEARANCE

ELI, PRIEST OF ZOUMAC.......... JENNIFER GREY
ELI'S DAUGHTER LIZA.......... DOROTHY MARKS
YOKO, THE WITCH DOCTOR....... ANNEKE' WILLYS
HIGHEST GAURD.......... ELIZABETH FAY
SPY.......... JUNE LESTER
ROBBER.......... ROSEMARY GILES
ANNOONCER.......... ANN LLOYD

WRITTEN AND PRODUCED BY
JULIA LOCKWOOD

BY KIND PERMISSION OF THE CHIEF OF THE SOUTH AFRICAN TRIBE ELI-ELI PRIEST OF ZOUMAC.

WRITTEN BY JULIA LOCKWOOD
DIRECTED BY JULIA LOCKWOOD
SUPERVISED BY JULIA LOCKWOOD

Today, I talked to Toots for the first time for years. She's just come back from many years of living in Spain. She's sitting in the middle of chaos and half-unpacked boxes. I tell her about writing this book. I ask,

'Have you any photos of the time?'

'Well how extraordinary!' says Toots 'I've just opened my mother's treasure box and on the top I see an *Alice in Wonderland* programme, and one of your drawings', What treasures!

The *Q Theatre* is one of the most important of London's small theatres. The play after *Alice* is *The Lady's Not for Burning* by Christopher Fry - starring Jean Kent and Michael Gough.

Alice in Wonderland

CLUB MEMBERS: The Club Room is now open for coffee and sandwiches until 10.30 p.m.

4D.

"Q" THEATRE VOUCHER BOOK CLUB MEMBERSHIP

Full Membership to Voucher Book Holders. Vouchers are exchangeable for tickets without further charge and can be used for any performance—except Bank Holidays—and including any Sunday performance

ISSUED AT THE FOLLOWING PRICES

27 Vouchers to 7/6 Seats £6 . 16 . 0 (Total Saving £3 . 4 . 6) VALID 12 MONTHS
15 Vouchers to 7/6 Seats £4 . 2 . 6 (Total Saving £1 . 10 . 0) VALID 6 MONTHS
10 Vouchers to 6/6 Seats £2 . 6 . 8 (Total Saving 18/4) VALID 6 MONTHS

NOW AVAILABLE FROM BOX OFFICE

MEMBERSHIP APPLICATION Date ______
Please enrol me as a FULL/SUNDAY Member of the 'Q' Theatre Club. I enclose herewith £ : : in payment of ______ vouchers (5/6 if Sunday Membership only).
NAME (Block Letters) ______
ADDRESS ______

SUNDAY MEMBERSHIP ONLY: 5/6 TO DECEMBER 31st, 1954

Printed by Cockayne & Co., Ltd., London, S.E.1 4151

"Q" THEATRE
OPPOSITE KEW BRIDGE STATION
Licensee: JACK de LEON
Under the Management of PLAY LIVE LTD.
Administrator: BEATRICE de LEON

PATRONS PLEASE NOTE
"Q" Productions are now advertised daily in *The Evening News* and *Evening Standard*.

Programme

Wednesday, 23rd December, to Saturday, 9th January

ALICE IN WONDERLAND
AND THROUGH THE LOOKING GLASS
by LEWIS CARROLL

4D.

EXHIBITION OF CHILDREN'S PAINTINGS
WILL BE HELD IN THE THEATRE
CLUB ROOM
THROUGHOUT THE RUN OF
ALICE IN WONDERLAND

TIMES OF PERFORMANCES
Matinees daily 2.15 Sats. 2.15 and 5.15
Evenings at 8.15
SUNDAY FOR CLUB MEMBERS 8.15 only

Wednesday, 23rd December, to Saturday, 9th January

ALICE IN WONDERLAND and THROUGH THE LOOKING GLASS

Characters in order of appearance:—

ACT I

Alice	JULIA LOCKWOOD
The White Rabbit	NORMAN OSBORNE
The Caterpillar	BILLY THATCHER
Frog Footman	FRANK ATKINSON
Fish Footman	DAVID SCOTT
The Duchess	MAIDIE ANDREWS
Cheshire Cat	GORDON WHITING
Cook	DAVID HOWARTH
Mad Hatter	PETER BUTTERWORTH
March Hare	BILLY THATCHER
Dormouse	ROSEMARY GILES

ACT II

Gardeners	ROSEMARY GILES, ANN NORCOMBE
Guards	SUSANNAH CLAY, ROSEMARY WHITEHEAD
Executioner	ANNEKE WELLYS
Knave of Hearts	DAVID SCOTT
Soldier	DIANE WEST
Queen of Hearts	WYNNE CLARK
King of Hearts	JONATHAN FIELD
Gryphon	GORDON WHITING
Mock Turtle	FRANK ATKINSON

ACT III

White Queen	MAIDIE ANDREWS
White King	NORMAN OSBORNE
Tiger Lily	ANNEKE WELLYS
Rose	DIANE WEST
Violet	SUSANNAH CLAY
Larkspur	ROSEMARY WHITEHEAD
Daisy	ANN NORCOMBE
Red Queen	WYNNE CLARK
Guard	DAVID SCOTT
Old Gentleman	ROSEMARY GILES
Other Passengers	ANN NORCOMBE, SUSANNAH CLAY
Horse	DAVID HOWARTH, NORMAN PEPPERELL
Signpost	ROSEMARY WHITEHEAD
Tweedledum	BILLY THATCHER
Tweedledee	JONATHAN FIELD
Humpty Dumpty	GORDON WHITING
White Knight	PETER BUTTERWORTH
Leg of Mutton	ANN NORCOMBE
Pudding	ROSEMARY GILES

Directed by **JONATHAN FIELD** Settings by **ELIZABETH TAPLAY**
At the Piano **CYNTHIA DELL** and **PHILIP KENDALL**
ACT I Alice in Wonderland
ACT II Alice in Wonderland
ACT III Through the Looking Glass
Lighting by **Michael Northen.** Special properties by **Phillis Jerrold.**

Toys by Galloways of Chiswick High Street. Teapot by Matthaies Café. Telescope and binoculars by Negretti and Zambra. Tea by Lyons of Cadby Hall. Milk by Carnation. Tyre by E. S. Motors, Chiswick High Street. Virginia Cigarettes by Abdulla.

Stage Manager	JILL RUSSELL
Assistant Stage Manager	CHRISTINA LAWTON
Scenic Artist	ANN RALEY
Property Mistress	PHILLIS JERROLD
Master Carppnter	HARRY PEGG
Electrician	N. S. PEPPERELL
Press Representative	GEORGE PEARON
Business Manager	BRUCE MONTGOMERY
General Manager	WILLIAM SHARPE

REFER CENTRE PAGE FOR FUTURE ATTRACTIONS

We girls have a crush on Jean Kent and leave her notes in the dressing room. We have an exhibition of our last terms paintings on display. My mother comes with Robin and I'm so excited to be able to show them *The Dutch Farm* in the foyer of the theatre.

Because of Alice, I have to stay in London for Christmas. The Craxtons have an enormous tree in the studio full of candles and we make a little Christmas scene, with Sylvia directing me. I enter the studio in my wispy costume, playing The Spirit of What's to Come and I 'dry' utterly, looking at this audience of Craxtonites. But I am gently prompted and finish my speech. So different from Christmas with Roy, who always gets drunk and ruins everything by rowing with my mother. Mrs. Craxton has given me a beautiful dress. It's a sort of blue tartan with a lace collar and I love it. I wear it for the Christmas party. The panelled doors to the study and interconnecting doors from the study to the studio all fold back so that the entire space is open and can hold at least five hundred people.

In the spring holidays we have to move the boat. This mooring has become too expensive. The boat hasn't got a motor so we will be towed a few miles downstream past Windsor and we have a new mooring just before the Albert Bridge in Datchet. This is cheaper, as there is no electricity. My mother is prepared for this and has bought some antique oil lamps. She will miss the television but has been given a wind up gramophone by a potential beau, seen off smartly by Roy.

'Huh! Going to woo you with Mozart is he?' He sniggers and taunts. The Beau doesn't return - she keeps the gramophone.

♫ *This old house ain't got no windows* ♫
- Rosemary Clooney

The day of the great move arrives and I'm thrilled to be inside while the boat is moving down the river. I'm writing a letter to Robin on my mother's typewriter.

'Dear Robin,
Guess what? We're moving down the river!'

At the first lock, as we slowly slide in, there is a ghastly crunching and cracking sound; all the windows that are wider than the boat have been torn off. Chaos and commotion! It takes ages to get these replaced, and my mother can't afford it, so we are an embarrassing eyesore with our makeshift plastic windows because this mooring looks out across the fields to Windsor Castle. It's on the edge of the golf course and it's much easier for me to get to by train on Friday nights. In the winter I get the tube to Waterloo and then the train to Datchet. I then have a couple of miles to walk across the golf course in the dark which scares me. I put on a deep cough and I hope nasty men don't know it's me. There are no streetlights and I always dread it. Sometimes my mother meets me half way and it's always a great relief to see her torch in the distance. I am stronger now, and I can row my dinghy down the stream to Old Windsor, and upstream to the Eton College playing fields. I go back to London early on Monday morning.

The River at Old Windsor

I'm beginning to want to spend all my weekends with the Craxtons, or with Toots and her mother. I love Toots's mum. But my mother is very good at making me feel guilty. It begins to be an ongoing battle.

Miss Lockwood - we children call her that as a mark of respect - loves to tell this story of how she is leaving her digs one morning in

Glasgow on her way down to the theatre. Her landlady calls loudly after her down the street,

'Miss Lockwood, Miss Lockwood! Would you remind removing the piss pot from under the bed? The steam rises and rusts the springs!' Sometimes Toot's mum sends the studio car to fetch us. We sit together, two inky-fingered giggling schoolgirls, in the back of a large chauffeur-driven Daimler.

Later that first year I appear in a television play - *Lost in Time.* It's made at the BBC's studios at Lime Grove.

Rehearsal rooms are etched in my memory. The tape on the floor, the chairs stacked denoting walls. If it's above a pub, then the smell of stale beer; the script holders we all had; the tea breaks. When I tell the mature actress who plays with me,

'Oh, I'm so nervous,' she says

'There's nothing to be nervous about, my dear.' But on the live transmission, she hands me a tea cup which is rattling, her hand is shaking so much.

I have snippets of memories … I'm at the BBC studios at Alexandra Palace, I'm sitting on the grass in an Elizabethan costume when I have this strong feeling and I seem to know how to sit in a Tudor skirt. I'm playing Lady Jane Grey. With Tracy Reed in Jane Eyre. A Victorian workhouse. A story about Mombassa in which I have to wear shorts and my kneecaps wobble in fear! Also, in a cowboy story where Australian actor Vincent Ball, has a line,

'Sure t'ing, boss,' which makes us all laugh.

I am being trained by the BBC and it is all live TV. In *Passage of Arms,* with Patricia Garwood, we have lovely costumes, because it is set in France in the 18th century. I have to ride a horse side-saddle. *Hooray!* I think but my excitement turns to dread when I climb up on a sleepy old hack. The director says,

'So Anneke, you will canter up to the camera …' *How am I going to make this horse walk,* I think, *never mind canter!* At the sound of 'Action!' however, my steed becomes a charger and I'm all but thrown. The horse is an old professional.

I go up for a part in a play called *The Mouse Trap*. Everyone at the audition has these shoes with a little strap across the instep. I can't afford them so I've cut and sewn a piece of leather onto a piece of elastic and then it looks as though my shoes also have a strap. I'm very pleased with my creativity! They are lining us up in order of height. To me they say,

'Can you take your shoes off?' Now I'm standing with my little straps showing. The director comes up to the footlights and peers at my toes.

'Hmmm, very ingenious.' I'm covered in shame, the other girls are smirking and I don't get the part.

Back at school, Mrs. Martindale presides at the reception desk. She has forties curls and a tweed suit with velvet cuffs and collar and nothing escapes her. She is a tyrant. One of the rules is about tied back hair. We love to have flowing locks and so we wear a band around our wrists that can be whipped on when we pass her desk and whipped off immediately afterwards. One day, she tries to catch me but I'm too quick, so seething with cruelty she punishes me because it is not the school colours, and gives me a thousand lines…

I must not tie my hair back with a green elastic band.

One. Thousand. Times.

Mr. Craxton protests and writes to the school. They compromise with five hundred lines. The whole class helps me and with a bold look in my eye I hand in pages of lines … all in different handwriting ...

A couple of Canadian sisters come to the school, Primrose and Claire Coulter. Claire will go on to become one of Canada's most-respected actresses. They tell us of a riding school in Norfolk. We are excited by this and a group of us go up in the spring holidays to Miss Lettice Bouwens's for the first time. Parents put us on the train at Liverpool Street, we change at Brandon onto the Watton Flyer, and we are met by Miss Bouwens who wears corduroy trousers and a leather jacket. She has round, metal specs, and a sweet face, and a withered arm from being run over by horses.

Robin and Carolyn Garnham playing croquet

Jasper and his elder sister, and Robin with his birthday cake in Eton High Street

We all pile onto the open, rubber-wheeled cart with our luggage and with a click of the reins we are off for adventures at Caudle Springs.

It's a very old farmhouse, with bedrooms full of iron bunk beds and horse blankets. It's all a bit rough and we love it. She has a string of assorted ponies which we will ride every day for two and half hours, after which we can do what we like.

We have to go into the fields to catch our ponies – I'm riding Tommy – he likes to stand in the middle of a patch of nettles grinning at me! We ride bareback to the stables where we groom them and saddle up and go off for our ride. There is an outside toilet – I don't want to go out in the dark so upstairs in the dormitory I pee into a jam jar that we use to put flowers in, but I can't stop, and it flows over and onto the floor! All my friends are giggling. A day or so later we are playing 'Racing Demons', when Miss Bouwens looks up,

'Hmm, a curious stain has developed on the ceiling!'

Miss Bouwens is a fanatic 'Racing Demon' player – no-one can beat her – she is so quick. She has found out that we've been scrumping in her neighbours' orchards – delicious English apples. So now she send us into Watton to buy some more, so we can return them with apologies. Grumbling, we set off on foot for the five mile round trip. When we get to Watton, it's half-day closing – everything is shut – no apples. We walk back and tell Miss Bouwens.

'Oh dear! I must have forgotten!' She is twinkling with amusement.

She cooks us fish pie and apple and blackberry crumble and gives us lots of tea and toast. We will go back there for years; in the later years, we are breaking ponies in for her and going to gymkhanas. She is breeding Palominos, and the stallion is an Arab called Prince of Orange. In the evenings we will blanket stitch the horse blankets that have rough edges. In the spring holidays I'm given a young pony to tame. Sitting in the corner of a stable reading my book while in the other corner a trembling wild pony who I ignore. After a while a soft velvety nose is inquisitively nibbling my ear. By the end of this year in the summer holidays I will have broken this pony in and be jumping him bareback. The sweetest relationship. A week at Miss Bouwens's will cost 11 guineas, which is a lot for my mother but she always manages.

At Miss Bouwens's

In the middle of the night at the Craxtons I am woken by a voice down in the road.

'Hello, hello! it's John! Come down, I don't want to wake mother!' I run down in my nightie to find John Craxton heaving paintings wrapped up in Greek blankets out of a taxi.

'I have no money!'

'Never mind …' Mrs. Craxton is there, behind me. 'Have you eaten?'

I sit in the kitchen with John as he tells his adventures. He has been living in Crete with Lucien Freud and Mrs. Craxton is feeding him soup and bread and treacle tart. It's love at first sight. I'm smitten. I will love this man for my whole life.

Now, life at the Craxton's has another dimension! John takes me everywhere, to wonderful markets in the East End, where we eat salt beef sandwiches in huge Jewish cafés early in the morning, looking for bargains. We go to Greek haunts in Soho, and sale rooms where we will find furniture that will be brought back to Kidderpore where it will be stripped of paint in the basement workshops and sanded and waxed and added to the house. We find the dining table, I don't think much of it but he excitedly bids for it.

It is terribly big, and black, but he knows, underneath it is very early Italian marquetry.

It's still in the dining room today.

He takes me to parties at the Royal Opera House, where he is doing the sets and costumes for Ravel's *Daphnis et Chloe* so I get to meet Margot Fonteyn who is his friend and one of his many lovers. And Lucien Freud, who John says will be very interested in me if he introduces me as Princess Anna Katarina, so he does - and he is! John smokes Gauloises, wears tartan trousers and a Matlow shirt. He paints huge canvases in his studio. He rides a motorbike, and speaks fluent French and Greek. Moira Shearer and Ludovic Kennedy are amongst his friends. He tells me about Peggy Ashcroft. How she is a wonderful actress, because her interests and knowledge are vast, and not just about the theatre. I hear this and I try to follow.

I go to parties in my school skirt because it's the best thing I have. So it's strange to think of John taking me everywhere – I'm thirteen! One time in the kitchen he says he will wait for me to grow up and he will marry me.

He is doing an exhibition at the Leicester Galleries so he's working on one of his canvasses, eyes squeezed up against the smoke curling from his Gauloise, his elegant hands with paintbrush, poised. Changing, altering, he will work on one canvas for months and months. And I love the smell of turpentine and linseed oil. It is fascinating for me to watch it change and evolve. He will have me model for him and will do a portrait of me, but he gives up because, he says I've 'got an impossible nose'! We go to see one of his paintings hanging in the Tate. He pulls the sleeve of his sweater down and with a disapproving 'Tut, tut.' – he dusts it! The gallery attendant comes rushing –

'It's alright,' says John, 'It's my work!'

At night I sit in my red baby doll pyjamas, looking at books of the great painters, El Greco and Velasques. He teaches me so much. Mrs Craxton will eventually come up at eleven and say,

'Now John, let her go to bed, she's got school in the morning.'

Mrs. Craxton has organised piano lessons for me. *Horrors!* Now I have to tinkle away, my foot firmly on the soft pedal, creasing up with embarrassment at the thought of the Craxton family listening.

She has a 'healer woman' called Mrs. Star who lives in Golders Green. The family are derisive, and love to joke about her. I have hurt my back riding so I go to Mrs Star. She massages me with herb oils, and wraps me in a warm blanket. I am to take some tiny homeopathic pills. Next day I forget I even had a bad back.

♬ *Cherry Pink and Apple Blossom White* ♬
- Eddie Calvert

I'm playing truant. Instead of studying the tin mining of Newcastle, I go the Baker Street Classic to see marvellous films like *Gigi, The Love of Seven Dolls, The Little World of Don Camillo* and *American in Paris.*

My mother and Robin become jealous of my life at the Craxtons' and of John in particular. So to put him down they tell me he is a homosexual. I say,

'No he's not! ... what is that?' They don't elaborate. So one time, coming home on the top of the 13 bus with John, I say,

'Are you a homosexual?' He is amused and teases me.

'What do you think that means?'

'I don't know. But are you?'

'Yes', he says, but also doesn't explain. One day Mrs. Craxton says,

'Call John and Spud down for lunch, will you?' Spud is John's friend, a lovely man and a great friend of the Craxton family who wears black leather and has a motorbike. I go up and knock on John's door.

'Lunch is ready!' As I put my head round the door, there is Spud, doing rude things to John.

'Goodness!' I think, and go back downstairs. I don't understand but this is John, and if that's what he does … well, it must be alright.

Homosexuality is illegal at this time. However, groping and flashing is rife and I suffer endlessly. In an enclosed carriage one day, on the train to London, I am crammed in with the other commuters. The man next to me masturbates to a climax under his newspaper, which of course, is *rattling!* No-one says a word … British reserve. And in the tubes, and on the buses, and especially in the deep fogs we used to have. There they are, the armies of 'wankers'!

We students are taken to see the Diaghilev Exhibition at Hyde Park. In awe we walk down a wide, white, marble staircase. Ahead of us, mounted on a marble plinth, is a beautiful woman draped in silk and flowers sleeping on silk pillows. Behind are deep dark woods with birds calling softly and a mist and all this behind layers of gauze so it's like a dream and there is haunting music playing. I'm totally spellbound. We see the designs and costumes and music of the Russian Ballet. I've got this funny feeling – like *I know it.* There's Nijinsky, the greatest dancer of all time, Karsavina's shoes, Leon Bakst costumes. On our way home sitting on top of the bus going around Hyde Park corner, the statue of Boadicea is lit up in the sunset. The horses are rearing. It's incandescent. I am transported.

After I've been in the TV series *The Prince and the Pauper* with two good-looking Welsh twins, I go up for a part where they need two girls who look alike. When I see a picture of the girl they're trying to match, I say,

'You don't want me!' to the surprised director, 'You want my friend Anna Casteldini. She looks just like this girl!' Anna gets the part. Even at 14, for me, it was more important to get the authenticity of the piece, than for me to get the part.

Christopher Beeny and I work together again in a series called *The Grove Family.* I play Olive - The Freak With Hair Like a Leek! I have my first screen kiss.

In 1955 I do a series called *The Blakes.* It's about a family who cut their losses and take off in a bus. I love the location, and being on this converted bus in the country lanes. It's like a holiday Robin and I had in Holland. We went to Texel, an island in the north; we stayed with a young woman and her older husband. They had a farm and we children slept in converted buses. We spent a day driving around the vast sandy beaches on a cart with a horse, collecting wood, and by the end of the day we were sitting with the old man on top of a huge pile. He got drunk and did rude dances with his

Billy goat. His wife picked plate after plate off the wooden racks and hurled them at him, and he swore appallingly in Boer Dutch, which Robin and I repeated verbatim to our mother to shock her when she met us at Harwich. On the London train she insisted, as she had no money at all, that we went to the restaurant car and had a 'feast on tick' -

'I'll just give the waiter my address.' I couldn't bear the embarrassment so while they tucked into a roast dinner with jam tart and custard I insisted that I wasn't hungry. As it happened, when we pulled into Liverpool Street station, our waiter was worked off his feet and forgot to give us a bill at all!

Chapter 8

Sketches of Spain

It's 1955 and I have told everyone,

'We're going to Spain!'

Spain! *So exotic!*

We get into the train and my mother wants us to have the compartment to ourselves. She takes out her lipstick and paints us with spots. The next unsuspecting passenger to open the door is greeted with three grinning, spotty faces and,

'Yes, come in! My children have chicken pox, though, do you mind?' We settle down to a pleasant and private train journey. This trick turns out to be so successful we will use it often in the future.

We go by boat and then get the train down through France across the mountains to Narbonne. We have a very long night on uncomfortable hard seats. At 5 o'clock in the morning we go to the restaurant car where Robin, because of his fluent French, manages to get us breakfast for 4 shillings each. We then catch a bus to a tiny little fishing village on the Costa Brava called Estartit.

Robin writes a letter to his girlfriend, Eva Lisa.

'As the sun dropped in crimson splendour behind pine trees laced with evening mist like damp gauze - climbing in a tiny bus out of Port Bou – we teetered on the edge - and could see the red mountains dive straight into the sea - bluer than blue - towns cling crazily on the edge almost as if the mountains might expand their chests and the villages would fly out into the Mediterranean like shirt buttons coming off.'

Robin, you were always the writer.

We see oleanders and hear cicadas at night, and Robin and my mother love to smoke celtas – black tobacco – 2/6d for 100. We watch the ancient circle dances, the sardanas, espadrilles dancing in the dust. There are white-washed villages and coloured washing lines. We see a festival in Gerona. They are all carrying candles and wearing pointed hoods, chanting in the streets. It's rather spooky. There are pots of magnolias and jasmine and there are geraniums everywhere.

Estartit has windy cobbled streets. Old ladies in black are sitting in their doorways. Everyone seems to own a donkey. There is just one bar, a sort of shack on the beach. It is a place of spectacular beauty. For us it is a revelation to see the countryside, the landscape changing and the people and the climate. Robin gets outrageously drunk on the first night we are there and my mother is furious with him. We all begin our love affair with that rugged coast.

My mother loves to tell everyone how she met Ernest Hemingway in France before the war. *The Old Man and the Sea* is her favourite book. And now she is determined that we should experience a bullfight. Nicholas is left with the adoring wife of the hotel owner, and we take a bus to a local town. The massive circular walls of the bullring are impressive in the late afternoon sunlight. Large crowds are piling in to witness this 'dramatic dance of death'. The brave bull, the romantic matador. The ancient stone seats are uncomfortable and Robin and I are laughing because the whole audience is munching away on peanuts and throwing the shells on the floor. At last, we hear the ear-splitting fanfares. The horses and riders enter and parade around. They are wearing flapping armour like 11th century knights. And I'm upset to see that the horses are blindfolded. More fanfares and the entry of the bull.

'But he's so small!' I say to my mother. And to me he seems bewildered. The horse-riders take an interminable time sticking lances into the bull's neck ... blood is pouring in the dust.

'Olé!' More fanfares and now at last the Matador enters to wild acclaim. This is just like the ubiquitous posters – (every coffee bar has a bullfight poster on the wall). The Matador wears silk stockings, patent leather shoes, high tight pants, his chest puffed up in white lace, the red silk cloak. He struts around to ecstatic cheers.

'Olé!' The bull can hardly see through the blood streaming down his face. A sweep of the cloak. The bull is staggering now, and the matador pierces him with his sword. Hmm, not quite good enough, so on the next pass he picks it out and has another go.

'Olé!' Now the bull is on its knees in agony and I'm being sick among the peanut shells. We beat our way out of the frenzied crowd. To hell with Hemingway, this is disgusting cruelty. I'm fourteen and I'm deeply upset. That night on the beach Robin quotes Tennyson's *The Revenge*,

'Then spake Sir Richard, to hell with the don and devildom....'

When we leave we are laden up with litres of wine and sombreros. We get on the train to Calais the customs officials tell us,

'You won't get away with so much wine on the other side.' It's going to be a very rough crossing so Robin, Nicholas and I make for the lounge to sit on the floor. We realise we haven't seen my mother, we search the boat which is not easy because it's heaving - and so are most of the passengers. We find her snuggled under blankets in a corner in the bows, blissfully asleep and burping happily!

'Well, I wasn't going to let the customs have all our lovely wine!' Now Robin and I have to get a drunken and protesting mother and a sleepy 5 year old Nicholas home to Datchet.

♫ *Just walking in the rain* ♫
- Johnny Ray

John Craxton takes me to see a review with Margot Fonteyn and Lucien Freud, it's called *Cranks*, written by John Cranko - Annie Ross and Anthony Newley are also in it. John Piper has done the sets - it's fast and funny, and I don't get half of it. We go to a party afterwards with Margot Fonteyn and Lucien Freud.

Professor Harold Craxton – this wonderful old man - and I will sit on stools behind the kitchen door and listen religiously to *The Goon Show* on the 'wireless' at nine o'clock every Thursday night. He and I also watch *Son of Fred* on the television with Spike Milligan, Peter Sellars and The Alberts. We love this. I am proud that Mrs Craxton trusts me to iron his concert shirts.

Left: Spike Milligan, Peter Sellars and The Alberts in *Son of Fred*
Right: Harold Craxton

I now have a friend called Tracy Reed. Her father is Anthony Pelissier, film director, and her mother, Penelope Dudley-Ward, is married to Carol Reed, the film director. I stay with her in an elegant house in Chelsea. I'm very envious of her lush petticoats, of her organdie-covered four-poster bed and her confidence. Her mother is delightfully forgetful – one time, when she steps out into the Kings Road to get into her car, her chauffeur says politely,

'Madam, your skirt.' She has her make-up and pearls but is in her petticoat. She makes us meringues. There is a walkway from their house through to Peter Ustinov's house and it has this vast aviary full of exotic birds, which is what I think Tracy is.

I want to show off my glamorous friend to Robin. He's 18 and definitely appreciative. She takes one look at him – he's very handsome – and says,

'I'll just slip into something more comfortable,' and comes down the stairs in a pencil slim skirt and high heels. He's impressed and I'm satisfied. Later, she and I become rivals at RADA.

Robin gets his call up papers - my mother and I are extremely worried about this, he will never survive National Service - he's so skinny and sensitive. We are greatly relieved when they refuse him on medical grounds - he's always had very bad asthma. So now he's got a job as a reporter on a local paper.

More trouble on the boat, this time the Dutch girl who's staying wakes up to find a foot of water around her bed. She paddles to the kitchen, makes a cup of tea, takes it into my mother and says,

'Good morning, Mrs Willys, I think we're sinking.' My mother makes headlines in the local paper - *CAPTAIN REFUSES TO LEAVE HER SHIP!* But as she says,

'Well, they were going to come and fix the hole and I had work to do so I just sat on a tall stool in my wellies to type my letters.'

Nicholas has beautiful blond hair, very long, dangling in his nose and lovely brown eyes. One day he gets fed up and takes a pair of scissors and cuts himself a little window in his fringe. He always has a dog at his heels. Robin also has these brown eyes, as do I. It all comes from my mother.

♫ *One, two, three o' clock, four, o' clock rock,* ♫

Robin and I love Bill Haley, and are practising this new 'rock and roll'! At The Craxtons, I now have a record player and I'm secretively listening to the Blues - John and I listen to Chet Baker singing *My Funny Valentine.* John will sit down at Mr. Craxton's *Bluthner* and extemporise - lilting mournful Greek type music - his long fingers dancing over the keys - a Gauloise hanging from his mouth.

We move again, to a mooring in a caravan park near Clewer, the other side of Windsor, which is more congenial for my mother as she has lots of neighbours along the towpath. Her sister Tilly has been living with Stanley Parker since the war years. They have a little cabin cruiser and we love sitting drinking tea in the open back bit while Stanley fishes. When I come home from school my mother has been showing off to her neighbours about her actress daughter and they tease her, saying,

'Well she don't look like a film star.'

'Well no,' says my mother. 'Do you think she should wear a mink coat?'

Friday April the 6th 1956. Back at Miss Bouwen's, Pat Garwood is writing her diary. I am 15. On the train going up to Norfolk, American soldiers are asking if we would like a drink.

The week is spent riding and catching ponies and eating fish pie and playing racing demons as usual but now there are some local boys who wait, with their bicycles at the gate. Andy and Killer (!). We are alternatively rejecting and egging them on and receiving little notes with bunches of violets and ragging around in the haystack.

On Wednesday the 11th we go to White Hall because they have a television and I am appearing in *African Holiday*. It's a lovely place and we feel out of place in our jeans. We see Dirk Bogarde in *Doctor at Sea* at the Watton cinema with Miss Bouwens and our week is quickly and sadly up

I have a friend called Naiad Ellis. She is very pretty with a thick fringe and sparkling blue eyes. She lives in a big posh house close by. I get to see the huge collection of shoes her mother owns. There are tennis courts and vegetable gardens and gardeners. She comes to stay the night on the boat and is telling us how her mother won't allow her to help herself to the strawberries.

'Right!' says my mother, 'Let's go on a raid!' So in the middle of the night the three of us walk to Naiad's house with torches. We let ourselves in through the big front gates. Whispering and giggling, we go to the vegetable gardens – we're lifting the nets off the strawberry beds and helping ourselves. With our arms full, we skidaddle back to the boat for a feast.

Chapter 9

The Railway Children

It's 1957, and I audition for Dorothea Brooking and Patrick Dowling for the part of Roberta – Bobby - in the BBC's eight week production of *The Railway Children.* I'm really thrilled when I hear that I have got the part - I read the book and I love the story. I meet up with Cavan Kendall and Sandra Michaels at Berman's for the costumes. I love this place, the wardrobes filled with costumes from all the ages - we are to wear the Edwardian style. They squeeze me into a sailor top which is too small, so they add on extra cuffs which will itch me for the next 8 weeks. Sandra and I have genuine boots of the time, not that comfy, but we love the long frilly aprons and tam 'o' shantas and red flannel petticoats.

Now we start the filming with our brilliant cast – Sandra and Cavan, Jean Anderson, Donald Morley, Norman Shelley, Richard Warner. The railway scenes are filmed in Kent on the Bluebell Railway - the old station - and the train! We film a few days with the train. The story is that we must stop this train, as there is an injured boy in the tunnel on the tracks. So Phyllis and Bobby tear up their red flannel petticoats to make flags. Standing in the centre of the tracks we ad lib,

'Stop! Stop! Please stop!' When we do the first rehearsal Patrick Dowling and the crew place a flag on the tracks to represent where *the children will be standing.* The train is around a bend in the distance so through megaphones they call,

'Cue the train!' and this wonderful old engine with a tall chimney comes puffing into sight. As it nears the spot its brakes are squealing to a halt, but it goes right over the flag and just manages to stop in front of the cameras.

'Don't worry.' says the engine driver, 'I'll get it right next time.' The next time it's a 'take'. Cavan, Sandra and I are very anxious and it's me who has to stand in the front.

'Action!' The train is steaming towards us getting bigger and bigger and is very frightening; we are madly waving our flags

'STOP! STOP! PLEASE STOP!' and it just manages to stop a couple of feet from where I'm standing. Then Bobby's knees buckle and she collapses on the line … *Yes!*

There are lots of different shots of us waving to the train, it is late February so it's cold but the sun shines and the station is all painted green. The production team takes great care to get the details right and are most upset when the BBC Photographer takes a picture for the front of the Radio Times which shows the modern signal box and also the white line which was painted for the blackouts during the war.

We children have chaperones, who will teach us to be punctual, travel with us on the buses and tubes, such patience they have during the rehearsals as they knit and watch the action encouraging and guiding us.

Our home is a huge set at Lime Grove and we have become a family. Jean Andersen plays our mother and today we are filming Bobby's birthday. I walk into our living room. Mother and Phyllis and Peter have decorated it. There's a pretty cake on the table and candles - our old gentleman is there and Mr. Perks. They are singing,

♫ Our darling Roberta,
No sorrow shall hurt her,
If we can prevent it,
Her whole life long. ♫

I say,

'Thank you, oh thank you!' with tears falling …

In the last episode, the moment when Bobby runs up the platform - the familiar figure emerging out of the steam - his face full of love and laughter - *Daddy, oh my Daddy* – into the arms of her long lost parent – has everyone in tears, including Michael Gough, who is watching it with his six year old daughter. He will tell me later how disturbingly attracted he was to this young, fifteen year old actress.

At the last transmission we have a party, and I am in floods of tears to have to leave everyone especially Pat Dowling who I have a big crush on.

Our production of *The Railway Children* will become one of the outstanding productions of its time.

Fifty years later I'm standing in a relative's farmhouse kitchen in Somerset when I'm told that a friend's father has never forgotten me. His name is Dowling.

'Patrick Dowling!' I say, 'He was the production manager on *The Railway Children*, this wonderful series I was in. I've never forgotten him either.' A few days later I am talking to him on the 'phone – he lives in Australia – and he's singing me the beautiful haunting music that was our theme tune, which I also have never forgotten. Grieg's Symphonic Dances. He says,

'It was the first major series I had worked on and I went on to do several more with Dorothea, until we did *Great Expectations*, which was too good! It got right up the nose of the drama department and an edict came down from on high forbidding children's programmes to do any more serial drama! Ah, happy days! It is so sad that all that early work is lost. And I think ours was a rather better production than the film, despite our having to do it on a shoestring.' He became an award winning children's TV producer with *Vision On* and *The Adventure Game*.

By this time I'm becoming recognised, people ask me,

'Were you in *The Railway Children*?'

'No,' I say. 'I know who you mean, and I do look like her, but it's not me.' I never wanted to stand out. I love anonymity.

The Craxtons watch me devotedly in *The Railway Children.*

This year there is a new programme on the television called *6-5-Special* that Pete Murray is introducing and on it, Lonnie Donegan sings *Rock Island Line* and Tommy Steele sings *I Never Felt More Like Singing the Blues.*

I'm beginning to meet boys. One is Kits Browning. His mother is Daphne du Maurier, the writer. Another one, Sean Hennessey, goes to Wellington School and sends me love letters. They land on the Craxton mat and are placed in that letter rack. These are innocent romances, a little kissing and lots of love letters. I've become a bit of a tease, I like to flirt but I don't want the boys to put their hands up my jumper because then they will discover my small breasts. It's a dangerous game. The boys at school – David Hemmings, Richard Gale – are pals. David Hemmings always has bogies in his nose, something I never forget. He is the first one of us at the Arts Educational to 'do it'

As far as we girls know, the boy will penetrate you, and it's very painful, and then you go into a sort of swoon - ever since I had my teeth out I've been afraid of being unconscious. The whole business doesn't sound very appealing - better to stick with crushes and secretive, delicious kissing. And if he isn't wearing a 'French Letter', you'll get pregnant. Abortion is illegal, and there are awful stories about *back street operations*; it's a dark and frightening prospect.

♫ *Que sera, sera* ♫
- Doris Day

I'm sitting in the boat doing the laundry with my mother one sunny afternoon when we suddenly hear a gurgling sound.

'Do you hear that?'

'What is it?'

'I don't know, lift up the carpet - it's under the floorboards.' We prise one up and see water trickling.

'Oh my God I think we're sinking, quick put something over it!' I get a book and put it over the hole and weigh it down with a fire extinguisher. With a whooshing sound both book and extinguisher are sucked down through the hole, which is now huge. WE REALLY ARE SINKING! My mother is running up the towpath calling for help while I still try to bung the now gaping hole. The fire engines are quick to arrive. They start briskly pumping the water out as fast as it is coming in. Meanwhile we are throwing everything onto the towpath: out of the windows, the doors and the hatches, we're chucking bedding and books, pots and pans, clothes and crockery – it's chaos.

I sit with her typewriter on top of the heap.

'Dear Robin … Guess what? We sank!'

When the boat is emptied, they call,

'Alright! Let her go!' and gurgling and bubbling, she heads for the bottom of the Thames. It's not that deep so the deck is just submerged. Before we can get the wreckers to come, it is towed to the other side of the river where it sits, listing forlornly, with the water lapping around the built-in table. It had been our home for seven years.

My mother has to pay a £200 fine for having a wreck in the river and as she tells everybody, it's all because she didn't bother to get her *bottom done!*

Diana Dors comes down the river in a motor launch and climbs onboard this 'wreck' with her husband, Dennis Hamilton.

It is true that over the years people have warned my mother that she should get the boat into dry dock and get the keel overhauled, but it was costly and as she always lives from one fiver to the next, she has simply ignored the problem and hoped it would go away. We are put up in a flat above the public loos in the caravan site until we find our next abode, which is little cottage near Chobham. The owners live down the country road in a huge Elizabethan barn by the side of a lake. They have a son – Jack – he becomes my holiday boyfriend. My mother has taken to sunbathing on tin foil …

'To get the sides done!'

In early summer. Jack's parents are on holiday in France. My mother persuades me to go with her on a snoop. Their gardens are ebullient with roses and delphiniums and we steal massive bunches. As we are walking back down the drive, Jack and his parents are driving towards us. I want to jump in the ditch and hide. My mother waves imperiously at them to stop, her arms filled with their flowers. They wind the window down,

'I'm so glad to catch you,' says my mother, brazenly. 'You must call a plumber, because the pipes are blocked. Had a nice holiday? Good, good.' And she dismisses them. Jack is winking at me from the back window.

During the winter holidays Jack and I are skating on the frozen lake. I have learned at Queensway Skating Rink in Bayswater – but this is something else! I feel as though I have wings – such freedom as we fly across the frosty expanse in the gloaming.

I have made Nicholas's teddy bear a passport – *Edward Bear* – because we are off to Rotterdam to stay with a friend in her large, modern flat overlooking the Maas. The customs officials, this time, kindly stamp Edward's passport. From the flat we look out at night over the twinkling lights of the huge ships – The Holland-America Line. On the harbour-side are brightly coloured cafés called 'poffertje kraans'. Over a fire, a chef flips many little pancakes. We get a pile on our plates, dusted with icing sugar. When we've eaten our first plateful, we are given another right on top. Some of the other customers have big piles of plates in front of them.

Back home, we have to move once again – this time we've found a lovely little white, Victorian, detached house in Datchet.

Chapter 10

Datchet Days

The owner of our new home is an artist, and he has painted it wonderful colours – the kitchen is yellow, the sitting room red. Robin moves in here as he's working now on the *Windsor, Slough and Eton Express.* Nicholas goes to the local school. Life goes on.

By the time we move to Datchet, Roy is no longer living with us. He will just return occasionally, like at Christmas or her birthday to get drunk, cause a scene, beat her up and then leave again. Robin and I are becoming increasingly exasperated with her.

On a Sunday night I get a tummy ache, and during the night it gets worse. By Monday morning instead of going to school in London, I'm rolling around on the floor in agony. My mother calls the Doctor, who takes one look at me and sniffs,

'Ask her what her first lesson of today is! - probably wants to get off school' - he leaves and I'm still in a very bad way. My mother calls another doctor. He comes. The next minute I'm in the ambulance, bells ringing on the way to Slough Hospital - emergency. They whip out my appendix which undoubtedly would have burst moments later and I'd have been dead. I lose all faith in Doctors. They show it to me because they are impressed with how large it has become. While I'm lying in the ward recovering I'm imagining them cutting my tummy open. I have a vivid imagination, and it scares me. Robin brings me a book by Spike Milligan which makes me laugh and this makes it worse.

'No! don't! I'll split my stitches'.

Opa comes to visit us in Datchet. Our darling old Grandfather, still in his beret, but now he doesn't remember who we are and it upsets us all very much. The family find him a home in Holland,

and soon after, he dies aged 68. Losing his wife and daughter and starving in the war had curtailed his life.

My mother has to go to the dentist – she's never had to go in her life. She never eats sweet things so her teeth have always been good. Until now. Robin and I go with her to the surgery in Windsor because she's very scared. We don't quite trust her. We are in the waiting room,

'Just going to the lavvy,' she says. She's been gone too long. In the ladies, the ground floor window is swinging open – she's gone. What a liability is this woman, my mother!

Our house in Eton Road, Datchet has a good-sized garden so my mother plants lots of vegetables and there are large apple trees which in autumn deposit loads of apples all over next door's garden. The neighbour is an uptight old fart and he dumps them from his wheelbarrow all over our front door. My mother says she's going to retaliate by pooping on his front step. She loves the idea of him setting off to work in his suit and … I hope she didn't.

Another time, she's reading her favourite O' Henry Short Stories and her specs snap in the middle of the frames so she dollops glue onto her forehead and sticks the specs to it so she can continue. Now someone is at the front door so she answers the door and pleads,

'You have to help me, my specs won't come off!'

The shops are quite a way so we take the wheel barrow to fill it up with the shopping. This is the brilliant idea of Robin's girlfriend, a beautiful Finnish girl called Eva-Lisa Kannikoski. He loves her for years, and one time, he dances on a table-top in a Cambridge pub declaring his love for her. She is the major love of his life. Although he has many girlfriends, Eva-Lisa is the most important to him.

Nicholas wakes me up with,

'There's a cow at the front door!'

'What? Go away, let me sleep.' He's insistent. We go down. Eva-Lisa, has left us a reindeer skin on the doorstep.

It is in Datchet that Robin shares his passion for jazz with me. Bix Beiderbecke and the Wolverines, Joe Turner - the boss of the blues, Coltrane, Chet Baker. We play all these LPs on his record player. He starts what will become his extensive collection.

My mother always loves to play Scrabble. We are allowed words in Dutch and French and later Spanish. Robin has passed 'A' level French so he is fluent.

'Come on, come on, what is *butterfly* in French?' They delight in this. I don't, I am hopeless at French. As his devoted sister, I am proud that Robin is so very bright. When he moves to London, she gets a lodger in the front room. He's a very reclusive man and never uses the kitchen or the bathroom, so she's always searching his room when he's out to see if he has a pee bottle, or what!

One day I go down to the students room at school and sitting on a table in a cloud of smoke is a strange creature with hair parted in the middle, very black made up eyes and puffing away with a long cigarette holder. Everyone seems captivated by her.

'Who are you?' I ask.

'Sarah Miles,' she drawls. 'I've just been expelled from Roedean.' We become friends. I spend weekends with her and her sweet brother Christopher, making home-made murder movies in her parents' lovely large and comfortable house in Ingatestone.

Sarah Miles is envious of my living at the Craxtons' - she's got digs near Baker Street. Now there is a major bus strike, it lasts for a week. Mrs. Craxton is in full swing - filling the Rolls Royce up with passengers. On the way home from school we stand at the bus queues and cars slow down to pick people up - one day it's a bubble car - Sarah and I both squash in. Next day it's a chauffeur driven Bentley with a crest on the side. No-one seems to dare so Sarah and I boldly jump in.

'Who's car is it?' we ask the young and rather dishy chauffeur - he's inscrutable and won't divulge the identity of the owner. We are shamelessly flirting with him and we set up a rendezvous at the Swiss Cottage Odeon. It's then that he tells us he works for the Rothschilds.

Sarah and I practise our autographs. She wants to change her name to Sarah Baskerville - she likes *The Hound of the Baskervilles*. I think that 'Anneke Delicatessen' has a good ring to it. She's a year ahead of me so she's off to RADA with Tracy Reed. Their parents can pay the fees.

I've met a boy called Guy Playfair. His father is a General. He's up at Cambridge, wears a duffle coat, plays jazz piano and trombone and writes me amazingly funny *Goon* type letters, which I love.

At school I sit next to Amanda Hoskyns-Abrahall. Her father works for the British Government in India so she has an address in Calcutta. This impresses me. She has a twin sister called Lucinda who goes to 'Tring', which is the boarding part of the Arts Educational in Hertfordshire. I'm fascinated that Amanda and Lucinda both get sore throats at the same time.

We students have formed deep bonds between us which will last our whole lives. Many of us will go on to have interesting careers within the theatrical world and we still have 'Arts Reunions'.

I get a part in a play. It's a new play written by Marghanita Laski and it's about life after nuclear devastation. This was ground-breaking stuff. I am to play the daughter. My parents and I are marooned in a devastated landscape with a black American soldier. They discuss the possibility that he and I will have to keep humanity going.

We rehearse in London and it will be premiered for two weeks at the Arts Theatre, Cambridge. *Goody goody!* I can get to see Guy Playfair - and his friends – I don't tell him about the play, which I want to keep as a surprise. So I write him a note to say I'm going to stay with Sarah Miles in Ingatestone and then I'll come and see him. He meets me off the train. Cambridge is plastered with notices for the play so he already knows! I'm wearing a sailor suit and a boater. He greets me with,

'And Ingatestones to you, too!'

Guy has got me digs and a bike. So now begins one of the most amazing few weeks of my life so far. I'm a very pretty teenager, I'm on the stage and I know some of the most talented students in Cambridge.

There is this wonderful pub called 'The Red Lion' where Guy and all his friends play jazz. Guy is at Pembroke College with Peter Cook, Alan Hickling, Roger Law, John Hopkins, Mark Hendy, Eleanor Bron, John Bird, Tim Birdsall, Bernard Philips, John Bulmer, John Fortune ... they are all here at Cambridge at this time.

The opening night is a moderate success. This is heavy stuff and it's definitely not going to transfer to London. But we get good reviews. Marghanita Laski is hugely respected. Gawn Grainger is in it. We have a grand party in the famous Art's Theatre green room on the first night. I get tiddly on cider for the first time. So I can't remember the combination lock on my bike and I have to push it home to my digs. I wear a large, man's pin-stripe shirt, tight jeans and sandals. I'm the first one on the stage and I always have to pee before I go on so they put a pot behind a screen for me. One matinee I'm looking out into the audience, and I see Mark Hendy, who I have a crush on, and my heart leaps and I'm off, dreaming. It's gone quiet on the stage, I turn around -

'Oh, it's me,' I say. A big lesson, I am so ashamed.

My mother comes to see the play. She's travelled by train. It's been a long journey. Now she's sitting comfortably in the dark when she hears me calling offstage

'Mummy, mummy!' So she replies,

'I'm here in the sitting room, darling.' Everyone around her laughs. She's so used to watching me on the television; she's forgotten she's in the theatre.

I love Cambridge. We go on the Backs in punts, of course. I meet John Hopkins – *Hoppy* - later famous for his 'Pot is Nice' placard in the Aldermaston demonstrations. Guy plays trombone and we dance and go to the pubs in the local countryside. At one party, we all fall asleep beside the river in the vintage car one of them has. It's very uncomfortable and, no sex yet, so sweet and innocent. Guy thinks he owns me and he can be violent and frightening. He persuades my mother that she should open my letters and keep an eye on me and report to him.

I am outraged! My letters, my life!

My mother has got me a holiday job. I am to accompany a famous circus owner - Billy Smart's son - and his wife and children, to Kitzbühel in Austria. I'm happy to be paid to go to the famous winter resort. On the outgoing flight I'm slightly disturbed because this nouveau riche couple are treating me like a servant. I am determined to make the most of it and try and get along with the two children who are very spoilt. I'm thrilled at the picturesque town in the snow and our lovely old fashioned Austrian Hotel. I'm also worried if this eiderdown thing on its own is going to keep me warm in this freezing weather - I have never seen a duvet before.

The parents are off to the ski schools so I take the children tobogganing. We heave our toboggan as high up the slopes as we can and when we climb on and start hurtling back down, we are hopelessly and dangerously out of control. Lines of ski classes are scattered like dominoes, everyone is shouting at us. So in the days to come we go to the skating rink instead.

During the two weeks I have made friends with the waiters and the other guests, one is old Lady Howard, and we get on very well. There is a huge wood basket by the fire in the hall which has leather straps and I give the young children in the hotel rides in it on my back.

The wife tells me 'not to speak to the waiters'. I am supposed to have my evenings free once the children have gone to sleep but these two spoilt brats never go to sleep. So by the time the holiday is over I've had enough. On the flight home the children are being sick and when I'm told by the parents to clear it up I refuse.

'My job is finished thank you.' When I relate this to my mother she's totally on my side.

'Well at least you got your wages before you told them to bugger off!'

At the end of the school year we have a day when school uniform needn't be worn. This is a torture for me because my school clothes are my best clothes. All the other girls come in cashmere coats and high heels. I persuade my Aunt Tilly to lend me hers. They are too small for me and I am in agony. When it is time to take my school certificate, it is nerve-racking. Over the years I have found a way of avoiding all the boring school classes - arithmetic and so on - spending my time with Mrs Scott in her domain, in the attics. She doesn't mind, I am her favourite. Or I'm hidden down in the cloak rooms. Or in the Baker Street classic. Or at rehearsals. Now I have these horrible exams to do. I fail miserably in all subjects. This will impact on my later life as I have to add up on my fingers and I am ashamed. But I do very well in art and literature, and get top marks.

For the Drama Cup, I do my 'Saint Joan' speech. When I'm finished, they are all in tears, and I'm amazed.

One of my best friends at school is Jennifer Creasey. She's very artistic. Her father is the author John Creasey. I love her. She goes on to Ealing Art School and I will go to the art school dances. Jiving, art-school style. Stompy, arms flailing, wearing black stockings and big long sweaters, wooden beads and hair in bunches, black eyes and pale pink lips.

She will go on to start Gingerbread - now a huge help centre for women and single parents.

My other friend, Philippa Coverdale, has a really fine family. They are Catholics. I love to go to Brompton Oratory for early morning mass. I love the beauty of the building, the candles and the incense … and the choir boys. One day, we are shopping and she realises that I have stolen a penknife. She gets hysterical and makes me put it back.

'It's a mortal sin, it's a mortal sin!'

Chapter 11

RADA

I really want to get into the Royal Academy of Dramatic Art because I want to 'learn to act'. I will have to try for a scholarship so now it's time to do my audition. I've been working hard on my three pieces and I go along to Gower Street and through the 'Hallowed Portals' and I'm very, very nervous. I do my pieces in front of the adjudicators in the Vanbrugh Theatre. It seems to have gone well, and on the top of the Number 13 bus, going up Finchley Road, I feel like I've got wings!

I am awarded the big scholarship of the year, fees, maintenance and everything.

On my first day there I'm so relieved to see Sarah Miles coming down the stairs but she loftily dismisses my greeting - I'm a new girl, not to be acknowledged. I'm very hurt by this and Tracy Reed isn't very friendly either. This first term is all about voice production, stage craft and all the things I'd been studying for the last five years so I'm sorry to say I am beginning to act up. I am unhappy at RADA, and I am rebelling against the 'old school' attitude. The Shakespeare teacher, Nell Carter, used to be in the Beerbohm Trees Company and has Sybil Thorndike's moves, which she follows down to the letter. She says,

'Now this is where you faint.' And I say,

'But why do I faint?' I'm objecting. Robin's taken me to see Marlon Brando in *On the Waterfront*, I've read about The Method. Stanislovsky. Acting teaching is changing. I want that. The only teacher I get on well with is John Broom, who is the movement teacher. Susannah York, Tom Courtenay, Albert Finney are all in the year ahead of me.

The aspiring 16-year old drama student, taken by Vivienne

I overhear Robin telling my mother that she should tell me the facts of life.

'Oh no', she says, 'she's far too young.'

I'm egotistically thinking,

'Ha! Too late, I know all about that!' But the fact is, I don't. There is no sex education, no information, no contraception, just this deep longing, wild urges, fear and deception. And yet virginity is definitely something to be got rid of, it is a stigma. *She's still a virgin.* So I get on with losing mine as soon as I can. There is a party in Slough. We are all quite drunk and I'm available. One of Robin's journalist friends, a married man, grabs me by the back door, and he rams himself into me. It's very painful and afterwards I feel sad and dirty and the next day when I look carefully into my eyes in the mirror, I don't look any different. *Everyone said I would.*

Robin buys me a dress. It's a blue wool 'Sack' - the latest thing - and I love it. He's the only man in my life to ever buy me a dress.

At RADA we girls wear pleated skirts and little high heels and dog-toothed-checked coats and scarves and little white gloves. We will wear roll-ons to keep our stomachs in but your skin looks all shrivelled when you take them off. We wear suspender belts. Soon I will wear a sweet little waspy which pinches my waist in.

I've fallen for Edward Fox. He has become a sweet gentle lover, and he has a lovely body. He is patient with my lack of experience as he is older than me. I take him to Datchet to meet my mother and they like each other very much.

After he leaves RADA he gets a part in *The Twelfth Night* at Dorking Rep and Robin and I drive over to see him on Robin's Vespa. He has wrinkly tights and isn't very good. We get drunk and laugh so much at the wrinkly tights, we keep falling off the Vespa on the way home.

There's a lot of rather pretentious *luvvie* behaviour at RADA,

'Daahling, did you seee Larry's perfooormance?' and so on.

At the end of the day the drama students will all gather in Olivellis. I prefer to go off to a coffee bar called 'The Partisan'. It is not far away, and it's where all the bohemians and political rebels hang out. There are tables with chess boards upstairs and down in the basement, jazz is played. I'm beginning to go to jazz clubs and I am jiving at Cy Lauries and Eel Pie Island, Acker Bilk's and Humphrey Lyttleton's - 'Humphs'.

Mrs. Craxton is wonderfully uncritical. She never says anything about the outrageous way I'm dressing, but will simply murmur quietly,
'Hmm, no need to gild the lily!'

When Mr. Craxton dies, in 1971, there is a huge memorial concert at the Festival Hall, with Princess Alexandra in attendance. For years my spirit will hover over that house in Kidderpore Avenue. Once again I will be running down to the front door in my nightie ... Many years later, in my commune days, I will be living and working in a house whose garden backs directly onto the Craxton's garden but I never walk around the corner, I'm too afraid to see it all altered. But it isn't, it's still there, run now as The Craxton Studios, with televisions still hidden in 18th century cupboards.

Between lying to Mrs. Craxton and my mother, I have been able to take off for illicit weekends to Cambridge with Edward Fox.

At RADA, all the first-term students have an interview with the Principal – John Fernald. At the end of which, he famously asks,
'Why do you want to become an actress?' Sarah loves to tell how she replied,
'An actress? I've wanted to be a *groom*, for years'. Now it's my turn. I am nervously twittering on about it 'being an act of love … you have to love the characters you portray …' John Fernald suggests that I do a secretarial course … just in case …
At the end of my first term at RADA my mother comes to see our end-of-term production. I'm playing a scene from *A Woman of No Importance* by Oscar Wilde. She thinks I'm very good.
'You really were that woman, I totally forgot it was you, and I felt her pain.' High praise indeed!
One sunny morning in the holidays my mother comes charging into my bedroom waving a letter.
'Get up! Get up! You've ruined everything! They've kicked you out!' I grab the letter, growling,

'You mustn't open my letters!' But here it is, my dismissal from RADA. I'm really shocked; I had pushed them too far with my rebellious behaviour … My mother is stomping back downstairs,

'Well, you'll have to get a job; I can't afford to keep you.'

So I get a job as a waitress in Eton High Street. There is a 16th century tea room called 'The Cock Pit', which is what it used to be. I wear a black dress and stockings and a little white apron and cuffs. I have a beehive and Louis heels, and I look adorable. I'm serving spaghetti to the Eton boys and their parents. The Eton boys wear top hats and look so sweet. I'm getting all the tips, so the old biddy waitresses decide to have a tip pool. Anyway, I don't care; I've made enough to get back to London.

I have to find somewhere to live, and get an agent. My time with the Craxtons is up. They are full with foreign music students. Guy's parents, General and Jocelyn Playfair, live in Ovington Square, and they will let me live in Guy's room while he is away at Cambridge. A huge, lovely room in the basement with its own kitchen and skylights, and I have it in exchange for cleaning their large house. They are another kind and intelligent couple and I enjoy drinking China tea with them in their first-floor drawing room, looking out over the plain trees in Ovington Square. Chelsea, full of temptations, is not far away.

Sarah has a little house in one of the pretty streets - *wouldn't she just* - and another school friend, Linda Bathurst, her father, Peter, a very good actor, has a coffee bar in the Kings Road called the 'Satortuga', with a pink round canopy over the door. This is the place to be!

I now have a yellow painted bicycle with a huge coconut basket in front so I can set off for any party that's happening, and there are lots. Later, we are referred to as 'The Chelsea Set' - we are notorious – Valentine Thynne, Brian Alexander, Suna Portman, Mim Scala, Johnny Gilbert, Kim Waterfield, the Campbell brothers, Johnny Summers, Katie Drew-Wilkinson (who I meet in California in the 80s – we have a dinner and we are rolling around on the floor in helpless laughter at the memories). They are heiresses and socialites and bums. And we party on the Circle Line, we party in St James's Square and we party in each other's houses. We jive in the nightclubs and in the jazz clubs – we are celebrating the beginning of freedom. The times are changing and we are on the way, breaking through the bonds of the old, stale, dead morality and the sixties are coming!

But freedom is not so easily achieved - while the boys are busy getting their ends away we girls will be secretly decorating the bedroom in our minds with our Dirk Bogarde look-alike husbands.

Much as I want to wander down the Kings Road in bare feet - with my Miles Davis LP under my arm - I have to get an agent, send off photos and letters from the lists that Equity has given me. I feel very alone. But one has replied and he seems nice so I go with him, John Varley. His outfit is small but he seems keen on me. The first thing he does is change my name. I've been working under the name of Anneke Willys quite successfully for 6 years.

'Better to try and Anglicise it,' he says. So it becomes Annika Wills which I don't like, and I won't use in this book! My mother has taught me to be very proud of my name. Occasionally, people would want to abbreviate it to Annie.

'No, no, Anneke is beautiful, she doesn't need a nickname.' But I just said *OK* to John Varley.

He gets me an interview with Michael Winner who takes me out to lunch in South Kensington, to discuss a forthcoming film. I think,

'Yay! this is it!' What a disappointment. I dislike everything about him, amazing that he can create that feeling in so many people however I need the work so I have to be polite. The film is about an Irish jockey and his love affair with an upper-crust girl. The actor they choose is a young Royal Shakespeare Company actor who is 4'6".

'Can you ride?' they ask.

'Yes,' he says, like all actors – say yes and then sort it out. He thinks he will get some lessons on Wimbledon Common before we start. We all fly off to a large hotel in Dunleary, Ireland.

Michael Winner is not popular. It's amazing because he knows it and his defence is to smile and smile. Keith and I do our love scenes sitting mostly on a bench – not very sexy but the height difference is tricky. Allan Ladd, a previous heart-throb, used to have his co-stars stand in a hole because he was quite short!

And then we are out on a race track and he is given a leg up on one of these huge, spectacular Irish racehorses who is trembling and with pink flaring nostrils and a ripple of muscles immediately takes off down the track. Keith hangs on briefly but then he's sliding sideways and crashing to the ground. All is angry confusion.

'You said you could ride!'

'Yes, well ...' When it is all sorted out he doesn't want to do it again and they have to get a double.

The crew and actors are planning a practical joke on Michael. The make-up girl and I carry it out. We get the maid to let us into his room. While we had been filming that day I had picked a plastic bag full of nettles. Now we carefully remake his bed 'apple pie style' - that is, the top sheet is folded under and back so you can't get in - but we put nettles in it, hugely pleased with ourselves. The next morning we are all down early for breakfast longing to see his reaction but he just smiles and smiles and doesn't let on. I never know what happens to that film. I think they ran out of money. There were rumours of Equity blacklisting it. It was all eclipsed by what happened next …

I'm flying home. The man next to me is reading his paper. On the front page is a photo of Edward Fox and Tracy Reed. They've got married. *Married?!* He is my boyfriend! How could he do that and not tell me? I've only been away two weeks! I'm devastated. This is my first heartbreak.

I go home to Datchet; my mother is also very upset.

'Huh, I bet she's pregnant,' she says, perceptively. I haven't heard a word from him and I'm sad. I've got another job, two episodes in a TV series starring Julian Holloway - *Don't Tell Father*. Julian is a sweetie and makes me laugh and I also like working with Noel Hood. We rehearse in London and the location is in the country. On my way to the rehearsal rooms in Hammersmith I'm hurrying along the Embankment, and leaning against the parapet is what I think is a sort of Teddy Boy. He's got scruffy Spanish boots and a leather jacket and long hair flopping over his dreamy blue eyes, and he's scowling.

'Excuse me is this the BBC rehearsal room?' I ask politely.

'Yes darling, you're in the right place.' Very posh, husky, voice.

I'm taken aback. Is he taking the mickey out of my accent? I go in and start the morning's work.

I'm working with Toots, so that's a treat. At lunchtime she says,

'I want you to meet my boyfriend, Simon Gough.' We go to the pub and I'm introduced to the Teddy Boy who turns out to be charming and funny and intelligent and son of Michael Gough.

'I saw your dad when I was nine,' I say. He and Toots are very much in love he calls her 'grey eyes.'

I get about £23 for a TV episode.

I've got two episodes in *Emergency Ward 10* with John Alderton, John Arnatt, Jane Rossington (later of *Crossroads*).

I've also got a role in *No Hiding Place*. It will be night shooting. And three episodes of *Probation Officer*. The stars of the show are John Paul, John Scott, Jessica Spencer and later, Honor Blackman will be in two episodes. I also work with Ian Hendry in Manchester on a *Television Playhouse* for Granada called *Ben Spray*. Work seems to be pouring in!

John Craxton has given me a special little waistcoat. It comes from Greece, dark brown goat fur inside, soft white chamois outside with little toggles. I treasure it. One of the guys in the Chelsea set I 'have a thing for' - Johnny Summers-admires it so I give it to him. *This begins a pattern – if I have something very prized, I give it away*. He also has nowhere to live at the moment, so as I have a small part coming up in Manchester I offer him three nights in my lovely room at the Playfairs while I'm away.

It's a TV play called *Three on a Gas Ring*, directed by Philip Saville.

He is a very enigmatic and sexy man. I'm attracted to and afraid of him. Alan Bates and Joanna Dunham are starring. I see a way of saving the expenses and getting a free train. I will hop on at Euston with Joanna; hide out in her sleeping carriage. When we arrive in the morning I sneak out and then walking down the corridor looking for the conductor, loudly asking,

'Do you know which is Miss Dunham's compartment?'

'Yes madam.' Joanna emerges, looking all surprised.

'Anneke! Darling! Thank you for meeting me!' And we are off to work. Very pleased with ourselves.

The writers are beginning to reflect and explore the new sexual openness and morally relaxed behaviour. We are enacting wild parties and louche carryings on. Alan Bates is so attractive; we all want to be in his company. Philip enacts a wall which I have to creep clingingly along. He's enjoying rubbing himself against me. This is beginning to happen more and more, the sex in rehearsals.

One time I'm working with Lawrence Payne when he says he'll give me a lift home. As we are driving through the streets of Ladbrooke Grove I notice that he has a damp look on his face.

'Do you like rubber?'

'Um … I'm not sure,'

'I have a lovely mackintosh that would fit you.'

'Oh, goodness!'

'Would you like to come home with me and try it on?'

'Let me out *here* please?!'

Three on a Gas Ring will be withdrawn by the Lord Chamberlain, because the unmarried mother in it 'was not contrite about her condition'.

When I note this today, it's hard to believe.

When I get back to Ovington Square early on Monday morning I can't get in, my front door is locked. A sleepy, half-clad strange girl comes to my door.

'What do you want?' I storm in. Johnny has had a party, booze and sleeping couples everywhere and the place is trashed.

'I'll give you half an hour,' I say and head off shaking with rage to the Kings Road.

The Playfairs kick me out - I go back to Datchet.

Chapter 11

The Alberts

Opposite me on the train from Waterloo sits an interesting-looking man. Sandy beard, blue eyes, white sailor's pants, a tatty old briefcase with a packet of spaghetti sticking out. We get talking, we can't stop. Before long, I have realised that he is Tony Gray, brother of Douglas Gray, who formed the hilarious double-act band known as The Alberts, and I had watched them with Mr. Craxton, in *Son of Fred.*

They are originals; they will be the inspiration for *The Temperance Seven* and *Monty Python*. Their father, a printer in the union, had got Tony and Douglas jobs driving newspaper delivery vans in the middle of the night. Douglas has a samovar in the back of his on which he brews his tea. They do this for three days a week which leaves them time to do their act, which is inspired lunacy. They are friends with Spike Milligan, and the marvellous Bruce Lacey. They attempt to fly the Hampstead Ponds in paper wings and leather goggles, all the while, dressed as 19th century figures, old Chelsea pensioner coats and boots. Douglas dresses as a Russian with boots and tunic and smokes a cigar. Tony plays trombone, Douglas the cornet. They invent the Dustbin Dance. They do their act in nightclubs off Trafalgar Square and they cause such a rumpus, the places have to be vacated, full of smoke and laughing people.

I go to meet Tony's family. They live in Windsor on the Kings Road, where I lived as a child, their house backing onto The Long Walk. Their son, Sinbad, will write a letter to the Queen.

'Dear Queen, I live under the shadow of your castle.'

Tony's wife Ann is a willowy blonde with hair to her waist and very direct eyes. Sheba, their white-haired baby. Their home is a revelation to me; I have never seen anything like it. They have knocked down all the walls, the space is open and full of colour and books and paintings and every bit of furniture is painted with flowers and designs. The kitchen walls have plates plastered in them. It is also in a permanent state of being finished. The yard has a mural with Mediterranean houses in the sun. One day they hear a knocking sound upstairs.

'Sinbad, what are you doing?' Sinbad, white haired, five years old, says solemnly,

'Fink I'll knock a wall down today.' He's got the hammer and the chisel and he's working on the wall *beneath his window*.

When this photograph was taken, Douglas's chair was too high. So Tony sawed the legs off.

This is a home of ongoing creativity and I love it. They have a Victorian hip bath in the garden. Ann will teach me how to sew. We make bikinis and peasant shirts and very full skirts. We go to the jumble sales and find Victorian night dresses and antique clothes, Victorian mugs, inlaid boxes, enamel coffee pots, old furniture to paint. They have a collection of old carts and the street is littered with Tony's vintage vehicles – the First World War motorbike and ambulance. The 1935 hearse. He will later help Lord Montague start his antique vehicle museum at Beaulieu.

The Aldermaston March is happening. The first leg from Oxford to Windsor is over. Tony and Ann's home is filled with friends camping, and the next morning we are all off to march to London. The Alberts are playing. I'm now dressed as a Russian with fur hat and antique boots. Sheba is in a Victorian pram. We all have our pictures in the local papers because we look so colourful. The feeling of brotherhood is inspiring. The weather is good and we walk to Chiswick and onto Trafalgar Square where so many politically aware people are gathered together to protest against the use of nuclear arms. I am proud to be there and I meet some amazing people – Christopher Logue, the poet, and Michael and Sheila van Bloeman who own The Troubadour Coffee House, who will become friends later. At the end of this historic gathering, we pile, elated and exhausted, into Tony's old ambulance and head back to Windsor as the sun rises.

One day, Ann sits on top of the fridge and announces that she wishes to explore the feelings she has for the husband of a couple they are friends with. This is discussed fairly reasonably. After all, *no-one belongs to anyone else.* We have to be free to *express* … this is an open marriage, and I am impressed. So, Tony and I become lovers. He will come to Datchet on the first train. We will leap into the back of the hearse and make love, and then I will walk home and he back to Windsor. We are enjoying each other very much. Lots of love and laughter and innocence.

They have a boat on the river. It's an old motor launch with a canopy so we take picnics and Douglas and Tony play the *Volga Boat Song*, and Douglas swims in his stripy Edwardian suit, holding his cigar out of the water. Such happy days. They fill me with light even now.

The Aldermaston March. In the photo are Michael Foot, J.B. Priestley, The Alberts, Canon Collins, Lord Montague, Ivor Cutler …

During their act, the explosions on stage are so loud that Douglas loses his hearing forever in one ear. One day sitting in the kitchen in Datchet my mother asks him,

'How old are you Douglas?' He always carries on as though he is an ancient old man and he reaches for his brass ear trumpet which he inserts into his ear and says,

'You said what ma'am? – you said what?'

They get their mother, Dolly, up on the stage when she can be persuaded. She is in her 80's, dressed in a 1920's beaded dress and flying boots and singing her First World War songs.

'Goodbye Dolly, I must leave you …'

The Alberts' act had to be seen to be believed. To say it was humour that swept everything away, to call it theatre of the absurd, nothing prepared you for the onslaught of The Alberts on stage.

They get me in the act, I dress up as a squaw, and Bruce Lacey, the extraordinary third member of the act, wears the most wonderful Victorian specs. He's painted circles in the middle of the lenses, so he can't possible see through them, and then he throws knives at the young squaw – *me!*

Ann Gray and Sheba, me, Dolly Gray, Sinbad and Douglas

They have a full size prop camel. They have made a door in its side, which they open like a flap. Inside is a xylophone, painted so that it looks like white ribs. They play *The Sheik of Araby,* then they take the camel's tail, wind it up, and two coconuts drop out of its bum. Bruce Lacey has built an amazing robot which stands on the side of the stage blowing soap bubbles. He has also made a huge foot that farts. This will later become an icon of *Monty Python's Flying Circus.* By the time the act is done, the stage is strewn with broken props and straw and dust and explosions and rubbish.

Tony's shift finishes at three o' clock in the morning. He can be back to Datchet and in bed with me by 4, then away to his home in Windsor before my mother wakes up. One morning he's late, so he's doing over 100 mph down the Great West Road to reach me in his vintage Daimler. So by the time we are happily mating away, it's near dawn, and my mother is banging on the door.

'Get up, get up!' As quick as a flash I bend my knees and Tony hides under the eiderdown, but the game is up. His overheated car has just exploded in the street.

I've had a row with my mother, so I jump on my bike with a few possessions and go and live with Tony and Ann. I love her and we are enjoying our life together. We go to Spain for a holiday, Palamos, the children on the beach, the old town. When we return,

Ann paints a portrait of Robin and me. She is an original artist, and another teacher for me - she is opening my eyes.

'What colour is it Anneke? Is it rose madder? Cerulean blue?' The house is full of instruments and Victoriana, pianos, magic lantern slides, penny farthing bicycles, and the aroma of Tony's cigars. In the bathroom, Ann has made a mural of a mermaid out of broken china. She picks up plates at jumble sales, just to smash them for mural making. The house is full of Sinbad's paintings. Using a leather punch and hides of thick leather we make sandals and bags and belts.

I make rag dolls. I stuff the bodies and paint the faces. They have black tights and little leather boots, and we call them 'Raggedy Anns'. I give one to Sheba.

There is a family run bakery on the corner - so the early mornings are filled with the delicious smell of bread baking - across the road are the barracks of the Queens Mounted Guards - every evening we hear *The Last Post.* Every day, columns of beautiful steaming horses - harnesses jingling ride up to the castle. When Robin and I were children we loved to join in at the back of the parading bands. Now I am with Sinbad and Sheba and we stand on the pavement and wave.

At the top of Windsor High Street, built into the castle walls, is The Grand Post Office. We continue up to the main square which has the statue of Queen Victoria in the middle. The famous Guildhall was built by Christopher Wren - we love this story. He wanted to build it with no support for the ceiling but the powers that be thought that it wouldn't hold, but Christopher Wren was a genius. He knew it *would* so as a compromise he built the beautiful pillars and left two inch gaps at the top which are still there today.

Opposite is Caleys – *Ooh, lovely Caleys* - the Fortnum and Mason of Windsor; a gracious store, catering for the gentility. The lingerie Department has pale green carpets and soft lighting. Expensive smells, pale oyster coloured silk chemises and slips, way beyond my means. But it's the atmosphere, the femininity which nourishes me. One day, I'm wandering around and I'm caught up in a waft of perfume. *What's that?!* It's *Je Reviens* by Worth. That's the scent that the lovely soft creamy lady wore at the party when I was three, when I had hoped my father would never come to pick me up. It now becomes my perfume for the next decade.

Near Caleys is The Tartan Room, one of the first coffee bars - I work there making espresso coffee in my student days. I will get the train back from London and it will come right into the heart of town. Windsor's Victorian station, beautiful wrought iron structure and the shops on the way down the hill, with the Theatre Royal at the bottom.

Just by the ancient bridge over to Eton is the cinema. What films we see there. Diana Dors in *A Kid For Two Farthings*, Laurence Harvey in *A Room at the Top*. The warm evening sunlight on the river, with all its life, the steamers going up and down with day trippers. For treats, we will visit the castle. The Royal Dolls House is magic for the children and we climb down past the 'trip-stair' and enjoy being scared in the dungeons of the round tower.

At the end of The Long Walk is the Copper Horse statue. It's a three mile walk from the Castle. The man who did the sculpture forgot to put the stirrups on; the feet are there; the muscles are all showing to be flexed as though the feet are in the stirrups. The sculptor was so mortified that he committed suicide. As children Robin and I were haunted by this story.

My spirit flies around Windsor for years to come.

Ann has had enough of Tony and me being together. She feels betrayed and closes her door to me, and I am heart broken because I love her as much as I do Tony, so I bicycle over to Windsor with branches of apple blossoms hung with little sorry notes and I learn a big lesson about hurting another.

Anyway, I'm off to London, and I still go on seeing Tony.

Chapter 13

The Troubadour

My friend Philippa has a new job in a clothes shop on the Kings Road, next door to our favourite pub, The Markham Arms. It's called 'Bazaar'. The woman who owns it is Mary Quant. The clothes are too expensive for me to buy but I love her style and later, when the shop moves to Knightsbridge, Alexander, her husband, dresses me up in a beautiful leather coat with fox fur trimmings and long boots and a placard which says, *'Bazaar Sale, Mad Reductions!'* and I have to parade up and down outside Harrods! I trade this with a grey wool sack, which I love to bits and wear to everything.

I spend quite a bit of spare time 'hanging out' at Bazaar. They do a fashion show. One of the lines is plus fours and tweeds. Alexander has bought pheasants from the fish and game shop Birketts, opposite Harrods and the models jauntily swing these as they trip down stairs, the pheasants dripping blood on the carpet

Eva-Lisa introduces me to her Finnish designer friends, who have opened Marimekko. Fantastic designs which I will wear throughout the sixties. Kikki Byrne opens her shop opposite the cinema in the Kings Road.

The Alberts have a friend called John Menasseh. He lives in Kensington and also has a huge house in Addison Road which he mostly uses as a furniture store. In the 1920's this house belonged to Mrs Van der Elst, who was famous and used to make her own potions and lotions for the face and body. John is willing to let me rent her bedroom for £2 a week. The Alberts help me move in. It's a large, beautiful room with a wall of mahogany fitted cupboards. Big windows look out over the leafy gardens. I paint one wall black and set up my new circular design wicker chair from Habitat. We go off to the Portobello Road on Saturday morning and buy a brass bed for a pound, and a Windsor-backed chair for 5 shillings. A pub table with a marble top, and this is it, I'm furnished. I make patchwork curtains for the windows and my Raggedy Ann is on my bed. At the top of the Earls Court Road, where it meets the Holland Park Road, is my favourite Lyons Corner House (the assignations in the Lyons Corner House!) and I can bicycle to The Troubadour …

In 1954 Michael and Sheila van Bloemen open their unique coffee bar, The Troubadour. It becomes a centre for West London's artistic and intellectual life. The first editions of *Private Eye* will be distributed from here. The Black Panthers meet here after they leave Paris in the 1968 riots. Bob Dylan's first London performance is an impromptu gig in the basement. He will be followed by such luminaries as Paul Simon, Long John Baldry and Jimi Hendrix. Ken Russell spends his evenings here and Richard Harris will meet his future wife, Elizabeth, while she's washing up in the kitchens.

Michael and Sheila are Canadians. They live above the coffee bar. Again, my eyes are opened. Their beautiful apartments are stuffed with antique toys, bicycles, penny farthings, all mounted up on the walls, bird cages, baskets, their kitchen table is round with six high-back rush seats, and little lights emphasising the drama. The coffee bar is the same – an amazing, lively atmosphere.

Michael van Bloemen has a big personality and he's always having great political discussions with his regulars. He is famous for it. He is forthright and dictatorial. He becomes highly animated and articulate when confronted with right-wing ideals. *No, no, you can't believe that! Get out! Go and have coffee with Enoch Powell!* But that was very much the atmosphere of the place, people like to come and get involved. Downstairs in the basement there is music. Eric Lister playing jazz. I work in the kitchens on Spanish Night because I like a Spanish dancer called Juan.

This magnetic place would become the cornerstone of my life for the next decade. *Time and Life* magazine do a piece on The Troubadour in the sixties and there I am in a photo, with Patsy Morton, in the candlelight in front of a panel of antique keys.

Down the road from The Troubadour is the Colehearn pub which is achieving notoriety, being one of London's first homosexual pubs.

Saturdays are always Portobello Road days. We go to the cheap end of the market at 6.30, collecting, collecting. The Alberts have loads of paraphernalia. It isn't just a theatrical act, they live it. Douglas's basement flat in Paddington is unbelievable. There are passageways between the piled up gear. One passageway goes to his bed, one goes to the kitchen and the whole place has antiques stuffed from floor to ceiling. There is a little Swedish wood stove where he sits in the middle in his smoking jacket, with a silk sleeping hat, drinking his tea. He is very happy that I'm living in Addison Road because he can come and practise his bagpipes, marching up and down the spacious hallway in his kilt.

I buy clothes, Mary Quant pinstripe trousers, boots, I have a fox fur collar and I carry a huge wicker basket everywhere. On Saturdays, after the Portobello market we go to Hennessey's to drink and later to sit in Eric Lister's first floor rooms with the windows open and watch all the people. Christopher Logue, the poet, lives across the road and we call to him. A great, colourful scene. And as always, The Alberts are playing.

There is a quiet couple who live in the top flat of Addison Road which is nice for me because the place is haunted. Famously haunted, I now discover.

After bicycling home late at night letting myself into the huge empty hall, washing in the marble bathroom with gold fittings and snuggling down into my brass bed, I sense a lot of nocturnal spirit energy which isn't all that pleasant.

I'm very broke. I sneak upstairs to the couple's flat when they have gone to work and steal a spoonful of their Nescafé. One morning I steal in and there is a note which simply says 'No, Anneke!' I go to Earl's Court Road and buy them a tin of the best. They had woken me up.

Robin and lovely, mad Eva-Lisa have split up and she's gone back to Helsinki. His heart is broken. He wants her back and starts writing very sad love letters and poems.

He's now working for *The Express* and being kept very busy. He's become a 'cool cat' with shades; he's got the new 'Mini' car. He calls himself a 'newshound'.

It's the beginning of the sixties and I've been to Annello and Davide to get some boots made - tall black with flat heels - they know how to make boots for dancers and the theatre - otherwise boots are not yet in the shops.

My mother has had enough, she says, of waiting for Robin and me to visit. She has learned Spanish and she is off to live in San Feliu de Guixols on the Costa Brava with Nicholas. As usual she doesn't have a bean, so she will try to run her agency from there.

When I go out to see her she's totally integrated, she's part of the town. *Señora Anna.* I get on the plane but I've forgotten to take her address. I get off the bus in this large old town and at the end of the paseo is a taxi rank, so I ask a taxi driver if he knows of my mother.

'Señora Anna? Si, Si!' and off we go. He becomes doubtful and has to ask someone else on a street corner.

Señora Anna? Si, Si!' and in they jump. By the time we get up into the back streets of the old town and we've come to another unsuccessful dead-end, the taxi is loaded with chattering townsfolk. I look up the street and sitting outside a doorway is our dog, Jacob.

'Jacob!' I cry, and he runs down the street grinning and wagging his tail. This is her *Casa.*

Chapter 14

The Strange World of Tony Newley

♫ *Half a pound of Tuppeny Rice*
Half a pound of Treacle
That's the way the money goes
Pop Goes the Weasel! ♫

I've got a part in a new series which Anthony Newley is making for ATV, *The Strange World of Gurney Slade*. He is one of our brightest young stars. In his last film *Idle on Parade*, he played a young singer and the songs became hits. Now, Tony has had two number one songs – *Why?* and *Do You Mind.*

Tony Newley with Dick Hills and Sid Green

I've got two episodes. I'm to play his dream girl. We meet on the bus going up to the location. Tony is very funny and sweet. We stay in a country pub and during dinner he is chatting up the make-up girl. Next day, out on a wind-swept aerodrome, we film our scenes. I am wearing a tightly-belted trench coat and little high heels. We look in each other's eyes.

Love happens.

When we do close-ups he turns his head away and yawns and stretches his face. His face then relaxes – *ACTION!* – I will use this trick myself from now on. It is hard to tell how *Gurney Slade* will come over because it is wonderfully bizarre. It is surreal and groundbreaking. This has not been seen before on British television.

Gurney Slade is now privately owned. It's sad that it cannot be seen because it should take its place in the history of British comedy.

Tony and I have to meet up again a few weeks later to do some dubbing. We are chatting and joking and enjoying each other's company and then he says,

'Come on Wills. Home!' as if to a little dog. So I go back to his flat in Earl's Court and that night in front of the mirrored cupboards in his soft, pinky-beige bedroom, we make love. *Well, now this is something else!* This man is a master lover, he has perfected the art. I am so green - enthusiastic, but green. A day or two later I move in, taking a few things from Addison Road. A painter at the Royal College of Art, Pauline Botie, sub-lets my room with bed and bike and ghosts and all and life with Tony Newley begins.

♫ *If I say I love you, do you mind?* ♫

- Anthony Newley

He's leading a very quiet, ordered existence in between working. He lives in a large third-floor flat off the Earls Court Road. It has green carpets, blue sofas and chairs, lots of photos of 'The Young Master' - as he likes to be called, and a baby grand piano, around which many of his friends – Lionel Bart, Gerogia Brown, Ian Fraser, and Leslie Bricusse gather, to create wonderful and original songs.

There is an office which his manager, Terry Cook, works in every day. His mother Gracie comes in and cleans and takes care of the very simple food we eat in the dining room. A little steamed fish – he has an ulcer and has to be careful. He hardly drinks, just a glass of white wine occasionally. After the business of the day and the flat becomes ours again we make love, and lots of it.

He is a fascinating man. I love his sense of humour and his laugh; I love the little boy that he is. He is a great sex teacher, he sleeps with a blindfold and he has the stance of an ancient Jewish magician. We are all very privileged to be around this talented being.

Tony wants me to go to Newcastle with him, as he tours *The Anthony Newley Show.* We walk along the beach and talk endlessly about aspects of theatre and television, where the reality expands beyond the microphone, proscenium or lens - and into other surreal dimensions. I tell him I saw him in *Cranks* when I was young, and all about The Alberts, the lunatic fun.

Now he has a new hit – *Strawberry Fair.* Leslie Bricusse and Tony love the Ingmar Bergman films. They decide to call each other 'Newberg' and 'Brickman'. Tony has made an album full of great songs – *Yes, we Have No Bananas, Drink to me Only With Thine Eyes,* and *Pop Goes The Weasel,* which becomes a hit in America as well as the UK hit parade. But he isn't happy being a pop star – he feels that it is not his world.

'Brickman and Newberg'

Jackie McGowran is a friend, as is Annie Ross - part of the unique jazz vocal group Lambert, Hendricks and Ross.

Tony calls me 'Face' or 'Facie'! He loves taking me to Harrods – he is the typical 'East End boy made good'. There, he has a deposit box. We are shown into the secret bowels of the store. In quiet locked cubicles he opens his box. It contains a film of him and his previous wife, Ann Lynn, making love. He buys me a leather shoulder bag and writes on the inside flap

'Wills – I loves ya, Tone.' I treasure it.

Leslie Briccusse and his wife, Yvonne Romaine, become very good friends and we all love *The Goons* so we're all tuned into the same humour. I've converted the spare room into my studio so while they are working, I'm painting large canvases. Listening to 'Brickman and Newburg' creating songs, they are so in tune with each other the songs just pour out. They can literally write a couple before lunch. We rarely go out in the evening but when we do it's to 'The Casserole' in the Kings Road with Keith Smith - *Keefers* - and friends.

One time we are in a friend's flat late at night and suddenly our dinner guests are 'at it' in front of us, inviting us to join in.

'No thank you,' Tony says politely, and he takes me home. This is the first time I've seen public sex.

Terry Stamp is at Tony's, draped over an armchair. He's just completed *Billy Budd. This man! I am here to tell you, they do not come more beautiful – the male species – than Terry Stamp. He is a fine, rare spirit.* He has a friend, Michael Caine, who I had already met on the edges of the Chelsea Set, when my friend Penny, on a Sunday morning after a party, sent them both out looking for a chemist in which to buy tampons. As it is Sunday, they are off to the East End to see their mums. *Meet you later in Humph's!*

Later, Michael Caine and I will be in a taxi. He lunges towards me.

'No, no, Michael, I'm a bloke, like you!' I mean, he's my buddy!

We watch blue films. They arrive in brown paper parcels. It is all very illicit. They always make me sad – the image of Father Christmas opening his robes with a 'present' for the girls – and the men usually wear vests and leave their socks on. I can't do it for days after watching those.

Tony drives a Jaguar, his 'Jewish Canoe' he calls it. It has a 'phone which please him greatly – he's such a kid.

We go to see The Alberts doing their show at the Fortune Theatre. They've called it *An Evening of British Rubbish.* Tony loves it.

The Alberts bring something very precious to the scene of the fifties and sixties. Their influence is massive - from Spike Milligan, Peter Cook, Michael Bentine and Peter Sellars to *Monty Python* and *The Bonzo Dog Doodah Band.* They are two very talented unique individuals with very little ambition and very sweet hearts.

I have a small part in an Edgar Wallace film, *Candidate for Murder.* We will film it at Merton Studios. I've got a cold and feel fairly under the weather. I have to get a cab to get me there so early in the morning - so expensive! I'm sitting in make-up when a head pops around the door and addresses the make-up lady.

'Be with you in a minute darling.' It is a wonderful, deep brown, voice.

'Who's that?' I say, opening my eyes.

'Michael Gough,' says the make-up lady. 'You're doing your scene with him today.' My heart leaps – Michael Gough! I've forgotten my cold and I'm wide awake and excited to meet him. He's another of those utterly charismatic beings that you cannot resist. We get talking. We are talking so much we've hardly got time to step on the set. We talk about everything – music, painting, photography, *The Goons*, horses – we have so much to share it's ridiculous. After the day's work he says,

'Would you like a lift home?'

'Yes please. Merton's hard to get to on public transport.' When we meet in the car park he's wearing a loud check suit and I have a sudden moment of hesitation, remembering *Do you like rubber?* but I push the thought aside as we get into his old Fiat, and off we go to Earl's Court where he lives.

Chapter 15

Glory be to God for Dappled Things

- Gerard Manly Hopkins

Our first meeting, in *Candidate for Murder*

Michael Gough lives in a basement flat in Earl's Court. He's been talking to me about life being a huge adventure. When he opens the door we are in a very large Victorian tiled hall, there's an upright piano, a rocking horse, and wonderful old French Chéret posters on the walls.

The long passageway to the loo - I'm dying for a pee as usual - is papered on one side with many front pages of *The Times* - when it was all the same format, and the other side is a patchwork of wallpapers. As he explains,

'All the leftovers from my friends' homes.'

We both have a great love for patchworks. The side of the Victorian bath, he has painted with fish scales and flowers. In the corner of the hall, a messy room, where Simon lives. The living room has rosy wallpaper, a wall of books, on top of which are a collection of Staffordshire figures. The sofas are soft green velvet. It is a most delightful room and reflects this man and his family. There is a large portrait of him, done by Bill Thompson, and I notice his bronze BAFTA for Best Supporting Actor 1956 in *The Last Reunion.*

And there is lovely Emma, nine years old, an enchanting child. It's hard to pull myself away.

'We loved you in *The Railway Children!*'

'I must go back to Tony. I'll see you again.'

I walk back up the Earl's Court Road bursting with joy.

Chapter 16

Stop the World

1961 dawns. I'm pregnant, and I'm scared. I want to go to Spain and see my mother but I'm broke, as usual. I am proud to pay my own way with Tony; I don't want to be seen as a gold-digger, so I keep a small account with Terry Cook. I'm sitting gloomily in The Troubadour; I ask these two blokes who say they are driving down to the Costa Brava later this week in their Porsche, if I can have a lift with them. They agree. We have a horrendous journey over the Alps in dangerously deep snow, and the windscreen wipers are broken and I'm feeling ill and they are cross with me because they are hoping for a gang bang.

When I get to my mother's casa, she's wonderfully uncritical and immediately discusses the practicalities.

'Sit down, have a glass of wine and let's have a look. What are your options? If you tell him will you lose him? Do you want this baby? Would you consider having it on your own?'

My head is spinning.

Having a baby outside marriage is absolutely not done, if you are in the public eye. As an actress I'll be torn to shreds. There is no support. I remember those school-day horror stories of back street operations.

We go to the bar to see her prostitute friend.

'She'll know what to do.' Later, sitting in the bath and full of gin, I think *Oh Lordy, I'm in hell.* The next day they've got me running half-heartedly across the mountains, with the prostitute and my mother on a scooter cheering me on … but nothing works.

So, I'm lying on the balcony sunbathing and notice a man on a hill opposite staring at me and masturbating. I protest to my mother,

'I'll tell José!' José is her protector and lover. So at lunchtime he comes over and we are out on balcony – we're going to catch him in the act! Behind the bush, sure enough, there he is.

'No, no!' says José, 'We can't get the police – this is my cousin!'

I go home to tell Tony about the pregnancy. I can't believe that his immediate response is overwhelmingly positive!

'We'll have a little Newley trotting about! We can make a nursery in your studio – darling Facie – I won't marry you – but I will look after you both.'

Chatsworth Court is busy with Ian Fraser, Leslie Bricusse and Tony working on some new songs. Bernard Delfont has given Tony an opportunity for a theatre in the summer. He's very excited, but Brickman and Evie are going to New York to work on a show for Beatrice Lillie. Tony and I have a brief check-in.

'Stay here Facie, mum and Terry can look after you and the new 'Young Master'. I'm off to get busy writing the new show, love you … back in a few weeks'.

I'm settling happily into mum-to-be mode. Buying all the books I can on childbirth. I'm doing paintings of white-haired children in Wellington boots, Christopher Robins …

Now, I'm fed up. My bump is beginning to show and vigilante old women in the bus queues notice I have no wedding ring, so an old friend of Tony's and I go off to Burlington Arcade to buy a wedding ring. The man in the shop is being all obsequious as though we are betrothed. This cracks us up and we go off to Fortnums for tea. This is one of Tony's favourite places for cucumber sandwiches and I'm flashing my wedding band, big, thick and gold, *see*!

One day I go into the office and see a note Terry has made by the phone, from where he talks to Tony in the States.

– Tell Wills to get an abortion.

I am 18 years old, and the bottom has just fallen out of my world.

I have crumpled into a state of frozen shock. I am already four months pregnant. Terry fixes up emergency appointments in Harley Street. I'm following like a zombie. We have to get two psychiatrist's letters, it's all horrible. The surgeon sadistically points out that he will have to *cut my belly*. Two weeks later, Robin accompanies me to a private nursing home in Hampstead. I take my Raggedy Ann to comfort me – I am so scared. I feel like a lamb being led to the slaughter.

I'm 18 weeks pregnant and I have to have a Caesarean abortion. They keep me in for ten days. The Irish nurse says,

'Do you want to know what it was?'

'No, please, I'll cry and never stop.' Robin and Terry Cook are the only people to know. I go home to the flat to mend this terrible, badly done, scar that I now have on my tummy… never mind on my psyche.

I never actually *speak* to Tony – he is hiding behind the transatlantic distance. Apart from Robin, who wants to kill him, I have no-one to talk to about the Caesarean.

When I go out I look longingly at babies in prams, lovely creamy faces, chubby-cheeked, gurgling bright-eyed babies. I feel so betrayed.

Robin has found a house to rent in Paddington. It's three floors above a shop. Peter Crofton-Sleigh will live on the first floor, Gavrik Losey on the next with kitchen and bathroom, and Robin on the top floor with a living room. There is a room for me, in case I need a bolthole from life with Tony. He's so excited, and he warns that it's hopelessly grotty, but I'm not prepared for what a shit heap it is – water coming in through the top ceilings, rats, ancient wiring – it hasn't been lived in for fifteen years. So we get to work. The electrics are rewired, leaks are fixed, and we paint all the way up the stairs white. Gavrik has a friend who does lovely modern canvasses and these we hang all the way up. The kitchen is blue and white with copper pans hanging. We sand and varnish all the floors.

One night, you are varnishing so late on your hands and knees after a long day at Fleet Street that you're kneeling over and you've fallen asleep, stuck to the floor. We go to the market and get you a £2 brass bed, and with your huge purple and orange cover and a fur rug, your room's done. Mine is tiny with a single brass bed because, I say, I'm not inviting anyone home. We climb out onto the roof, to sunbathe among the chimney pots.

After a while Tony comes home. He is sympathetic, but says it wasn't the best timing.

'Facie, this show may take me to the States – it wouldn't have worked out anyway. *Stop The World* needs all our energies at the moment; we must get it cast because rehearsals start soon.'

We hear the new songs written by Tony, Leslie and Ian, songs which will go on to become standards, sung by many great singers - *What Kind of Fool Am I, Just Once in a Lifetime*. And they have written it all in just a few weeks.

We go to see a review called *And Another Thing* which stars Joyce Blair and Anna Quayle. We're both struck by Anna and Tony asks her to be in the new show. We are spending a lot of time up in Stanmore with the Bricusses as *Stop the World* begins to take shape. I've done a drawing of Evie in orange trousers and a brown top.

Leslie tells me, in 2002, that she still treasures it. He also says,
'You were the best thing that ever happened to Tony'. Hearing that was like a massive bandage over the ancient wound.

Tony wants Lionel Blair to do the choreography for the show, but Lionel is very hesitant, so I suggest my lovely old ally from RADA, John Broom, as he does movement more than dance, and Kiki Byrne to do the costumes. We already have Sean Kenny working on the sets; he's just finished his famous exploding stage for *Blitz* by Lionel Bart. I love Noel Coward's quote,
'Twice as loud and twice as long as the original.'

We start to do the auditions; I love to be next to Tony as we whisper,
'No, no, yes, that one.' The beautiful Baker twins, great jokes about Tony leaving a trail of lollipops leading to his dressing room. Prophetic …

At this time, Tony has me dressed in a school tunic.

Tony is getting frustrated with Sean Kenny because when he comes with his drawings for the stage design, it isn't what Tony wants. The show revolves around the character Littlechap's journey, his rise to riches, marrying the boss's daughter – who's pregnant – she gives birth to two daughters. But Littlechap longs for a son, who dies at birth. So he goes on meeting other lovers, all of whom are played by Anna Quayle. Eventually he has conquered all except himself, so he offers himself, instead of his baby grandson, into the hands of death. It seems to me that everything Tony writes is autobiographical – but what else would he write about, but that which churned incessantly within him? It is all Tony's journey – I am just part of the scenery.

Tony wants a set like an egg-shape – out of which, the action will emerge. Sean has come up with a circus set and arguments are happening about Tony playing a clown. I love the idea, but they are worried. John Broom and Tony are working on a mime sequence that will start the show.

We are all off on the pre-West End tour. We play in Nottingham – where the cast find their feet. Anna is so sweet because she's as blind as a bat, and very afraid of falling into the orchestra pit. Various people have come to see it, and some are frankly bemused. They can't make out whether it's brilliant or awful. It's in Manchester, while we are sitting out front watching a rehearsal, that the idea comes for Tony to step out of the action with,

'Stop The World … '

David Merrick, the big American producer, has given Tony truly excellent reviews and offered Broadway as soon as the London run is over, so Tony is feeling confident.

I'm back to work and it's a big one, a P*lay of the Week* called *The Primitives.* I'm playing a teacher who has a conflict with the Head of the school. Scott Forbes's character and I will have a sexy kiss. After what I've just been through, the prospect of kissing a stranger is not an appealing one.

A still from *The Primitive*, my psyche scarred

While working on *The Primitive* I am still feeling vulnerable, and I am embarrassed by the sexual innuendos. The director will say,

'OK, we'll call it a day. Anneke and Scott stay behind, we'll just run your kissing scene.' He makes me do it this way, and that, then he has a go himself, they both have erections and I'm becoming more and more miserable.

The Primitive is well received and I get some good notices. One in particular from Bernard Levin (such an intelligent man!).

I have a black velvet suit with a white Victorian lace shirt to wear for the first night at the Queen's Theatre on July 20th. The Bricusses and I have a box. We laugh because as the Royal anthem starts, we stand up and there is exquisite Evie, in a white sequined evening dress with shoulders back and her monumental boobs proud. Every eye in the theatre is on her chest! The audience love the show, the press are not sure. Once again, Tony has come up with something so unique; there is no point from which it can be compared. The songs became legends. The show is a huge success and will run for many years all over the world. I am happy that it changed John Broom's life as he goes on to accompany it to the States later.

Sammy Davis Jnr. sees the show and asks Tony if he may sing *What Kind of Fool Am I* at The Prince of Wales Theatre. Tony is very flattered, and Sammy's recording goes on to sell a million copies in the following year. This is the beginning of a life-long friendship. Sammy, the one-eyed black kid in the apartheid of the USA; Tony, the illegitimate cockney from the London slums. Both are multi-talented. They have a natural bond, and they really love each other.

Meanwhile I have my paintings hanging in Tony's dressing room and they are selling. Sammy buys one and we become friends. We go to see him at the Prince of Wales Theatre. One night, while Sammy is singing *What Kind of Fool Am I*, Tony accompanies him, from the wings. There are grand parties at The Mayfair where Sammy stays. The Mayfair is the only hotel to admit a black guest.

While Sammy is at The Mayfair, he overhears some snobby white person in the foyer say,

'Look, there's a coloured person!' Sammy leaps up and says,

'Where?! Where?!'

He has many inner scars from all the discrimination he has suffered. One night I ask him which eye doesn't work. He takes a match and *tap, tap*,

'This one!' he says. We go out to dinner with Nelson Riddle and his group of blue-rinsed American women and I talk to him about Miles Davis. Sammy loves me and calls me 'The Countess', because, he says, I talk like the Queen. We go to see Tony Bennett. I walk into the Talk of the Town on Sammy's arm. The photographers are out. They think I am Mai Britt, a Swedish film star, and Sammy's wife. That night, Tony Bennett sings -

♫ *Fly Me to the Moon* ♫

Ever since the abortion, I'm sleeping more and more at Robin's flat in Spring Street. One night I'm missing Tony and I turn up at the flat. He's not expecting me and he's sitting eating a boiled egg on a tray in bed and all over the bed are photographs of Joan Collins. I now know it's over and I'm hysterical,

'I'll kill myself; you don't love me any more!' I run to the kitchen, and take a butter knife and pathetically saw away at my wrists. He's very sweet and calm.

'Now now, Facie, no scenes. I'll call you a taxi.'

I go back to Spring Street.

Peter Crofton-Sleigh who lives with us is a dear friend, a be-whiskered free spirit, and he's mellow and wise. He plays cello all night, sleeps all morning, lunches in The Troubadour and in the afternoon he is a master decorator and gets very good jobs in nice houses in Notting Hill. I begin to work with him. I learn how to brush walls - no rollers for Peter! Olive greens and pale pink exteriors. I will hang off cradles with him, chip off old paint and repaint railings. He joins The Alberts when they go to America, and he tells everyone,

'Hello … yes … I'm a star! How do you do? I'm a star you know!' He's dressed in his Victorian gear. Tony Gray spends the next few years blowing him up on stage, because he is jealous of Peter's friendship with me.

Gavrik Losey, son of Joe Losey the American director, also lives with us. He has startling blue eyes, a black beard, rides a Vespa and works in the production side of films. A while later, he will go on to make films with The Beatles. He's crazy, and has a great laugh.

I'm having my roots done in Vidal Sassoon's, when to my horror I realise it's Joan Collins on the other side of the mirror I am looking in. Wicked Vidal knows this and is having fun.

'So, Anneke, do tell … how's Tony?'

Later, under the dryer, I'm reading *Queen* magazine and I'm completely absorbed by this article about Peter Cook who has opened a new satirical nightclub called 'The Establishment'. I'd like to meet him.

Sean Kenny and I have become mates since *Stop the World* and I've been to a party or two with him. He always gets hopelessly drunk. Now he is inviting me to go with him to see *Beyond the Fringe*, the most talked about review of its time. It is hilarious, we are falling off our seats with laughter and afterwards Sean takes me to The Establishment and I meet Peter Cook. Later that night I am twisting in the basement to the 'Dudley Moore Trio'.

Chapter 17

The Establishment

Beyond the Fringe has opened at the Fortune Theatre. It's directed by Eleanor Fazan and Sean Kenny has done the set. It is an overnight sensation. The nation falls in love with these four university graduates. Peter Cook, Dudley More, Jonathan Miller and Alan Bennett. Of course this form of lampooning the establishment was nothing new, it was rife in the 18th Century but it seems fresh to our generation. The word 'satire' was attached by the ecstatic press and the four became the most renowned satirists ever. Riding on this success Peter fulfils his dream, and he and Nick Luard buy an old strip club in the heart of Soho and transform it into 'The Establishment' - the first satirical nightclub.

Its membership fills up at once. Sean Kenny does the décor. Lots of black. There is a stage and dining tables for twice nightly shows. A great long bar where the members can drink. All along one wall are the wonderful cartoons of Roger Law and downstairs in the basement is Dudley's jazz club - wild, hot, and sweaty - twisting and jiving. On the floors above are the offices. Sean Kenny has a lovely light studio where many young and beautiful people will sleep after a late night and Lewis Morley, in his studio, will take *that* photo of Christine Keeler naked astride *that* chair.

Royalty to politicians, ballet dancers, actors, writers, film directors, cartoonists, poets, Duchesses and drunks - all gather, night after night, to partake in this heady atmosphere.

Jeremy Geidt, John Fortune, John Bird and Eleanor Bron are the main stay performers. Annie Ross and Jean Hart sing. Peter will come back from the theatre and be in the second show. Dudley plays the blues in the basement.

Among the regulars are Rudolf Nureyev, Margot Fonteyn, Paul McCartney, Peter O'Toole, Michael Caine and Terry Stamp, Christopher Logue, Mary Quant, Kikki Byrne, Francis Bacon, Georgia Brown, Lionel Bart, Alma Cogan, Barry Humphries, George Melly, Danny La Rue and April Ashley – the first person to have a sex-change. And of course, Robin and Anneke Willys! I haven't got a membership card but I'm always let in. I also can't afford to eat the supper so sometimes I join friends, but often I am just standing at the back, of nearly every show, loving the moment when sensual Annie Ross climbs on a stool in the spotlight and says in her husky voice,

'It's melody time.' Every night is different – totally alive, and the audience participation is volatile. The casts of other shows in the West End will come to the second show so every night is a *happening*. Sometimes some of us actors who 'aren't working' go to Jimmy the Greek's, where down in the green tiled basement we can get a wedge of good Greek bread with olive oil and garlic for a shilling, and that will fill us up. And then we go back to The Establishment to dance.

There is a pub crawl I am sometimes taken on. It starts at the Coach and Horses in Soho, at lunchtime, this bunch of Irish actors and poets, and me, start drinking and continue till closing time. We then stagger to the Langham Club opposite the BBC to continue. Louis MacNeice, Jackie McGowran. Finally, it's on to The Establishment. This is sincere drinking. *And what company!*

Robin and I go to see the most wonderful film - *Orpheo Negro.* It's shot in Rio at the time of the Carnival. We have never seen anything quite so colourful, or so human and sad. This becomes *our* film. *It still is.* The music stays with us forever.

Robin has always loved films. When he was two years old, before war broke out, my mother had taken him to meet his Grandmother in Holland. One afternoon he climbed out of his bed, when he was suppose to be having his afternoon rest, and trotted down the street, naked except for a vest. A kindly passer-by asked this little two year old,

'Waar gaa je na too?' *Where are you going?*

'Ik gaag naar het bioscope!' Robin replied. *I'm going to the cinema!*

Robin and I spend every night at The Establishment. We are talking to Peter O'Toole about butterflies. He has just finished *Lawrence of Arabia*, and his face is tanned and he has amazing blue eyes. One night I meet Peter Cook's girlfriend, Wendy Snowdon. *Aha*, I think, *the woman behind the man.* She's very attractive and also very direct – I like her at once and am invited to one of their splendid dinners in their flat in Prince of Wales Drive, Battersea. She has marvellous taste – a large refectory table, lots of Bristol blue glass, she is an excellent cook and hostess and the company is nothing less than scintillating. Peter is holding court, so quick and funny and bright, so much laughter around him, and Wendy grounding it all with,

'But what do you *really* think about that?' She is the strength of this relationship. He'll be gobbling up all the attention, he can't help it, but every now and then he will glance across to Wendy, checking in. They are an irresistible couple. Such excellent company in Prince of Wales Drive. It is a large flat and many people stay there, including me. One day we go to Battersea Funfair which has been there since the festival of Britain. In one of the sideshows, there is a surreal image of a beautiful face in the centre of a flower, which is suspended in space. We are trying to figure out the illusion, when Peter says,

'Look, there's a mirror there!' and so he explains away the mystery. Suddenly the Flower Face says, in a broad cockney accent,

'Well thanks. That's fuckin' charmin'!'

Peter and Wendy

It's all a great distraction from my wobbly emotional state – I had just lost a baby at four and a half months, and I now have this huge unsightly scar right up the centre of my belly – I'm damaged for ever.

So, it's wonderful to sit next to Dudley as he plays his piano. He confides in me one day he would like to play real dirty, deep-down blues; so he would have everyone writhing on the floor, and then he would walk out over the top of them – *and feel the power!*

I teach Wendy and Peter 'The Twist', the latest dance. I'm wearing hipster pants and high black boots. I often walk home through the streets of Soho at two o'clock in the morning with a string of guys panting behind me. Back home to my little brass bed. Will Tony call? When he does, our love-making is urgent. It's satisfying for me to feel he still needs me.

In early 1962, Tony and I have a secret place where we sometimes meet. It's Nikki Byrne's luxurious flat in Chelsea. I wear a totally simple 'little black', with pearls - just the way he likes me. I'm drenched in Je Reviens and hoping to be all that he's missing. I will cry a lot and it's all very poignant.

Later I meet his mother, Gracie. We talk in the Earl's Court Road. She doesn't like Joan and she's fed up with having to wash the bath which is full of her oil. Much later, I discover he is still married to Ann Lynn and that he keeps my letters with him always. He leaves them to a library in Boston.

I am jealous of Joan Collins for years. In the 1980s, I would see images of her doing Dynasty while I'm on my knees cleaning houses in California.

Chapter 18

Spring Street

In Spring Street, we have lots of parties. At one of them, I'm tripping down the stairs. Michael Gough is coming up with Simon behind him.

'Well darling, how lovely to see you, what are you doing here?'

'I live here.' They are with Jill Bennett and are out cruising the scene.

Robin loves Jules Pfeiffer cartoons. He and I go to see this new French mime artist - Marcel Marceau. Pure magic. Also we love *Les Enfants du Paradis* with Jean Louis-Barault – 'Acting is Loving' is his famous statement.

Sean Kenny talks about being invited to do a show in Las Vegas. He's got great ideas, I love him when he's creating and his arms wave in the air and his wicked Irish eyes are twinkling. He wants to, and will, have the girls floating around the audience on little round moving discs. He has designed a church in Ireland with no altar, just a big window looking out onto the nature because that, he says, is what is holy. And he plans to electrify his windscreen wiper in Greek Street so when Lovely Rita Meter Maid comes …

He tells me of an amazing adventure he has had. After architectural college, he and a group of fellow students decide they want to go and study with Frank Lloyd Wright – the master architect in America. One of them has a small sailing boat off the west coast of Ireland. So, they equip it and study maps, and winds, and set sail for New York. This has attracted quite a bit of publicity. Only one of the three is a sailor, so they are risking a lot. Sean says,

'It was great. We were making good headway, and our spirits were up – she was a grand little craft and the winds were with us. Just a few days before we were due to get into the harbour in New York, we hit the most powerful storm. We just managed to get the sails down when this huge wind snapped the mast and we battened down the hatches to ride it out. We began to say our prayers but the storm abated, and when we opened the hatches, the little boat was stripped - even the fockin' paint!' They have been blown way off course, so with improvised oars and faint now with hunger, they limp into the first harbour, where immediately, the customs are onto them;

'Where are your papers? You can't just land here!' But the three young men explain their plight, and the American press are alerted, and then they are celebrated and sent to Frank Lloyd Wright's studio where they get to meet the great man and study with him.

Peter Cook and Nick Luard are going to meet Lenny Bruce at the airport. Should they hire a limousine? He is a big American star.

'No, no we should just get a cab – he's a man of the people.'

They choose the limo and are feeling quite apprehensive about Lenny's reputation as a heroin addict … what would he be like … well he's high, and crazy. He has been recording conversations of fellow passengers during the flight. He is blown away by the poignancy of humanity. Peter and Nick don't quite know what to make of him. In the limo on the way back to Nick's flat he shows them his special briefcase which is all fitted up with all his hypodermics and gear - this addiction is like something not previously seen in London - and this will become the main drama of his stay - getting him enough drugs. This is not a world that these Cambridge graduates have previously encountered, and the sight of Lenny collapsed in a heap before his fix, and the sheer excitement and delight of being with him after he'd had it, was a real eye opener to the Establishment crowd.

I'm talking to Peter about The Alberts. He's fascinated and I take him to see their act. Now he's going to get them to appear at The Establishment. I'm proud as a cat with nine kittens. *My friends! It's wonderful.* Naturally, they cause complete chaos.

Such magic has happened around the writing of this book. Today I've been on the 'phone to Tony Gray - he now lives in France - and he tells me how he wrote a love song for me which he sang every night on stage in *The Three Musketeers* - with an orchestra.

'Shall I sing it to you?' He clears his throat 'Farewell my love …' This wonderful 86 year old friend is singing me a song across half a century, and he can't go on because he's choked up.

When they are playing at The Establishment, Peter Cook explains that Lenny Bruce is doing his gig that night, and says,

'Since you make such a mess on the stage, would you mind appearing after Lenny?'

'Yeah, yeah, that's fine' said Douglas and Tony. But Lenny hears this and said,

'Hey man this is your country - you should be first!' so he has to climb over all the straw and the smoke and the old dustbins and the props of The Alberts, and he goes on to do a whole piece all about them, saying how great and wild and anarchic they were. This, coming from Lenny Bruce. He invites them to come to the US which they do. They play New York and California.

I'm wearing a great product called 'Tanfastic' – it makes you brown, and I love my new lipstick, Italian Pink by Gala in a gold stick. I put my hair into rollers. I've been invited for supper at Au Pere De Nico with Norman Parkinson – he wants to take photos of me. He is *the* photographer of the moment. When I come to take the rollers out – *disaster!* I haven't tucked the ends around properly and it's all kinky, and not in a nice way. I have to catch a bus to Pimlico, there's no time. I grab Robin's trilby and put my hair inside. When I meet him 'Parky' he's intrigued, and he's very good company. We end up at the Markham Arms. Robin is there with Julie Christie. I can see he likes her. I hope he doesn't get hurt - I always worry about Robin - my mother and I both do. Is it because he was born on Friday 13th? He knows that the old superstition comes from historical fact, that the Knights Templar were rounded up and massacred on that day. The Holy Grail fascinates him and he talks of it often, especially when he and I get stoned, then he goes off into other realms. Parky doesn't photograph me, John Cole does. More of him later.

My mother and Nicholas are back in England. He now has long blond hair and is swearing in fluent Catalan and writing sick poetry. He's going to live with Roy and go to school in England. The last time my mother was in the UK she had been hassling her local health authority to give her a facelift. She could be so convincing.

'I have the energy of a younger woman,' she says, 'and I could get work, you know, speaking five languages and being so intelligent! It's just that my face has fallen down!' With that, she pulls her face up with her hands and smiles coquettishly, fluttering her eyelids. She wears them down. They've agreed. And now they are here, with a car, ready to take her to the hospital to have it done. But in the reality of this moment she's very afraid.

'I can't go through with it. Tell them I've gone to Spain!' and she's under the kitchen table, hiding.

'No, we will tell them that you're afraid.' They leave, shaking their heads. She goes back to her young boyfriend in Spain. He's called Björn. He's a blond, 30 year old, Danish musician with a Volkswagen bus. He's totally handsome - like Frederick of *Nina and Frederick*. He loves her and they travel all around the Mediterranean living in the bus, making fires on the beach, laughing and drinking wine. One morning, early, on a deserted beach, she's stoking her little fire, wrapped in a blanket, when a peasant comes up and addresses her, in Catalan, as

'Old Woman of the Hills'. My mother says,

'That's it! I've achieved!'

Later, Björn will go off with a young girl, and once again her heart is broken and she never has another lover.

I change agent. I've been told about Terry Owen and Bernard Hunter who have an agency called *Leading Players*. I go to see them, I like them and them me. Now they've sent me to meet an American at an address behind Marble Arch at seven o'clock in the evening.

'Why can't they see me in office hours?' I ask suspiciously.

'This suits them; they're seeing lots of people.' Apprehensively I turn up. They're very polite, they're American, the film is about Freud, and they will be in touch. A few days later Sam Spiegel is on the 'phone.

'Will you have dinner with me?'

Have dinner with Sam Spiegel! He is one of the biggest producers in Hollywood and I panic.

'I can't, I can't, I'm busy working.' He calls one more time.

I hold my nose,

'Sorry, I carnd, I've god a coad.' He says,

‘Can I send my physician? Would you like a hamper from Fortnum’s?’ Robin is leaning in to listen. He says,

‘Say yes to the hamper!’

‘No, no …’ I just feel I can’t handle it. What if he comes onto me? I feel sure that those men were vetting me.

As it happens, Susannah York has already been signed up. The story goes that the next girl to have dinner with Sam, Henrietta Tiarks – who will go on to become the Duchess of Bedford - admires a painting and is then given it as a present. It was a Renoir.

My friend Venetia is staying with Nick Luard. On a warm sunny Sunday we are both returning to his flat and the back streets off Hyde Park square are quiet and empty so we immediately become aware that these persistent footsteps are following us. We quicken our pace and are relieved when we arrive at Nick’s front door - *quick, get the key out* - but her bag is full of clutter and we are laughing and panicking. Now he’s right behind us -

‘Have you got the time?’ We turn to see this man with a strange smile, his coat open and his parts exposed. She’s found the key - we open the door and tumble in together in hysterics.

Nick is determined that we should pursue the matter, so he calls the police. A while later they catch the man in the act; he is a Cypriot with a large family. Venetia and I feel sorry for him and do not press charges.

Robin hauls me out of bed in the mornings and takes me to the little café across the road for breakfast but I am already on a diet. I’m always on a diet. *I’ve been on a diet forever.*

Over the years to come you will go to Spain often. You loved Formenterra best, empty beaches, the pines, and the lavender. You’re now working in Fleet Street, writing long letters to Eva-Lisa. You want her back and you’re offering her marriage and life in Australia, all sorts of ideas. But she never comes.

You really love exotic Carlotta, the dancer. She’s very sweet. You and Gavrik will go on his Vespa to Swanage and sit with Carlotta’s grandmother in her old wicker bath chair looking out over the bay. And Simi - whose parents were royalty in Africa - you wanted to marry her but her parents prevented it. How many of your girlfriends I’ve met up with in my life, and each one feels you *really* loved them.

Chapter 19

Some People

February 1962 and I've got a part in a film directed by Clive Donner. It's being made entirely on location in Bristol. It's about a group of kids whose lives are turned around when they get involved with the Duke of Edinburgh's award schemes. Kenneth More plays my father, who runs the youth centre which the story focuses around. David Hemmings - *remember the bogies* - David Andrews, Ray Brookes and Angela Douglas, a great team. We all go to Bristol and it is freezing cold. We stay in the Grand Spa Hotel. We live and work here for a few weeks before shooting so that they can get an idea of the Bristol accent. I like this way of working. We are taken to youth clubs and factories and really become a part of the scene. We rehearse for a few weeks at Filton Church Hall. We are nearly ready to start the shoot. Kenny arrives – what an absolute charmer! He has his jacket over his shoulder - this man is so famous and yet so relaxed and jolly. I have a special scene to do with him - I will spend a whole day sitting in a bath tub full of dry ice - smoking a Gauloise with my skin going wrinkly. I don't mind any of it though, because of the sheer delight of working with someone as present and warm as Kenny. *What a blooming great gift for me!* Clive Donner is a dream to work with, really professional, down to earth, inspired and funny. What a happy shoot it is.

At Bilsten Airport they've built a raised platform for the second unit which Nicholas Roeg is directing. We are waiting for one of the planes to take off and 'break the sound barrier'. This is the first time that this has ever happened and we are going to film it.

Angela is very nervous because she's playing the singer of the group – miming to Helen Shapiro who sings the film's title song. Ray Brooks will have to mime the guitar part.

On St. Patrick's night Kenny is having a big party in the Hotel. Angela and I are tarting up - she's applying mascara with a shakey hand - spitting on the little cake of Max Factor - we're excited and planning our conquests.

'You can have Kenny and I'll have the Duke of Edinburgh!' I say. In her case, she did.

I am torn between waiting for Tony to ring, and Nicholas Roeg who is just the job - intelligent, sexy and good looking. But when your heart is still yearning for another … I do the bath scene with Kenny where I am lying in the bath shrinking my jeans; I have to be sown into them to make them totally skin-tight. He hands me a towel. As my father, Kenny knows I am becoming sexually aware and this touches him. I look into his eyes and there is the most tender look, of love and tears. I am humbled. This man can act.

Angela and I have become intimate friends. We love to order room service – prawn cocktails – and hang out in each other's rooms in our dressing gowns after the day's work, relaxing and sharing our secrets. We all have to go to a doctor's surgery to have smallpox jabs – there's been a scare. I'm also worried because I think I've got crabs – *don't ask me how*. We all sit in the waiting room and go into the doctor's room one by one. The walls are very thin and everyone hears me say,

'Oh, and I think I've got crabs.' The entire unit cracks up and I am teased mercilessly. Angela is sweetly obliging. Later, I am spread-eagled, and with her beautifully manicured fingers, she prises the little buggers out and with a satisfying -

'Yes!' - she presses them onto the soap. *Such is friendship!*

I have some sweet love scenes with Ray Brookes which I enjoy because he is dishy and I like him – he's not some old fart with an erection. It's a happy shoot and we have a grand wrap party and I've made two very good friends, Angela and Kenny. I will work with Clive Donner again, on *Nothing but the Best* and *Pleasure Girls.*

The Cuban crisis looms over us. There are protests happening all over London. People are afraid, putting food and water in their basements in case. On one particular day we are not sure if we'll still be alive that evening. I decide in my last moments to buy and listen to Nina Simone's album, *Forbidden Fruit.*

With Ray Brooks – and shrinking those jeans.

April 1962, and I'm pregnant *again*! By my calculations, it's Tony's. After the Caesarean, I swore to myself that if this *ever* happened to me again, I would keep the baby, no matter what. Can I keep my promise to myself? Do I dare? It will be risky, and I will be judged. Can I manage financially? I run it by Nick Luard. He seems to be a very grounded person. He talks to me about being responsible for this new life. I'm getting excited by the idea. It feels right and I won't tell Tony, damn it, this is my baby, I want nothing from him, I'll go it alone. When I tell my mother, she simply says,

'Well maybe this will make you less irresponsible!' And with that, she goes off Copenhagen with Björn.

I put it about that Sean Kenny may be the father, to deflect the truth away from Tony. I am quite ashamed that I have been caught out again. I don't have a doctor nearby, I am registered in Datchet with the one who nearly killed me by misdiagnosing my appendix - so I can't ask him for this new form of contraception called The Pill. He won't approve. Instead, I go to a clinic in Paddington and buy a Dutch cap, hoping that it will fit ... hopeless really ... but the help and support simply isn't there. Yet those later, clandestine meetings seemed to have such an urgency for the two of us. Tony was with Joan Collins, yet our love was still so alive.

The cast of *Some People* has been invited to tea at Windsor Castle and I'm not allowed to go because I'm in a disgraceful state – I'm showing my bump, and I'm not married. I'm so sad about this, partly because I love Windsor Castle and I would love to see the private apartments. Angela tells me all about it.

'We waited ages in a large, grand room. When the Duke of Edinburgh came in I promise you he was wearing a Tootal tie with a Van Heusen shirt. My high heels sunk into the lawn and I stumbled against His Highness; I'm sure he thought I was doing it on purpose and I was so embarrassed. David Hemmings was very busy schmoozing!'

For the premier of *Some People* in Leicester Square, I'm having an A-line dress made with stiffenings so that it disguises my 'shameful' state, this being a Royal Premier. We all stand in line, me trying to remember to hold my tummy in. Prince Phillip is devastatingly handsome when we meet him.

'I liked you in the bath,' he murmurs.

'Thank you, Your Highness,' I say politely. Afterwards we go to the Caprice. Someone at our table says,

'There's Sarah Miles'. I turn and see Sarah and James Fox entering the restaurant.

'Sarah Baskerville!' She walks grandly across, as though she owns the place, and dumps her leopard-skin coat on my head! I am overcome with embarrassment. David Hemmings saves the day. He calls a waiter, and sends the coat back

'To that bitch over there'. I try to brush it off with,

'We are old school-friends', but it does dampen my special night, as I never go to places like the Caprice or the Ivy.

Some People is very well received, and becomes a cult new-wave film dubbed into many languages. I have an Argentinean poster of it! My mother sees it in Spain, dubbed, and is amazed to see me speaking fluent Spanish! Bernard Levin, once again singles me out in his review.

August 1962, Marilyn Monroe dies in peculiar circumstances. This upsets us all. The papers are full of it.

Robin and I go to see the film *Jules et Jim* by Truffaut. We think it's a masterpiece. Jeanne Moreau in a triangle of love. A turning point in film-making. Afterwards in the kitchen, we talk. He doesn't think that Spring Street is a good place for a baby. I'll have to find a new nest.

I talk with Wendy Cook about my situation. They are off to the States very soon, and I'm feeling a bit abandoned.

'Do you know anyone who might have room for you?'

‘Michael Gough,’ I say. ‘He has a very big flat and loves babies.’ So I ‘phone Mick and ask if I may come to lunch because I have something very important to ask him. When I go to lunch, I wear a turquoise mumu from Fenwicks - I think it hides the bump. He cooks us a little ‘chikkie’. We eat at the scrubbed pine table in the kitchen. When he has washed up in the Victorian scullery, I finally have the courage to launch into,

‘I’m pregnant; I need a nest, can I rent a room?’

‘I knew that,’ he says bemused, ‘and yes you can.’

I get a job working at Kikki Byrne’s shop where Jaegar used to be in the Kings Road. This is handy, because now I can pay Mick my rent and buy all the necessities for the baby - twelve soft terry-towelling nappies, 4 woolly vests etcetera. I like working here among the lovely clothes and interesting customers. One day, Sean Connery’s wife Diane Cilento comes in with Sean Kenny. We go for coffee - Kikki is indulgent towards me because I’m pregnant. Sean Kenny is telling us how he has put his young sons into a ‘survival school’ in Switzerland. They will learn how to survive in the wild. I’m struck by how brilliant that is - true knowledge … if my baby is a boy …

Chapter 20

On my 21st birthday. Mick and his old friend Edward Fox have got a little cake for me. By this time, Edward has left Tracy Reed and now has a daughter called Lucy. I've gone off to Ladbrooke Grove to get drunk on Babycham in some huge pub with Robin. I've bought myself a rug from that lovely Spanish shop in Pimlico called Casapupo. My brass bed is moved into the little room at the end of the long passage. Wendy has lent me an antique wooden cradle on rockers and I begin nesting.

Mick has a very old Siamese cat that he 'utterly dotes on'. His name is Boysie and he doesn't like me. He creeps around with his belly hanging on the floor and yowling. I'm relieved when he dies and we get a new kitten.

Mick does the most wonderful drawings - very fine and spidery, pen and ink drawings of ships and flags and people and horses and carts, almost Dickensian. Everyone who has ever received his Christmas cards knows what a joy it is to receive one of these treasures. He will do drawings of 18th century ships dressed 'over all' with little coloured flags and a key on the side which explains how to read the code. On deciphering the code, the greeting within the flags – 'Merry Christmas' or 'Happy Birthday to You' - is revealed. He also spends hours doing jigsaw puzzles. He will do a lovely series of different sailing boats painted on cardboard boxes and I get them mounted into maple frames.

He's still at it, over ninety years old, drawing for the 'crippled jockeys club' in Ireland …

He is into Transcendental Meditation. Every morning and evening he goes into the bedroom and meditates for twenty minutes. I want to find out about this. We go to a large house in Knightsbridge where two actors live. They are initiators for the Maharishee. I like them and I am given training for a few weeks until one day Mick takes me for my initiation. There are offerings and rice, white handkerchiefs, flowers and incense, and I am given a mantra. Now we meditate together morning and evening. *It's the beginning of a very long journey, but I don't know that then.* Things go 'better' when I've 'sat', even though often I don't want to, or I fall asleep, and other things keep popping into my mind.

Emma, by John Cole

I'm feeling very grounded and healthy. Setting up my little sewing machine on the kitchen table, I'm making Emma cloaks and little shifts. I buy her black tights and she wears a little Marimekko hat of mine. John Cole, who is one of the top fashion photographers and lives with my friend Patsy, gives us a family session.

Jonathan Miller has introduced me to his friend Norman Morris who is Professor of Gynaecology at Charing Cross Hospital. He is a charming man with a twinkle in his eyes. I can see in his face that he is horrified at my caesarean scar. He asks me who did it - so I was right – that surgeon *was* a butcher.

I join Erna Wright's Natural Childbirth classes. Prior to this childbirth had been rather old fashioned - *clinging to the bed posts in agony*. Now, we are taught psycho-prophylaxis. As we become aware of each stage of our labour we know which gear of breathing to employ so instead of focussing on the pain we are focussing on our breath.

As the months progress I've become friends with the other mothers in the class. There are students who are invited by Norman Morris to attend my examinations. This is a training hospital so I just have to accept that these young men will be peering attentively at my privates and prodding my belly. They have a brand new policy of allowing the fathers to be at the birth, but I will be on my own.

It's January 1963 and it's the coldest winter since 1947. My contractions are coming fast and furious so I'm off to the Charing Cross Hospital. Angela Douglas is there supporting me. We eat mince pies and chat to the nurses in between my contractions.

Now, it's thirty-six hours into the labour and I'm exhausted. I'm stumbling up the corridor, panting, when a young doctor gives me some encouragement.

'Don't be nice to me, I'll cry!' I am afraid to lose control. The pains have been going on for so long, they want to give me drugs but I insist on being compos mentis. And then, at last, it's really happening and I'm pushing. The supreme effort … the last push … extreme agony … I just think it's going to kill me.

With a mirror at the end of the bed, I can see the head coming. I'm crying, I'm laughing and, Polly is born. January 14th. She weighs 7lb 5oz. The moment when Polly is first put into my arms, a mother is born. I love to hold her ... I never want to put her down ... this little being ... how can I protect her forever? ... my baby girl, Polly. I am put into a heated bed and sleep the sleep of the deeply satisfied. I spend ten days in hospital learning to look after her.

When I leave the hospital, the fountains of Trafalgar Square are frozen over. Polly comes home and into her little wooden crib. I don't breast-feed. I've got to get back to work as soon as I can. Mick is enchanted by her (and increasingly by me).

Five weeks after Polly is born, I get a part in *No Hiding Place*, so I put her into her old-fashioned pram, which I've painted bunches of flowers on. Covered in her patchwork quilt, with bottles of milk and nappies on board, I push her around to a friend and I'm off to rehearsals.

Afterwards I pick her up and bring her home for her bath and bed, make supper for Mick and Emma, learn my lines and fall asleep listening to her breathing beside me. My darling, precious daughter.

I write to Tony telling of the birth and to tell him that I'm 'going it alone', so he needn't concern himself, which I am sure he is relieved about.

Mickgough is doing *Six Characters in Search of an Author* at The Mayfair. The hotel decides it doesn't want the actors coming into the lobby, and they should use the kitchen entrance. This is Ralph Richardson and Barbara Jefford! Mick is delighted.

'It's right,' he says, 'we have always been rogues and vagabonds, not Lords and Ladies.' He has a bottle of Irish whiskey in his dressing room, and he has noticed it is going down faster than he is drinking it. Is it his dresser? On the last performance, he pees in it. I am shocked by this deed but my only conclusion is - well, Mick is - Irish!

Vincent Price has invited us to tea at The Mayfair. He is the most elegant and charmingly soft-spoken man, and a great art collector, so we talk about his paintings.

We are invited to Nick Luard's wedding, a big posh society affair. I take Polly, her first outing. A smiling journalist says,

'Lovely baby, Anneke. Who's your husband?'

'I don't have one,' I say.

'So who is the father?'

'I don't want to talk about it. Please leave me alone.' She's hassling me. My heart is pounding and I move away. The next day Mick's 'charlady' looks upset as she lays *The Daily Mirror* on the kitchen table. There, across the middle pages, a Marjorie Proops article, with the headline,

A WORD TWO GIRLS SHOULD REMEMBER:
ILLEGITIMATE

It was an evil piece about me and Catherine Deneuve, and how irresponsible we are to have babies out of wedlock. Mick is incandescent with rage. We talk to our friend, who is a lawyer at *The Daily Mail*,

'Is this libellous?' we ask.

'Yes, you could sue them.' I'm happy to let it go, after all, it's what I expected but Mick is insistent, so for the next seven years, a large part of my earnings are poured into the pockets of be-wigged QCs in the Inns of Court.

Mickgough and I have succumbed – we are lovers – it was inevitable. I am very shy about showing him my scarred tummy. I leave his bed in the early hours. I think we should tell Emma *before* she finds out – he's prevaricating – now it's too late. One morning, I'm still in Mick's bed when a cross little face wakes me up.

'What are you doing in my father's bed?'

'Well, um, he needed a cuddle.'

'That's my mother's job'

'Well … um … she's in Mallorca!'

That holiday, when Emma goes to see her mother in Palma, she doesn't return. Mick is very sad about this and I feel guilty. He calls me his 'Petite Oiseaux'. Over the next few years I will be his 'Little Bird'. Mick's son, Simon, returns from his travels. We walk together to the off licence in the Earl's Court Road.

'So darling, who's your latest beau?' enquires Simon.

'Well, um, actually, Simon, it's your father.' We don't see him again either for months.

Mick's two dearest friends are both called Michael. Michael Wallis is a photographer, who is waiting to 'inherit' - *he will wait his whole life and die before it comes to him.* He lives next to the 'Classic Chelsea' and often pops in for a matinee in his slippers with a cup of tea. He loves to lie stretched out on our living room floor, lighting his farts. He has a stammer so he calls Mick 'Mmm-Gough'. And then there's 'Mmm-Johnson' who is a wild Cornish artist and later will live with us. So 'Mmm-Gough' becomes 'Mickgough'.

On 1st October 1963, we go to a first night at the Royal Court Theatre, the opening of *Chips with Everything* by Arnold Wesker. We leave Polly in her Moses basket in Elizabeth's restaurant just behind the theatre. Elizabeth is a volatile Russian woman whose restaurant is very popular. She cooks delicious food and whatever she cooks is what you have, there's no menu. When it's time to pay the bill, she sits down with you, adds it up and, if you happen to be an MP or simply well off, you may well be told,

'And you're paying for that man over there, he is a struggling artist.'

We get to the theatre and there's a real buzz in the foyer. We're sitting in the circle. I'm wearing a black velvet trouser suit I've made and it's ahead of its time so I want to show off. I'm wearing *trousers*! So I put my feet up on the back of the seat in front. Mickgough is doing a stage whisper in my ear,

'Put your feet down darling. Darling, now!' Princess Margaret is in the seat in front.

When we get back to Elizabeth's there's Polly, tucked up in the arms of Arthur Davidson MP, being given her bottle, and everyone is cooing over her.

Tim Craxton is now working in the Jaguar showroom in Sloane Square. He looks dapper in his bowler hat with his moustache and his passion for 'honeys' and cars. It's been hard for him to adjust to a regular life since flying his Spitfire during the war. That was a present danger and feeling of *being alive* that can never be equalled - the bravery and the camaraderie unsurpassed. When he talks about it he gets a look in his eyes ... but for us it's rather boring, sadly, and a bit embarrassing. Soon he will leave for California.

I am going to Hampstead to see Mrs. Craxton. And Sammy Davis is on the 'phone.

'I'm in town for a few days, there's a party tonight, want you there Duchess!'

'I can't Sammy; I'm going to see an old lady ...' He is very put out. No-one says no to Sammy. When he's having a party everybody drops everything and gets there. I'm a bit afraid he won't call again. A few days later he invites me to dinner. Just him. Later in the sixties, I meet Sammy after he has left Mai Britt, and he's joined the Black Panthers. He's together with a very beautiful angry black woman who looks me up and down and I feel like a small ... white ... worm.

Mick goes to the States to make *Phantom of the Opera* with Herbert Lom. He's relieved to be leaving as he's deeply in debt – he has two previous wives to support. One day I notice his bank account. He has 6/9d, the price of a bottle of red. Now he hasn't even got that. He's bundling into the taxi and taken off to the right side of the square, and on the other side, the bailiffs are coming.

'Michael Gough?'

'Yes,' I say, stalling, until I see that taxi's gone off into the Earl's Court Road.

'Yes, ah, *noooo*, not here. I don't know when he'll be back, actually ... um, he's gone to America.'

Polly comes with me everywhere in her pram – to The Troubadour, and to Finch's in the Fulham Road. She begins to have her own group of friends.

I've got the part of a jazz xylophonist in *Sentimental Agent.* I go to Humphrey Lyttleton's and meet up with Tubby Hayes - a top jazz xylophone player – and he very kindly helps me with the piece I am to play. I'm miming it, but I want it to look authentic.

When Mickgough returns from the States he gets a contract with the Royal Shakespeare Company. They will take a production of *The Hollow Crown*, an evening of music and writings of and by the royalty of England from Arthur to Victoria all around the States for three and half months. And, he says, I should definitely accompany him, it's the chance of a lifetime. The chance to see so much of America. I'm torn – my baby, my man – but I have already got a live-in mother's help and Olaf Pooley is lodging with us and will keep an eye out with his sweet lover 'Jillybeans'.

I love the Irish shop in Bond Street. For Mick's birthday I buy him an Aran sweater which he loves and wears forever - he always talks of 'upping sticks' and going to live in Ireland. It is his childhood home and he is always longing to return. They give actors a tax break in Ireland. We dream of getting a Georgian rectory and giving Polly the kind of upbringing Mickgough had, barefooted and free …

November 23rd, Mickgough's birthday, and I am lying on our brass bed on the 'phone talking to Angela when she interrupts me.

'Anneke, something's happening. My God, put your telly on!' John F. Kennedy has been assassinated.

The world is utterly stunned. The President of the United States.

That same day, The Beatles release *With the Beatles* and *Doctor Who* is broadcast for the first time.

Mick is rehearsing with John Barton, one of the gems of the Royal Shakespeare Company. I think he is Shakespeare come back again. The company also includes Ann Firbank, John Nettleton and John Warner and two musicians.

I'm getting a new passport – to fill in the form I have to have it signed by a 'professional male'. I say,

'Can I put Michael Gough? – he's an actor.'

'No, no!' *As Mick said, rogues and vagabonds.*

'Well, he's in *Who's Who*!' I say proudly.

'No, it must be a solicitor or a doctor."

'Ah!' I say, 'I know a crooked solicitor or two, never mind the doctors …' I also have had to get a male signature for my bank account. How ridiculous!

Mickgough

Chapter 21

Christmas in New York

I am utterly amazed by the size of everything in New York. I spend the taxi ride from the airport into town with my neck cricked, in awe of the skyscrapers. We will stay in one of Peter and Wendy's friends' apartment in Greenwich Village. The amount of locks and bolts on the door makes us a little uneasy; we fall into a jet-lagged sleep. We are woken in the early hours by a woman screaming outside in the hall and then a shot. We are glad of the many bolts! Next morning when we put the radio on, we can't understand a word of this incredibly loud and furiously fast way of talking, intermixed with jingles, gospel music and bible thumping. It all seems very far removed from the dulcet tones of the BBC. Our broadcasters are still talking like George VI.

We go to the corner drugstore for breakfast – bright lights, very busy – we join the customers sitting up at the counter.

'Whaddya wan'?' barks the cook. Mickgough, in his theatre voice, replies,

'I wonder, could I have a little fried egg?'

'How ya wan' it? Sunny side up, easy over?' We can't understand him, we're not used to this accelerated pace. When we walk down Madison Avenue, people come out of shops to take photographs of us because we look so unique – Mickgough in his long Irish tweed coat with a beaver fur collar, me with my Charles Jourdan thigh boots. I am looking forward to seeing the American sixties style but there doesn't seem to be any. The cool kids in the village seem to be wearing sneakers and jeans, walking in the street with rollers in their hair.

We go to see Peter and Wendy. I've bought a bottle of Guinness for Wendy to put in her Christmas cake – it's her special recipe - and also an album of the new rave band in England, the album's title is *With the Beatles.* A few months later the US will see the biggest crowds ever seen, as they mob The Beatles.

Peter and Wendy have an apartment in a brown stone building in Greenwich Village. Wendy, of course, has grafted her style onto it. Now, we are in New York hanging out with Peter Cook and the other *Beyond the Fringe* boys, who are the toast of the town. We stumble through the snowy streets to jazz clubs, and shop in Bloomingdales. Wendy and I buy these marvellous long knickers with a velvet bow and a lace trim. Roger Moore will fall in love with these when I work with him in *The Saint*, and call me 'Knickers'. They do look enticing with a leather mini skirt. Lacy stockings – we are still wearing suspenders. I love the button-down-collar men's shirts. It's not until we go further west that we go 'cowboy'.

Mickgough is playing The Hollow Crown in Princeton. The evening is very well-received.

The knickers from Bloomingdales

Tony Newley calls me. We will meet for dinner. He sends his driver to pick me up. I'm wearing my cream lace Marion Foal and Sally Tuffin dress. White stockings, gold shoes. I want him to think,

'Shit, what have I missed?!' We're happy to see each and the love is still there, so we enjoy and swap pictures of our newborns. I tell him about Mickgough adopting Polly. He says there's no way he could have anything to do with her because of Joan. We part with love.

John Krimsky is working with Peter on a Broadway review, based on The Establishment, which will show at the Strollers Theatre Club. Peter Bellwood and Roddy Maude-Roxby have come from London to appear in the production.

Mickgough wants to go to Harlem to see a 'black' concert. Peter is enthusiastic and so are Roddy and Gaye Brown. So a bunch of us take a cab to The Apollo Theatre which is right in the heart of Harlem. We are the only white people there.

It's a fantastic show starring Gladys Knight and Little Richard. We've never seen such energy and dancing. As we come out into the foyer we get the distinct impression that we are being hemmed in menacingly by the audience and are relieved to jump into cabs. It is quite a dangerous thing to do at this time. I am horrified and fascinated by the people sleeping in the doorways in the Bowrie. One day, right in front of us, there is a shooting, and the body is sprawled over a car. And no-one's doing anything!

'Why don't they call an ambulance?'

'Because if you do, you're the one that pays for it.'

This is a weird place.

That Christmas is the best ever. Wendy has an enormous tree and I am astounded to see the presents are nearly as high. Her food, of course, is the best and Peter and Dudley are on top form. They are doing the *Dead Sea Tapes* and we are aching with laughter.

We go to see Roddy in the American version of The Establishment at Peter's Club, The Strollers.

On New Year's Eve there is a huge party in a very grand house, belonging to one of the New York elite. New York high society is extremely grand, the atmosphere is electric. We are making our way through the seething masses down a passageway. It's a tight squeeze. A being looms up, an extraordinary face peering inches from mine. It's Salvador Dali! - *An intense moment.* Dudley is in the centre of the party at the grand piano, and he's inspired, lit up, drunk. I sit with him on his piano stool, we all toast in the New Year, New York style.

Excerpts from my journal:

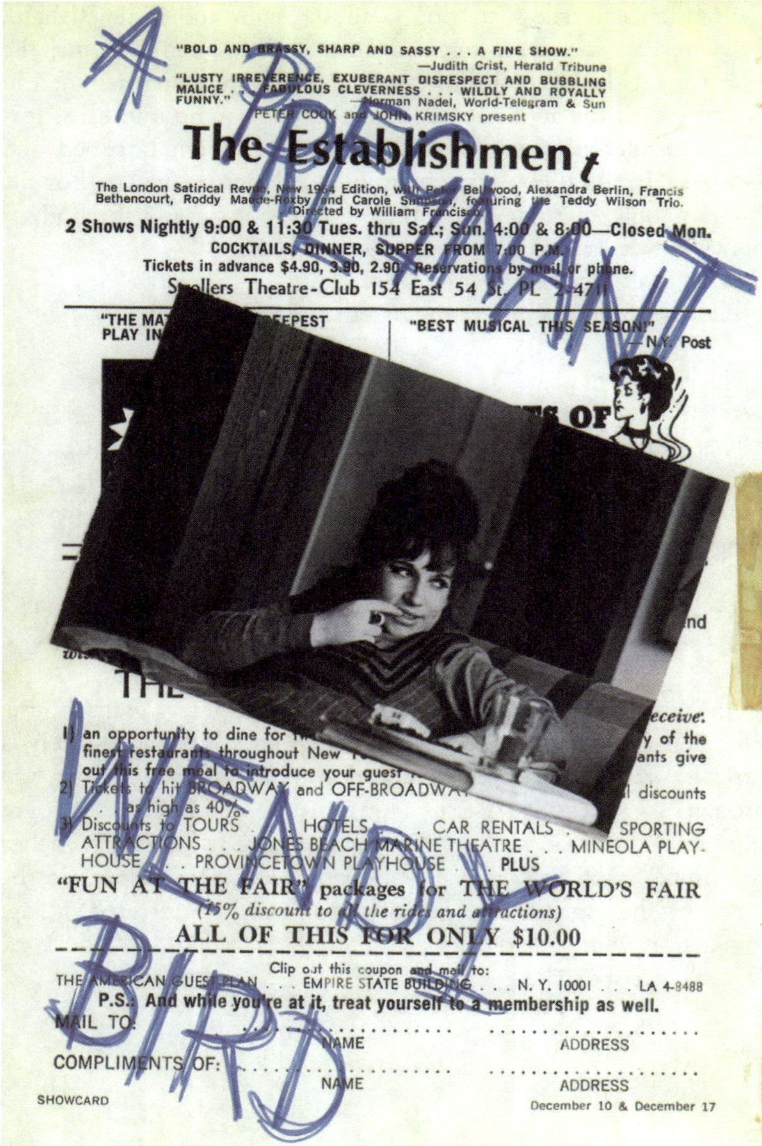
A PREGNANT WENDY BIRD
"BOLD AND BRASSY, SHARP AND SASSY . . . A FINE SHOW."
—Judith Crist, Herald Tribune
"LUSTY IRREVERENCE, EXUBERANT DISRESPECT AND BUBBLING MALICE . . . FABULOUS CLEVERNESS . . . WILDLY AND ROYALLY FUNNY."
—Norman Nadel, World-Telegram & Sun
PETER COOK and JOHN KRIMSKY present
The Establishment
2 Shows Nightly 9:00 & 11:30 Tues. thru Sat.; Sun. 4:00 & 8:00—Closed Mon.
COCKTAILS, DINNER, SUPPER FROM 7:00 P.M.
Tickets in advance $4.90, 3.90, 2.90. Reservations by mail or phone.
Strollers Theatre-Club 154 East 54 St. PL 2-4711
"BEST MUSICAL THIS SEASON!"
—N.Y. Post
"FUN AT THE FAIR" packages for THE WORLD'S FAIR
ALL OF THIS FOR ONLY $10.00
Clip out this coupon and mail to:
THE AMERICAN GUEST PLAN . . . EMPIRE STATE BUILDING . . . N. Y. 10001 . . . LA 4-8488
P.S.: And while you're at it, treat yourself to a membership as well.
MAIL TO:
NAME
ADDRESS
COMPLIMENTS OF:
NAME
ADDRESS
SHOWCARD
December 10 & December 17

RODDY MAUDE-ROXBY. A graduate of the Royal College of Art, he took part in many college revues and productions, writing his own revue material. With Annie Ross and Roger Price, he made up the company of *Three at Nine*. He was also in *One to Another, One Way Pendulum, J. B.* and *Salad Days* in the West End. He appeared at London's Establishment and has had small appearances in the films *The Wild and the Willing, The Party's Over, In the Dog House,* and some television parts. He has continued painting and has exhibited in London and Nottingham.

CAROLE SIMPSON. The only original member of the London company still in the United States, she joins the acting company in this edition of The Establishment, after establishing herself initially with American audiences as a singer. Prior to her two years with this London revue, she was much in demand in England as a vocalist with several popular bands. As both actress and singer she was regularly seen on such British video series as The Saint and heard on her own radio series. She went to Southaw school for girls, but found time during her school days to begin her singing career at the age of 14.

Your host: Ralph Santoro
Manero's
STEAK HOUSE
"ONLY RUSSIAN NITE CLUB IN NEW YORK"
Two Guitars
• Fine Food
• Exciting Floor Shows
244 East 14 St. AL 4-3838
Entertainment Nightly
OPENS DEC. 20
Oscar BRAND
OPENS DEC. 27
Woody
To quote Jean LaMarche, Lord of Meucet, during a visit to Limoux, before "The Burning" in the Year of Our Lord 1321:
"a JENO MATE HUNGARIAN SOUVENIR LP ALBUM* will enhance the Noel Gift List of the meek and the mighty, even 642 Years from now, when JENO MATE portrays me in the 1963 re-enactment of "THE BURNING" at the York Playhouse, East 64th Street and First Avenue, TR 9-4130 ...."
*(c/o Hayes, 155 W. 46 St., NYC, PL 7-6300)
tional quality a long association with Benny Goodman, climaxing it this past summer making a government-sponsored trip to Russia with Goodman. Having struck out on his own as a recording artist and then as a bandleader, Mr. Wilson has become known for his own style of technical mastery and dazzling inventiveness. He is now a permanent fixture at the Strollers, featured in The Establishment and playing after the show in the Pub, backed up by Gene Ramey and Arthur Edghill.
PETER COOK. He was born at St. Chad's Nursing Home for Gentlefolk, Torquay in mid-November 1937. Two years later he was saddened to see the beautiful iron railings outside his home sawed off to be melted
to be amongst
to set the flag of freedom
Havana.
JOHN KRIMSKY. He is the organizer-owner of the Strollers Theatre-Club. He had a long career as originator of venturesome entertainments including Cranks which introduced Anthony Newley to America. In the Thirties, he and Lucius Beebe ran the American Music Hall (Chez Firehouse), where beer and wine were imbibed during the presentation of heart-rending melodramas. He introduced Kurt Weill and Berthold Brecht to New York audiences with the original production here of Threepenny Opera as well as the distinguished German film Maedchen in Uniform and Eugene O'Neill's The Emperor Jones.
WILLIAM FRANCISCO (Director). Recently represented off-Broadway as the director of Color of Darkness, Mr. Francisco headed Quartet Productions for whom he produced, directed and co-authored the off-Broadway musical Sap of Life. In Boston, he designed
SHOWCARD
December 10 & December 17

and directed a widely heralded production of *Fantasticks*. He had, after graduation from Amherst, earned a three-year scholarship to the Yale Graduate School of Drama, after which he accepted a teaching assignment there. Later at Yale, he stage managed the original production of Archibald MacLeish's *JB*, an assignment he also handled at the Brussels World's Fair. In 1959, he became a staff director for the Williamstown Theatre Fund and the following year came to N.Y. as a member of the CBS-TV Director's Workshop. Among his television credits, he lists the spectacular, The Gershwin Years on which he served as producer Leland Hayward's assistant.

THE ESTABLISHMENT

The 1963-64 Edition of The Establishment marks the second completely new production of this satirical revue from London at the Strollers Theatre-Club. The London Company, which had debuted in Soho on October 5, 1961, opened here on January 23rd, 1963, with John Bird, Eleanor Bron, John Fortune, Jeremy Geidt and Carole Simpson as the resident cast. The troupe came to New York via Chicago and Washington and during a summer respite from New York this year, the group played in Toronto, Montreal and in San Francisco. The unique entertainment which has been in the vanguard of the movement satirizing people and events of importance has also found its way into American television. Broadcasts on WNEW-TV and sketches from the show on Ed Sullivan's video offering have introduced The Establishment's special brand of wit to millions. Originated in London by Peter Cook and Nicholas Luard in their own nightclub, the revue is presented here by Mr. Cook and John Krimsky. While the original company, with the exception of Miss Simpson, returns to home base in Soho, the producers have imported Mr. Peter Bellwood and Mr. Roddy Maude-Roxby from London, Miss Alexandra Berlin and Mr. Francis Bethencourt from the ranks of local talent, to join Miss Simpson in the new offering.

STAFF FOR PETER COOK and JOHN KRIMSKY

General Manager .... Ivor David Balding
Publicity Director .... Ruth Cage, Samuel J. Lurie Associates
Business Manager .... Jane Slay
Stage Manager .... Robert MacGowan
Restaurant Manager .... Joseph Frangie
Box Office Treasurers ...... Catherine Duerden, Leslie Daniel, Carol Keefe
Master Electrician and Sound .... Norm Simonsen
Decor .... George Dunkel and Diane McCoy
Chef de Cuisine .... Haydar Guzeyer
Miss Simpson's costume by James Holton

There will be a fifteen minute interval between the first and second acts to order refreshments.
Teddy Wilson and his Trio play in the STROLLERS PUB (back room) after the second show each evening.

Chapter 22

The Hollow Crown Tour

Mickgough, Brian P and the bus — John Nettleton, me and John Warner

Now we are packing, to start our big journey. Our luggage is restricted. We will be on this bus for three and a half months together. I'm going to keep a journal. There are twelve of us including the driver, plus costumes and a few props. Four musicians, four actors, one under-study, two partners in tow, two sparks and a carpenter. We drive up through New York state – it's January, lots of snow. We will play in university campuses and theatres all the way.

Wherever we go we are welcomed and feted by wealthy socialites. We are given grand dinners in every new town.

TORONTO

THIS PICASSO WAS ACTUALLY IN THE CLEVELAND ART MUSEUM - BUT ALL THE COLOURED PICASSOS POSTCARDS WERE SO BAD.

THESE FRIGGING AMERICAN TELEPHONES

So here we are now then in Toronto at the King Edward Sheraton Hotel and very nice it is too. The Royal "Alex" theatre is nice but the audiences are atrociously bad. We had all the photos developed - most of them didn't come out! We had everything cleaned and I washed things and we did generally get sorted out. →

We start to become 'bus-wise' – when we are in a big city it's time to do laundry, and spread out. On the road we stay in motels, but in the cities we are in big hotels.

In Toronto, we play the Royal Alexander Theatre. I write in my journal -

We have turned up at 2:00 for a 2:30 show, discovered the show is actually 2:00!! - I have never seen Michael Gough Esquire get so quickly into his dinner jacket and fly straight on with no dress shirt, no make up and no breath. And the gallery is full of school boys throwing paper clips.

It is such a privilege to see Mick playing every night. He is a master of his craft. He had been trained at the *Old Vic* with Alec Guinness, under Michel Saint-Denis. When we go to the theatres I have to help him with sound testing. I move around the auditorium, so he knows how strong to pitch his wonderful voice. As he says,

'You want them just to sit a little forward to hear you.' Women fall in love with his voice. He lets the words ... just … come. This always makes me very nervous because I always think he's just dried. Alec Guinness says about acting,

'You can't be swimming with one foot on the ground. You've got to jump in and trust.'

The Hollow Crown is an enchanting evening and the students amaze us with their knowledge of English history and Shakespeare. In Toronto, there is a buzz – Richard Burton and Elizabeth Taylor are in town, staying at our hotel. Mickgough had known Richard as a young actor so he is most put out when we are searched and identified before we can get to our floor. The whole of Toronto is turned upside down because of these two.

In Montreal we play the *Place des Arts*, a huge, ultra-modern building – we have never seen such architecture, in London, we don't have buildings like this yet. After the show, we go to an upstairs club and listen to Miles Davis. In between sets he's at the bar. Mickgough and I shyly go up to introduce ourselves as British fans. Miles turns, big smile on his face,

'Man,' says Miles, 'I know you, I've seen you in the movies!' The other musicians are laughing around us. It seems they love to watch

BEDROOM WINDOW in MONTREAL
CN
CANADA
7 cents
CANADA
20 CIGARETTES 20
MOCASINS FOR POLLY
FRAPPEZ AU VERSO
JANUAR
JAZZ
UPSTAIRS
JAN. 16, 17, 18, 19
MILES DAVIS
AND HIS QUINTET
94 ST-CATHERINE E.
UN 1 - 8213 (Upstairs)
UN 1 - 6105 (Downstairs)

horror films. Many of which, star Mickgough. This is a thrilling moment for us both.

In Chicago we meet the legendary radio interviewer and lovely man, Studs Terkel. He interviews Mickgough on his morning show, I'm there as well. We enjoy meeting his other guests so much that we go every morning while we are in town. He has just been on the Freedom March, a massive anti-racism demonstration in Washington. He's made a documentary about it called *Born to Live*, which he has won a medal for, and the BBC have bought it.

There was one great old grandmother who he spoke to. Below is a moving transcript, that I kept in my journal.

Terkel: Do you think heaven is going to be integrated? How do you feel about the whites on this train?

Old Negro Woman: The white man's heaven? (laughs merrily) Nooo! If a white thought he had to sit next to a coloured through eternity, why, I believe he would rather be in hell.

The whites on this train are wonderful. If every white man in America got on this train and saw all this good fellowship he would either suffer a stroke or a change of heart. These died-in-the-wood, no-good, grey white men who think they are so great and God's gift to the world, I got news for them: they ain't.

I know that things will be alright someday. But when white folks ask me,

'When you come back from Washington, will you be satisfied?' (very sassy, sarcastic.) 'Or will you people keep fighting?' I got news for them: we will.

Negroes got love. White man doesn't know the love in a coloured heart. Too much love, maybe. That's why Negroes have gone along with this crazy American pattern for so long. (cackles, merrily.)

Studs tells us he can't ride a bike, he can't swim, he can't type, he can't do anything, all he can do is talk. And when he talks to you, he really listens, empathises and often weeps.

At the Art Institute, I see Van Gogh's painting of his Blue Bedroom. I sit down in front of it, and cry. My grandfather's family had known the Van Goghs in Paris and my mother is fiercely protective about Vincent.

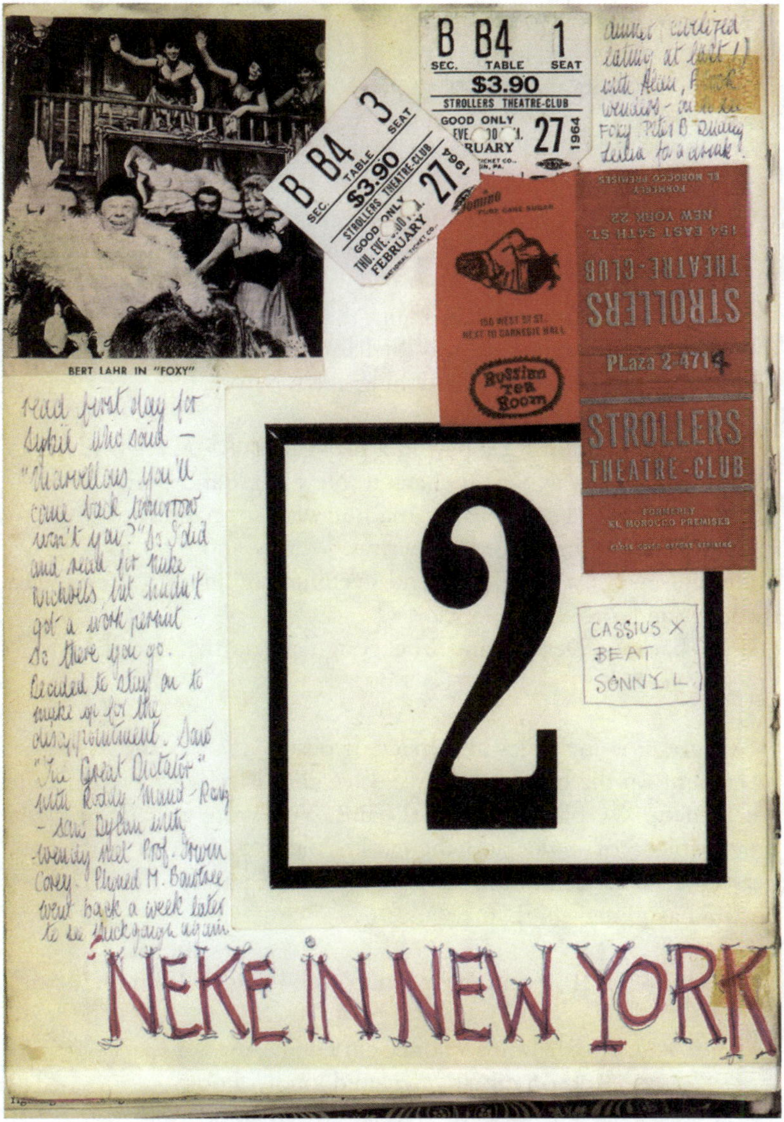

BERT LAHR IN "FOXY"
B B4 1
SEC. TABLE SEAT
$3.90
STROLLERS THEATRE-CLUB
GOOD ONLY
27
1964
B B4 3
SEC. TABLE SEAT
$3.90
STROLLERS THEATRE-CLUB
GOOD ONLY
THU. EVE.
FEBRUARY 27 1964
Domino
150 WEST 57 ST.
NEXT TO CARNEGIE HALL
Russian Tea Room
STROLLERS
THEATRE-CLUB
154 EAST 54TH ST.
NEW YORK 22
FORMERLY
EL MOROCCO PREMISES
PLaza 2-4714
STROLLERS
THEATRE-CLUB
FORMERLY
EL MOROCCO PREMISES
2
CASSIUS X
BEAT
SONNY L
NEKE IN NEW YORK

We hear the J.J. Johnson Quartet. I've got the album, back in London. I'm sending loads of postcards to Robin. We love old town Chicago with its arty bookshops, bazaars and loads of cafés, 'Troubadours' - early-American style. Our favourite is called The Crystal Pistol.

Winnipeg is so cold, our breath freezes and we can't walk in the streets.

We read about the pandemonium that The Beatles have caused at the London Palladium. It was bedlam; they didn't know how to handle it. They'd never seen anything like it before.

I have an audition for a part in a play called *The Knack* – it will be played off Broadway. So I fly back to New York and I read for Mike Nicholls. They're keen to have me but with so many Brits working in New York, I am refused a permit. Wendy and I go to see Alec Guinness in *Dylan*, and we spend evenings in The Strollers – with Roddy Maude-Roxby.

I fly back to Denver and Mickgough meets me, dressed in full cowboy gear.

We are crossing miles and miles of desert in Colorado, there are mountains on the horizon and we drive and drive but never seem to reach them. We play games in the bus. You write a made up word on the piece of paper and then fold it and pass it on – the next person writes a definition, folds it again and passes it on. The last person has to make a rhyme.

'Schpook' – an '18th century spittoon', (courtesy of John Nettleton)

Doctor Johnson once aimed at a shpoock,
And on missing declared loudly 'Fook!'
That's the fifth time today so I'm going away
And Boswell can clear up the mook.

We cross the Rockies to Salt Lake City, my journal noting everything – the amazing snow-capped mountains. We go through Nevada and on to Lake Tahoe, which we love.

FISHERMAN'S WHARF • SAN FRANCISCO
Souvenirs and Gifts
Sea Captain's Chest
SAN FRANCISCO
Domino Club
"World Famous for Cuisine, Gloria & Galaxy of Paintings"
Evelyn
One of more than 200 oil paintings adorning the Domino Club dining room
BRENDAN BEHAN DIED
CONCORD COACH
THE STORY OF WELLS FARGO
SANDAL

Then, we are in San Francisco where we stay two weeks playing at the Curran Theatre. We fall in love with San Francisco. There are orange trees in the streets. We go to Finochios to see the female impersonators. Art Blakely and the Jazz Messengers, the American review, *The Committee*, Kenneth Williams and friends in *The Private Ear and The Public Eye.*

We walk around what is just beginning to become Haight-Ashbury - the colourful centre of San Fransisco's Hippy Movement. We go to the Hungry Eye where Bill Cosby is performing and Mick and I love him so much, we go every night.

Story has it that a year earlier, a young Barbra Streisand had given an audition and when she was rejected she retorted,

'In a year's time I'll be back and you won't be able to afford me!' A year later she returned - and they couldn't!

Across in Sausalito we are wandering around when we see a charming little theatre – we are in the foyer looking at the photos when around the corner comes this larger than life character wearing a wide-brimmed hat and a cloak and boots and he welcomes us in a deep Irish brogue, his dark eyes flashing. This is the actor-manager, Jack Aranson. Off we go to the nearest bar and listen to tales of the Irish Theatre and all the old character actors at the Abbey. Mickgough and I relishing the stories. He lives with his wife and many children in Mill Valley in the redwoods. We run barefooted on Stinson Beach. We don't want to leave. I've been reading Jack Kerouac's *On the Road.*

On down to Los Angeles. I'm not attracted by it at all, too big, too violent, and there are too many cars. We see these freaky women on the streets downtown, with huge picture hats and fur stoles. Rich lawyers everywhere. We see the kids on the make, trying to get a part in films. Mickgough says,

'They want it handed to them on a plate- they don't want to work for it … '

As soon as we get settled in our hotel in Hollywood, we call everyone we know – Sammy Davis, Pete Sellers, Lenny Bruce, but we can't get through to any of them for days because of their protectors. Eventually Sammy calls, cross because we hadn't been in touch with him earlier.

SAMMY DAVIS

called!!!!!

THIS LADY IS AN ATTORNEY - - - - - - - !

You see this kind of lady everywhere on the street

We swam in the pool of the hotel which was *freezing*! It was very sad to see all those pathetic kids on the make in **PJ's** who are there to sell themselves and maybe get discovered. But they are not prepared to work for it. They want it handed to them on a plate. One tastes the rat race of Hollywood of old and "movie making" and I long for the old fashioned sweetness of secure old London.

PASADENA was alright, an *enormous* auditorium and I bought a pair of shoes.

When we go to his beautiful home, to meet Mai Britt, I am wearing black velvet trousers and a white Mexican shirt. When Mai opens the door – so is she! So we laugh and hug – she is a warm and lovely woman. Sammy shows us his basement playroom. He sits in his Master's chair, from which he can control the screen coming up and down and the movies being played. He has some of Mick's horror movie films, which he loves. A stage rises out of the floor and there are swords on the wall so he can have Errol Flynn-type fights. Mai and I talk babies in the kitchen while she's feeding their children, Mark and Tracey. I'm really missing Polly.

Then I'm called into Columbia Pictures to see about a part in the film *The Collector* with Terry Stamp. I read the book and I get very excited because I think,

'I could really play this part – right up my street!' I don't get it, but I do get taken all around the Universal studio lot. So strange to see cowboy streets, old English, Spanish and French towns. We see Rock Hudson, working on a British picture in a British street – a mews flat, pissing rain, red buses. It makes us feel homesick.

Mickgough and I go riding 'cowboy-style' in the Hollywood hills.

We're off across Arizona, miles and miles of desert and cactuses. At The Grand Canyon, New Mexico we are simply astounded at the vastness. It's too much to take in. I see what I think is a bird flying below us – actually it's an aeroplane. In Tulsa I go to see Mickgough's film, *Horrors of the Black Museum*, in which he plays a sadistic villain. I can't let him touch me after that for quite a while. He was really frightening in it.

When we get to Dallas we hear the most extraordinary rumours – apparently there were parties already planned by the Republicans *before* the assassination of John F. Kennedy.

We drive through Oklahoma's fields of horses, Palominos and Pintos.

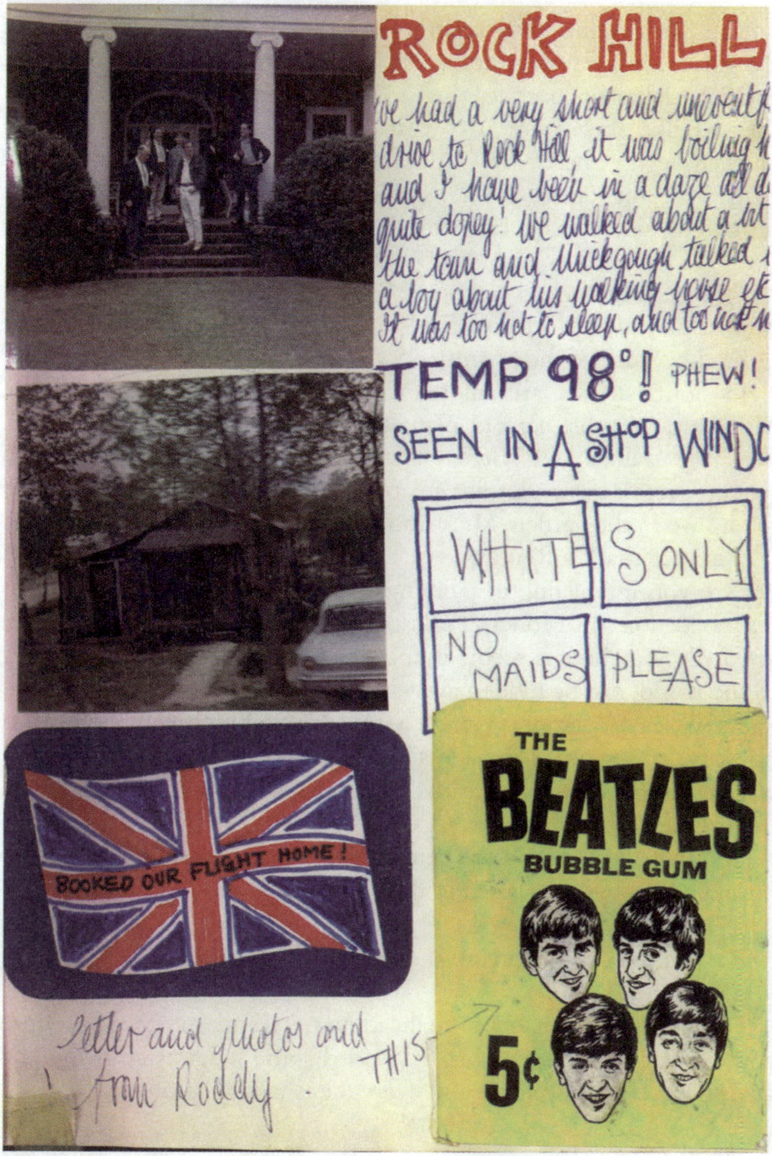
ROCK HILL
ve had a very short and uneventf
drive to Rock Hill it was boiling
and I have been in a daze all
quite dopey! We walked about a
the town and Mick gough talked
a boy about his walking horse etc
It was too hot to sleep, and too hot
TEMP 98°! PHEW!
SEEN IN A SHOP WINDO
WHITES ONLY
NO MAIDS PLEASE
BOOKED OUR FLIGHT HOME!
letter and photos and
from Roddy.
THIS
THE BEATLES
BUBBLE GUM
5¢

The Rock Island Line, swamps and catfish, Uncle Tom figures in dungarees, images straight out of *Huckleberry Finn*, old grannies in rocking chairs on porches, just like Nina Simone's songs. Women dressed like they were fifty years ago, beautiful black kids, and chickens everywhere. We notice poverty-stricken shacks along the road with the latest car alongside, and the old abandoned cars heaped up side by side. Huge modern fridges on the porches.

In Memphis we go to Beale Street – *The Beale Street Blues*. In Mississippi, we see cotton fields. They bury their dead above the ground because of the swamps.

In contrast, we are invited by the owner of the theatre in Memphis, who has an old plantation house, to see his dogwoods. We have walked into *Gone with the Wind*. The black servant with white gloves serves us mint juleps. On our way, escorted through the house to the garden, Mick notices a painting.

'I'm sure that's a Renoir,'

'Are you interesting in paintings?' says the owner, and shows us his collection of Monet, Picasso and Toulouse Lautrec. We are stunned. Somehow it seems immoral, these paintings should belong to the world, not be hidden away in a private collection.

As we leave Memphis we see a little white church with a crowd of black people standing outside silently praying, surrounded by Police with pointed guns. It makes us both sad. When we stop for lunch, the owner of the drug store says,

'See that flag? That's the cemetery where the Yankee soldiers are buried. Our boys are buried in the ditch.'

We can feel the history on our heels.

Next day we visit a police headquarters and see the American equivalent of a county court. It's weird – the judge is smoking and talking into a microphone, and everyone is talking at once …

We see chain-gangs working on the roads and endless miles and miles of flat desert and prairie lands.

leading members of the
Royal Shakespeare Company
in
The Hollow Crown

Only if you do this journey do you really understand the vastness of this country. We touched the history. In the cowboy films we had seen, it was always the men who were glorified – Wyatt Earp, Jessie James – now, we meet the grandchildren of the early pioneers. They have photos of their grandmothers – such tough women, standing in their aprons on the wooden porches of their cabins, fiercely wielding huge shotguns, in their dangerous world. We see photographs of 'Red Indians', these wonderful faces. We see their outfits, touch their feathers and beads. Sadly most of them are now on reservations becoming drunks.

We love the music that emerges from the soul of the black people in the south. Singing The Blues is how they express their ancestral pain. Bessie Smith, Coleman Hawkins, Big Bill Broonzy, John Lee Hooker, Muddy Waters, BB King, Lightning Slim ... wonderful names, and the list goes on.

We drive on through Georgia, Atlanta, we see the poverty along the way. We notice, in a laundrette, a sign saying 'Whites Only and No Maids Please'. We are deeply disturbed by the racial prejudice and we are included in this because they see us as liberal 'nigger-lovers'. *Yeah!*

Charleston, West Virginia, more cotton fields, and up to Pittsburgh, which we dub 'Pissburg' because we have our final party there. About time. I just can't wait to get home to my little baby girl. I have been away from her for three and a half moths. I've bought her some tiny Levi jeans and a jacket, and some Indian moccasins.

It has indeed been a 'trip of a lifetime'.

Chapter 23

Home to Polly

Polly, in her antique pushchair.
Taken by Michael Wallis

London seems so small! They've put flags out around our front door and there is my lovely Polly looking bigger – within a few moments she's clinging to me and being very demanding. She know's I'm her mum and *where have I been?!*

We sit in Finch's with a warm pint – proper beer at last!

Mickgough has a John Mortimer play to do. He will be playing an MP so we go to the Houses of Parliament to sit in the public gallery and hear a debate. We dress up smartly – me with my rose-pink straw hat – and we take our seats. We are astonished by what we see. A bunch of fifth formers interrupting each other, throwing darts and jeering and shouting each other down. This is serious! The country is being run by schoolboys. After a while, one of them notices a pretty girl in the gallery wearing a pink hat, and nudges his friend. Now, a few of them are distracted by me. We leave in disgust and disappointment. Later, as *Private Eye* is being distributed for the first time from The Troubadour, instead of the usual notice you put in your window advertising your chosen political party, we have 'DON'T VOTE – IT ONLY ENCOURAGES THEM!' and 'GUY FAWKES – THE ONLY MAN WHO ENTERED PARLIAMENT WITH HONEST INTENTIONS!'

I have a dear friend, Barney Broadbent – he is a designer of environments. Over the next decade, Mick and I will spend much time with him and his family in Lincolnshire, Dee and Roy his parents, Julie his sister and James his younger brother.

James – *Jim* - will come to us and talk about the possibility of acting. Mick is teaching part-time at the London Academy of Music and Dramatic Art so he advises Jim to go to LAMDA, and then to do rep, which is exactly what Jim does. And now he has become one of Britain's best-loved, Oscar -winning actors.

On one of my forays up the Portobello road I find a little Edwardian silver cigarette and match case with 'Ernest Reid' inscribed. He's one of the old characters who inhabit the Portobello Road scene. So I've told everyone, and at Hennekeys on Saturday lunchtime, when he comes in I present it to him. He is deeply touched; it was part of his grander Edwardian days. On a stall, I see this group of sepia photos. I'm drawn to them – a little boy in a dog cart, a group of maids in Edwardian costume. When I bring them home and show them to Mickgough, he says,

'Wait a minute; I think that's my father. Yes. When he was a little boy!' He will show them to his mother.

'Oh yes,' she says, 'There's Beck, and there's Hannah, one of our maids, ooh, I remember her, she was tyrant!'

Mickgough has been on tour in a play and I'm going to meet him at Liverpool Street Station. I haven't seen him for a couple of weeks and I've been missing him badly. I am wearing my new pink and mustard Marimekko dress and a cloche hat. I walk down the platform, everything goes into slow motion – *I know this scene* – the echoing announcements, the busy passengers, my heart is pounding with anticipation.

In the distance, emerging out of the steam, the familiar figure. His face is full of love and laughter.

He is going down on one knee. We are suspended in this moment.

'Dear Heart Darling, will you marry me?'

The other passengers are cheering and clapping and we are off to the pub to celebrate. Of course, we will have to wait for his divorce to come through. I am 22 and he is 47. He wants to adopt Polly.

Mickgough gives me a Mexican silver engagement ring, two huge balls twisted on a band of silver.

'It's what I think of marriage - a load of silver balls ha, ha! We will celebrate our anniversaries 'cause I don't think we'll have many, ha, ha!'

I'm so excited about getting married to Mickgough I tell an actor friend, but they are less excited,

'He hasn't got a very good track record'.

My Scouse friend, Stevie, has got a job being a wench the Gore Hotel in Kensington. Huge Elizabethan feasts, everyone in costume

– she looks luscious in hers. But the costumes give the punters a licence to touch her up. She asks

'Ey, Mickgough, what's Elizabethan for fuck off?'

I write to Wendy in America, checking up on her pregnancy.

Sarah Miles has invited herself and her husband, Robert Bolt, to dinner. I'm not wildly enthusiastic. I think she's only really coming because she wants to meet Mickgough. She's a big star now. Anyway, I've gone to some trouble to cook chicken with walnuts and Mick and I are awaiting their arrival when we hear a huge commotion. Instead of coming in through the front door, she's launching herself down the area steps and as we open the sash window, this huge white Pyrenean Mountain Dog leaps over the window ledge and starts checking out our home, wagging its tail and knocking everything flying. Sarah is following and exclaiming,

'Addo! Addo! Dahling!'

Robert is also climbing over the window ledge and she's heaving this huge cast-iron pot, which is darling Addo's dinner. Now our supper must come out of the oven while the dog's is heated up. *What a carry on.* Robert is a quiet, northern school teacher and we like him because in spite of his fame, he seems so ordinary.

We have annual sessions with our accountant. He marks up actors' expenses - telegrams, flowers, entertaining, bags, shoes - all fantasy - I feel really depressed when we've finished - do people really spend so much money on luxuries? When I was a child, if we saw a swanky car go by, my mother would say

'Must be crooks. Nice people never have any money.'

We also now have a financial advisor, Peggy Thompson. She has many actors on her books; since we are unable to handle our money because of the feast or famine nature of our work, plus the fact that we are taxed very heavily, things can very easily get out of hand. So we give her all our earnings and she handles our bills and 'outgoings' and she gives us pocket money to live on. It's the only way.

We hear that our flat is to be divided into two and our rent will be doubled. *Hells bells, now what?* I come up with the idea of buying a house and filling it with lodgers to help pay off the mortgage. Mick is very doubtful but Peggy agrees so we are house-hunting. We look at some dilapidated properties in Islington but it looks rough and ugly to me – not the sort of place that I want to push a pram around. Our friend Noel Harrison says there's a house going in his street in Fulham. We love it, a Victorian terrace, opposite a large park. It's £9,000. We put down a deposit and in the autumn we move into Hurlingham Road.

I do a drawing of how the interior will look once we've knocked the wall down, opened the fireplaces and sanded the floors. Naturally, there will be a jungle in the window. Later, when it's finally done, Mickgough fishes out the drawing and is surprised at how accurate it is.

We visit Noel and his wife Sarah, who live down the street and have renovated their house, which is lovely and light – we are inspired and can't wait to move in to our own home. Noel is Rex Harrison's son. He's a very sweet, talented musician and Sarah is a very bright blonde. They have two children.

Mick is doing a play – *Jackie the Jumper* – in which he is brilliant, although he is very worried about forgetting his lines. During the dress rehearsal, he falls into the orchestra pit. John Dexter, is directing, and says,

Napoleon picking his nose, and me with Pat Macnee

'It was very funny. One minute you're spouting away on the stage very nicely thank you, and the next, there is a loud clash of cymbals and a cry of *Oh Shit – I'm not dead.'*

I have an episode of *Our Man in St Marks* to do. Leslie Phillips plays the Vicar, and lovely Joan Hickson is also in it. She is a close friend and neighbour of Mickgough's mother in Wivenhoe, so I'm on best behaviour. She is everything she seems, wonderfully dithery and very perceptive.

After that, I get a part in *The Avengers* – I will be working with Honor Blackman, Pat Macnee and the wonderful Leonard Rossiter. Honor wears black leather, does judo – *the new woman is emerging*. Pat is a very witty sweet man. The action takes place at a New Year party on a train, and I wear a pussy cat costume.

Although much of my work has been lost over the years, I am pleased to say that this episode – *Dressed to Kill* -is still in existence.

Robert Graves, the great poet, is standing in our hall! He has a Roman nose, long silver hair, a wide Spanish hat and a cloak. He is on a visit from Mallorca. Mick's first wife is a cousin of his. He takes one look at me, and tucks me under his cloak,

'You are my family!' and we all march off to The Troubadour where he presides. People are reverential, listening to his every word, which of course, he loves, so he's on top form. It's a very, very special evening and one which those of us who were there will never forget.

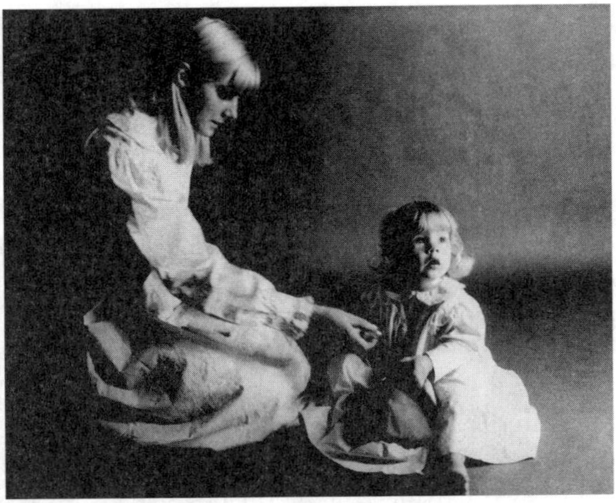

Polly and me in Victorian nightdresses, taken by John Cole

Chapter 24

Hurlingham Road

♫ *The times they are a changing'* ♫
- Bob Dylan

Our new house in Hurlingham Road has been lived in by an old couple since before the war. We are going to renovate it ourselves over the next few years. We'll knock down the major wall on the right as you come in so that you step straight into a living room, with stairs ahead. Then we open up the doors between so now you have one large room with windows out onto the garden. The 1950s fireplaces come out. It's all very dusty but we're so happy to have our own home. The garden has a concrete path down to a shed full of rubbish Why do I always inherit sheds full of rubbish? Why is it that previous tenants never take responsibility for their garbage? (Where's my soapbox?!)

Polly can have a little nursery. There is a room for the mother's help and the two top rooms are for our 'lodgers'. We paint our bedroom 'Gauloise blue' with the brass bed and the patchwork quilt. *The little kitchen! What dinners we have there! What guests!* The walls are terracotta; a Victorian brass lamp hangs over a scrubbed pine ship's table with benches. One day Mick and I are trawling around the junk shops of Fulham when we see a young man struggling with some very large pub mirrors. We chat to him, and buy them for £10 each. Now we have two huge eight foot Art Nouveau mirrors. Ogden's Flake, says one, and the other, 'Lower Prices Than We Charge Are Impossible If Satisfaction Is To Be Given'. Mickgough says it should be in a brothel! And a Wills Stars Cigarettes for the kitchen. It takes us most of this autumn to strip off the forties wallpaper that's been varnished onto the main wall. We choose a lovely 'Coles' hand-printed wallpaper with roses and birds – really exquisite. We have a green leather Chesterfield and a Victorian chaise-longue, a wall full of books, the Staffordshire on top, and the rocking horse. It's very attractive - eventually!

I buy my first-ever washing machine – what freedom! I can wash the nappies myself! I have a garden and a washing line. Not everyone has washing machines and we still send our sheets to the laundry. Wonderful baskets full of ironed sheets and pillow cases, men's shirts all clean and folded once a week.

Our two lodgers are not there all the time. They are with us when they have work in London. One is dear friend Olaf Pooley, actor, and the other is Arthur Davidson, MP for Accrington. Olaf Pooley and his sweet girlfriend Jillybeans collect early 19th century paintings. He's marvellous at restoring them. She is another inspiration for me. I thought, that when you get to forty, you get fat and wear twin set and pearls but here she is in boots and jeans and Fair Isle sweaters, and so slim! Alright! There's hope for me later then!

Mickgough and Arthur Davidson both get stinking colds at the same time. I'm getting fed up with running up and down the flights of stairs to look after their needs, so I get them in the brass bed together during the day. So, there is this MP and this old actor, together under the patchwork quilt, reading newspapers and blowing their noses. Peter Cook loves this image and expands the story with,

'Nurse … NURSE!!! What about a change of sheets?'

Every time I make a bit of money from now on it will all get ploughed into making our home comfortable and paying the lawyers for the beastly ongoing lawsuit. We have a birthday party for Mickgough in November. We empty the living room except for a makeshift table covered in a red Conran bed sheet, candles everywhere. The friends all come and I'm anxious that the goose cassoulet will be alright. Wendy approves – *the Royal Seal!* We have a raucous dinner at the end of which we all have to help change the scene ready for the sanding of the floors the next day. The floors are Victorian and have been covered in lino for years so they will come up really well. After that I paint the walls 'library green' and it's all looking great for Christmas. Although, I forget to put a top coat of paint on the front windows.

My spirit never forgets this and in my dreams it wants to return to Hurlingham Road and paint that final coat.

We leave each other little notes

Henry Grossman from Time Magazine comes to do an article on Mick and me. We go to a lovely old ruin in the country and they take pictures of us, in the sunset, Mickgough dressed like a cowboy.

That Was the Week That Was is transmitted for the first time. We think that Millicent Martin is a poor man's Annie Ross.

Mick is doing some night shooting so I've gone to bed. I'm woken up by the sound of grunts and thumps and I am immediately wide awake and in fear. I'm afraid of the sounds of violence - shadows of my childhood. *What's going on?* I pull on my dressing gown and go down to investigate. Now, Mick drinks but I've never seen him legless. He never loses control of himself. But here he is, very pleased with himself.

'We've been filming in an old ruined house, Dear Heart!' He is struggling with two ten foot plaster pillars with ornate tops that he knows,

'Will look really good on either side of the opening between the two rooms.'

Our first Christmas in our new home. Mick has a collection of Victorian glass baubles so our tree is exquisite and the wood stove is crackling. We have a Dalmatian puppy called Hector.

Clement Freud has produced the most marvellous article in the Sunday papers – *The Days Before Christmas.* He has worked it all out for us, the shopping and preparations are all planned so on Christmas Day all I have to do is light the oven. I keep this article, and will use it for years. When I meet him, I thank him.

I have found Polly a little Victorian doll's pram. She sleeps in a black, Art Nouveau iron bed that Stevie has lent me. I make curtains for all the windows. We have no central heating, it is too costly, so we have gas fires. It's not warm so we simply wear more clothes.

Mickgough is playing in *The Prime of Miss Jean Brodie* in the West End, and I am rehearsing during the day, so at the moment, we are like ships passing in the night.

Alice Pollock and Ossie Clark have opened a shop in Chelsea called 'Quorum'. They are my friends and I love their clothes.

I've booked myself driving lessons with a lovely out-of-work actor. His face is stuck in a permanently anxious state. He is terribly nervous. But because of all the lessons I had with Tim Craxton, driving in his Riley all over the countryside, I progress well and book my test in Ealing. I pass, first time. I buy myself a second hand Mini Traveller. It costs me £60. *Now I'm free!* We can park outside the shops, Harrods, Peter Jones, Christopher Wrays and Pollyanna in the Fulham Road. The roads are still relatively empty.

By the time we leave in the 1970s the traffic is beginning to pile up.

♫ *To know, know, know you…is to love, love, love you,* ♫
- Adam Faith

Mickgough's divorce has come through! We book the Fulham registry office for Valentines Day. We plan a party. We have a wedding lunch with the Van Bloemen's, The Troubadour cheering us on. Quorum has made me black coat with yellow trim and yellow trousers. Michael Wallis and Stevie will be our witnesses - but Wallis is hopeless, and gets lost on the way, so we ask a couple of strangers. The Registrar speaks the immortal words,

'Do you, Anneke … ' and I've flown out of my body. I'm watching the scene from above, thinking that our transcendental meditation initiation ceremony was much more magical than this! Then, I'm back in my body again, and we are off home to get on with the party preparations. Polly looks adorable in the party dress I made her, the house looks lovely, all the friends are smiling and we have a bath full of Spanish champagne on ice. John Craxton, our agents, Noel Harrison and family, Robin and new girlfriend, The Alberts playing music, so many friends.

In the early hours we drive to Aldborough in Essex where Jillybeans has lent us a holiday home. Mickgough of course doesn't want to spend any money. We have Hector with us. Very tired, we arrive to find we have just the basics. We shuffle the single beds together, and exhausted we sleep, with Hector on top of us. The next day we walk on the beach, and it's very cold. I say,

'There's a little restaurant in the town. Shall we book a table?'

'No, we won't, it'll be too expensive.' Replies Mickgough. That night I cook us supper. It feels like he is punishing me – but what for?

Had I made too much of a fuss of John Craxton? I hadn't seen him for years. John will come to supper later and Mick will say what a privilege it is to meet such an endearing and knowledgeable person. John can speak of symphonies and canvases and Greek peoples and art history and antiques. Anyway, it is my honeymoon, and I don't want a row. Each time something truly hurts me I cocoon myself in numbness.

Next morning, we hear the 'phone ringing. Who can it be? It's very early … it's our 'mother's help'.

'Oh, I'm so worried! I think Haze has taken to the bottle.' Hazel Terry, actress, has landed herself on us for a while. She's an alcoholic and Mick's trying to help her, so we've got to go home.

We have lunch with Mick's mother (Gran-Gran) in her lovely house overlooking the harbour in Wivenhoe *en route.* Mickgough has taken Hector for a 'pee-break', so Gran-Gran and I are washing lettuce together.

'I hope you'll make him happy, Anneke. He fought so terribly with his other wives … ' I promise to do my best.

We stop off at Flatford Mill as I want to see Willy Lot's Cottage which Constable had painted so often. As soon as we get out of the car, Hector is off madly running around in ever increasing circles until … plop! We drive home with a stinking dog and I am feeling forlorn and also very nauseous - my honeymoon.

Mickgough is famous for his stinginess. But I understand where that comes from. When he worked as a young actor in New York with his first wife Diana Graves, he was in a play and they were so utterly broke they would steal the knives and forks from diners and pawn them. Alec Guinness gave them both some money and a talking to.

'British actors should not be seen to be so hard up'

Willy Lot's Cottage in oils

We get home to find Hazel utterly sozzled, powder all over her face, clutching her bag, dousing herself with eau de cologne but actually swigging the vodka hidden inside. In a theatrical drawl, she croaks,

'Po-o-lll-y? Come he-yah, de-yah.' Polly is frightened. This is not good, Haze needs professional help. Mick arranges for some nurses from a clinic to come and pick her up at nine o'clock next morning. Hazel has agreed but Mick knows her too well. Before we go to bed he puts the rocking horse in front of the door. We sleep with our door, and one eye, open. Sure enough, in the early hours we hear her creeping down the stairs to escape. Mick is marvellously patient and talks and talks to her until the doctor and the nurse arrive. There is a scuffle, the Irish nurse is saying,

'For God's sakes, don't stroike her! Don't stroike her!' but Hazel has ducked under their arms and she's scuttling off up the back streets of Fulham and disappears totally.

She has a habit of going round to friends' houses when they are out working, and getting the nannies to leave her alone in the living room, so she can nick the vodka and leave. She would be found later in area steps or in the gutter. She is a beautiful actress, with a long career, and is related to the famous Ellen Terry.

She doesn't return to us, she's not long for this world. Poor Hazel.

Now I know why I'm feeling nauseous – I'm pregnant! We are both delighted. We somehow know that it's a boy. And our darling Polly is becoming such a little character – happy families.

But one night, she won't settle. She has been quite impossible - Mickgough takes over, and I go downstairs exhausted. The screams are only getting worse, and when I go back upstairs I see Mickgough shaking her roughly, dangling her out of the third floor window. Polly is hysterical. I rush to rescue her. Mickgough slopes off in a guilty sulk. Later when I ask him about it, he admits that when he loses his temper he loses it totally, he's afraid of what he will do. That's why I rarely see him drunk. He had a friend at school with red hair and sticky out ears who he was fighting, and if the teachers hadn't pulled him off, Mick knows he would have killed him. The boy's name was Jasper.

I do an advert for Topic, just me, straight on to the camera, cut off just above my bump.

'This is my Topic for tonight!' It is still considered a bit risky for an actor to do commercials, but it doesn't seem to do me any harm – I get quite a lot of work from that advert.

Chapter 25

Walking Back to Happiness

I look in The Lady magazine for a new mother's help. Verena comes – a beautiful girl from Dorset. I love her at once and she will be with us for a while. They will come to us all innocent and mousy and leave us to become models or go trekking in the Himalayas. This will be our family, and we all eat together. When Arthur moves on, Michael Johnson comes for a while. A wild, drunken Cornishman. We buy a big stew pot in a new shop open in Fulham Road and take it next door to the butcher. Michael says, like Robert Newton in Treasure Island,

'A-har! Fill it up with steak and kidney, my darling!' And we're off home to put it in the oven and open the wine.

He is marvellous, and expansive. Every morning he will crawl, hungover, around the corner to our lovely chemist who will fix him up with a small draught – *ah, medicine!* – and then off on a bus to the advertising agency J. Walter Thompson in Mayfair, where he is the art director. When he went for the job he joined all the other smart, well-dressed applicants with their neat portfolios – and there's Johnson, with all his drawings and work held together with kitchen twine, his trousers tied up with a tie well below his beer belly and he's sweating profusely. But they choose him because he's an original. He created the *Kodak* series in which Mickgough was the original *Kodak Man.* He had lived in St. Ives, and left his heart there.

He is also working with Tim Craxton's erstwhile love, Sam Arnold-Foster at J.W.T. She is such a rare beauty, with blue eyes and very short hair. She's sitting in on a meeting, trying to create the name of a new scent – everybody's ideas are very veiled illusions. Sam cuts in, in a flat posh drawl,

'Why don't you call it Lust?' *To the point, but too daring.* This is the early sixties and the Lord Chamberlain's shadow is still hovering …

Robin is now working for the *Exchange Telegraph* - a press agency. He's becoming quite respected in his field but he and I will argue because I don't think it's right to intrude upon another's pain. The foot in the door and,

'How did it feel when this tragedy happened?' I think it's immoral and I wish he would become a writer. He writes lots of poems - one begins 'Slumped Beer-wise in a Soho Pub'. He's got his own flat now behind Marble Arch.

Mickgough and I are having riding lessons in Wimbledon with an inspired Russian teacher, Captain Sumowski. Mick is a great rider; he was brought up in Ireland by his uncle who was the Master of the Galway Blazers. Miss Bouwens had taught me to have 'light hands', but Captain Sumowski is tough – much trotting, no stirrups, over uneven ground, over jumps.

'Anneekah, don't look at me, votch your horse, he's already killed three people!' He will eventually keel over in his saddle with a heart attack and die.

We love to see show-jumping at the International Horse Show. A blanket, a flask, and Harvey Smith in his prime.

Peter and Wendy have moved into a large Georgian house in Hampstead and are busy making it beautiful. They can now afford the best. I see it's not as much fun to simply go to a shop and say,

'I'll have that, and that!' as it is to go on a search for bargains in the junk shops. But when their house is done it is exquisite - a beautiful sixties home. Some American friends are stepping over the Georgian oak floors upstairs,

'*Pederr*, you paid *how much*? *Twenny four thousand pounds*? But the floors are uneven! You were conned! '

They are riding their wave and they fill the house with beautiful, creative people. At one of their dinner parties I'm wearing my silver paper mini-dress. I'm talking about The Alberts with Peter, and showing off because among the guests is John Lennon and I want him to notice me, so when I see him going down to the kitchen – I follow him. He is alone and helping himself to strawberries. He gives me a wink.

'While the grown-ups are upstairs getting pissed, let's you and I eat the strawberries?' So we do. He wants to know more about The

Alberts. *Had I really lived with them?* He had heard them recording at Abbey Road and it has obviously had a massive effect on him.

'Are they for real? I mean, like true eccentrics?'

'Yes, and all the clothes they wear are authentic, not Carnaby Street copies!' pointing to his military style jacket. 'And Douglas can play any instrument – harps, fiddles, bagpipes, trumpets … Too soon, we are interrupted by other guests who want his attention.

The Alberts are recording an album at Abbey Road with George Martin, when The Beatles arrive at the studio. John Lennon in particular is struck by this raucous sound and, inspired, will later use a similar sound *Yellow Submarine.*

♬ *And the band began to play..* ♬

When The Alberts arrive in New York, off the boat, sadly Lenny Bruce is in prison. So the English contingent - *Beyond the Fringe* - is at the docks to receive them. Alan Bennett cracks up with delight at the chaotic scene. It has become an *Alberts Happening,* the entire dock taken up with old wardrobes skips, ancient wicker baskets camels, pianos, the penny-farthing, and other bizarre props. The massed Alberts and wives and girlfriends and children. Douglas playing the bagpipes. What a wonderful scene.

♬ *Hey, Mr Tambourine Man* ♬
- The Byrds

Mickgough is doing *Dr. Terror's House of Horrors*. He tells me how, at the end of a take on these horror films, the first assistant will call out,

'Time for the Japanese version!' and out will come the tomato ketchup. We do not show blood or excessive violence at this time but the Japanese don't have these restrictions.

Hurlingham Road is up, with new drains replacing the Victorian ones so we have noise and road works, but also no cars, doors are open, Hector is flying in and out, and we are chatting to neighbours. Joan Sims lives down the road, Stephen Yardley round the corner. We've tiled our garden with York stone and we have an old kitchen table and odd chairs. I'm growing bigger and Polly's painting crazy paintings. We don't have big umbrellas yet, so I have slung a canvas awning over the washing line, and we are eating *al fresco* in the shade. The nasturtiums are creeping everywhere, the sound of Wimbledon on TV comes through the open French Windows, and the roses are abundant in the back gardens of Fulham.

Verona has taken Polly for a holiday to her parents' home in Studland, Dorset. Mick is away again on tour. So I go to spend some time with Peter and Wendy. I sleep very well in one of their attic rooms. Our days are filled with Cook life. People arriving, interviews, Dudley and Peter in closeted sessions of work. The house resounding with laughter. Expensive goodies being delivered. I help Wendy prepare the evening meals. The writers, the actors, the cartoonists, the musicians, you name it; they come to dinner at the Cooks. It is a special time for me, a feeling of brief independence, but now Mickgough is returning.

'Come and spend one night at Peter and Wendy's, join the grand dinner?' I'm telling him about the darling maid's room

I've got up in the attic and how deeply I've slept in it.

So Mick comes and we have a grand party, and later we snuggle up together in the lovely bed. In the early hours (it always is, isn't it? The veil then is very thin) - I am suddenly shocked awake, heart pounding, something deeply malevolent. I have the distinct impression that had I not woken up, this 'energy' would have destroyed me. I talk to Mickgough and he comforts me. Eventually I fall asleep again. It happens again! That's it. Not wanting to disturb Mick I go down to the kitchen and make tea. When Peter comes down eventually we talk about it, he says.

'*Funny!* … perhaps it was one of the old servants and he was jealous when Mick came.' I think,

'Lord, even the ghosts are jealous of me!'

Peter has a theory that British Airways employs actors to pose as the handsome, tanned pilots that the public see walking across the tarmac. If we saw the actual pilots, the neurotic drunks, we wouldn't be so keen to fly.

We close friends of Peter all think that David Frost has been stepping into Peter's shoes while he was in America. He had known Peter at Cambridge and he poached a lot of Peter's original work. It will rankle with Peter for years and eat him up inside. Wendy tells me how David Frost nearly drowned in the pool of a holiday home where they all stayed in upstate New York. Peter will talk of how he will always regret fishing him out!

Now it's autumn, and I'm feeling even bigger and Mickgough is having a dalliance with someone. Again. As usual, I know this, but at the same time, I don't want to know. Ever since we've been together there has always been some woman on the edges. I didn't want an open marriage – I wanted to be loved – *just me!* I would look down the cast list of his scripts and make a note. Hmm, her, definitely, and maybe her. I will meet him after rehearsals with Polly in a pushchair, to put them off the scent. But he is a charmer, and they are charmed. Mick has one particular girlfriend, an intellectual, who will often be in my home, playing with Polly, when I get back from work. I go to rehearsals and share my frustration with one of my friends – Douglas Wilmer. He says I should challenge Mick by saying that unless he stops seeing this woman, I won't go to work.

'Please stop seeing her! Otherwise, I am not going to go to rehearsals!' Mickgough laughs dismissively. But later I will find photos of her, which he has taken, in his sock drawer. It is as if he wants to be found out. This is what people had told me to expect. Do I listen? Do I learn? *No*, I think, it will be different with me. *He really loves me.*

Chapter 26

Jasper

It's early November, and Mick is doing a series of *The Count of Monte Christo* with Alan Badel. I'm ironing after supper when

'AAAGHH!' That's a huge contraction – right on time.

So I call upstairs.

'Olaf, can you baby-sit? I'm off to have a baby!' Mick takes me round to Parson's Green, which is an offshoot of the Charing Cross hospital, in the Mini Traveller. The big black nurse hardly has time to prepare me because -

'I'm pushing!'

'No, no, you're only three fingers dilated … '

'I tell you, I'm pushing!' The doctor comes hurrying. The standard lamp's switch is bust so Mick has to hold the plug in the wall, but he's there when, with very little fuss, Jasper is born big and healthy and happy. 8lb 6oz. This was the first birth Mickgough had been present at and he would say to Olaf later that he felt humbled. When we get home, we have a present for Polly, a tricycle from her new brother so there will be no envy. Polly is fascinated by this baby. They are connected in love forever, these two.

After Jasper is born I try the pill, but it makes me blow up like a balloon, and very weepy. I rely on my Dutch cap instead.

Since Angela and Kenny got married, I have seen very little of them. Our lives are so busy, and Mickgough is 'snarly' about Kenny so it's awkward. She's on the phone asking how I'm doing with my new baby and all – at last, a lovely woman friend to talk to.

'I'm feeling overwhelmed ... the nightly feeds with Jasper … Polly's very demanding … my finances are strained … the court case with *The Mirror* has cost me a fortune and is dragging on … and I can't afford to buy my lovely baby the best powdered milk … '

A few days later, I'm coming back from the park with the children; the neighbours are out looking for me – very excited,

'Kenneth More and Angela Douglas came to see you in a Rolls Royce and they left these.' Huge cartons of the best milk and a bucket full of peach-coloured gladioli.

We go to have Sunday lunch with Olaf in his country home in Surrey. We are always excited to have a day out in the countryside. As we pile out of the car, hugs and greetings, and then a ghastly squawking and yelping. Hector has had his lunch – Olaf's prize chicken!

Rex Harrison is on the 'phone. 'Rexy' lives in Portofino. We have seen him in *My Fair Lady* with Audrey Hepburn. He and Mick go way back to Kay Kendal days and I know that Mick's last wife was a friend. I'm hoping he will take us to a posh restaurant, but no! Mick is inviting him to ours for supper.

'It will be nice for him to have home cooking, he's always in restaurants …!'

I go into overdrive. I start at Peter Jones. New plates, napkins, a tablecloth, the best ingredients bought from the butcher opposite

Harrods. The house is spring-cleaned from top to toe. At the eleventh hour, the children will be in bed, the flowers *just so.* Our kitchen at the back is on a slope, as is the gas stove. I'm cooking veal, and I have to wedge forks under the pan to keep it level. He's late. Mick and I are waiting - waiting. He's even later. I fuss and put the food on anyway.

'Where is he now? Damn it!' He finally calls, at about ten.

'Sorry old dear, got held up, we'll make it another time.'

'Don't worry, Dear Heart, no problem,' says Mickgough.

After all my efforts!

♬ *Baby love, my baby love,* ♬
- Diana Ross

I have landed a huge part. It's a *Play of the Week* called *No Baby, No Baby At All.* I'm starring opposite Richard Vernon. I play his secretary – she's a bitch and a sexpot. She drives her boss mad, breaks up his marriage and revels in it. John Frankau is directing. Richard Vernon, what a dear man. He invites us to dinner and in an upstairs room, we have to duck, and come up in the middle of a vast model railway set. It has everything – trees, mountains, stations, villages – complete magic and it's his obsession.

I am having difficulty letting rip with this character. We have to record me shrieking with laughter which is played over the boss's face as his life falls apart. On the day of recording up at Wembley, John Frankau announces that he is going to pick me up and drive me to the studio. I am surprised, because Richard lives in Putney, and he usually gives me a lift. But John insists. On the way, he demolishes me, telling me exactly why he thinks I am no good as an actress. I can't believe my ears and I get out of the car feeling about a foot high. I go into make-up, a blubbering mess. The wonderful make-up people work their healing magic as always and I walk, fairly wobbly, out onto the set. As the day progresses my rage comes to the fore and when we record I *am* that bitch. Afterwards, in the bar,

'Darling,' says John, 'I knew you could do it.' Well, he had taken a risk, and he's gone into my black book next to Mr. Winner. (However, I will use that same device later, when I am directing.)

Mick and I are on a train for a little break, alone. I'm tired and want to sleep; he's leaning over me in the carriage.

'Rest my darling. I'll just pop and get a drink.' He kisses me. The door slides open and a fellow traveller says,

'Is this man bothering you?'

'He sure is, he's my husband!' When we get to the little country hotel and sign in as Mr. and Mrs. Gough, the receptionist winks at us knowingly. People mostly think he's my father.

My mother has come to see me and her Grandchildren and our new life. Unfortunately, Mickgough takes a dislike to her which will only grow over the years. This makes things very awkward, and me very sad. She stays with friends in Putney.

As the children grow, they love having holidays in Spain with 'Oma'. She's magic with them, because she's so magic and child-like herself. They have great adventures, like I did when I lived with her as a child. She loves to take them to the big local bar where they make friends with the local prostitutes and musicians, the old man who sleeps with his donkey and sweet Pedro who is a smelly fisherman with a simple heart who loves Jasper, and Jasper him. My mother loves Pedro more than anyone else because, she says, his heart is pure. She also has two gay friends, Alex, who's German and has an existential angst and is always saying'

'Scheiße! I have to go to Malaga,' (Like the tramp in *The Caretaker* who has to go to Sidcup). Then there is Axel, who's Danish. He makes outrageous jewellery, which my mother wears, huge clusters of juicy, dripping beads, which I'm mean about. He will cook them all exotic meals which get more and more elaborate as he gets drunker, and he starts decorating the dishes with branches and beads.

The Alberts are doing *The Three Musketeers* with Valentine Dyall and Rachel Roberts at The Mermaid Theatre. They nickname it *The Three Musty Queers.* Ann Gray is doing the design, and since we are friends again she's using a room at ours to get 'some space' while she works on it. Tony's chuckling away because they can have their collection of Edwardian shirts washed and ironed by the wardrobe ladies at the theatre – he loves that! When Ann eventually leaves him, he will get a double-decker bus and fill it full of all his children, and drive them up and down from Wisbech to London's Theatreland.

The Playbill for the follow-up to *The Three Musketeers*. Designed by Ann Gray

Mick is having a suit made by Dougie Hayward. I'm thrilled for him because he deserves it. But, *oh dear*, it's too tight. I think and he looks silly and it's cost us seventy quid, a week's work.

Peter and Dudley have written a film, called *Bedazzled*, based on the Faust legend. Eleanor Bron and Raquel Welch are in it. Peter's very apprehensive because, he's also got a lead role, and as he says, he's not really an actor,

'I don't know what to do with a script. Can you help me?' Mick is busy, so Peter and I spend a couple of weeks working on his part. When we break the script down into the phrasing of the thoughts -

' - it's not prancing about and showing off, Peter!' He relaxes and begins to inhabit his part of the Devil! What a privilege to coach Peter Cook. Of course most of the time we're falling around with laughter, the man is so very funny. As Eleanor Bron says,

'Peter Cook is the funniest man in the world.' And, he is a performer. Now, the studios are trying to mould him into a heart-throb. *You can't mould Peter Cook!* The powers-that-be mishandle this genius totally. He is never given the vehicles and the breaks for his talent that he deserves.

The doorbell rings – a messenger with an enormous bouquet of flowers – and a thank you note from Peter.

Robin comes for supper, in need of a story. Great groans from me and Mickgough. He does a small piece for the *Radio Times*. He's very drunk when he leaves. I'm worried about him drinking so much. Is he becoming an alcoholic? In the pub, after seeing the Three Musty Queers, I talk to Rachel Roberts about alcoholism. Rachel says, in her Welsh accent,

'No, he's not an alcoholic – he's a drunkard!' So Robin is a drunkard.

He signs his letters *Drunken Robin*

I'm called in to see the film director Antonioni; he's making a film called *Blow Up*. I have heard that he speaks perfect English but he likes to hide behind an interpreter. I walk into a large hall and they are all behind a long table. He's whispering in Italian. The interpreter asks me,

'Can you turn to za left-a … ' There is more whispering. 'Now can you turn to za right-a … ' Interminable waiting. I'm beginning to feel very self-conscious and silly. More muttering.

'Now can you take off your hat-a … ' My *Britishness* comes to the fore… I hate being told what to do! I whip my hat off, toss my hair out and say,

'Yes, and I can talk as well! Good Morning!' and I march out. I don't get the part, Vanessa Redgrave does.

We are improving our bedroom by adding a bathroom in the small back room. This is not strictly legal. We can't afford to put in another supporting beam so we will do what Ann and Tony did, which is to leave the studs in and just remove the plaster. We have painted the bedroom a beautiful deep plum colour. The brass bed has been silvered. The bath has been raised up and set across the corner with mirrored tiles and steps leading up to it. I find the most beautiful set of etched chemist doors and they become the front for our built-in wardrobes. The building inspector is coming to approve the work. He only sees the bathroom, which is accepted. He leaves. Mick immediately takes huge hammer and with delight, starts removing plasterboard walls. The doorbell goes – the inspector is back! A moment of panic - he's left his papers on the kitchen table.

'Yes, yes, thank you!' and we wave him off.

'That was close!' We get on with our demolition. We create a unique and beautiful room.

I'm returning from one of Wendy's sumptuous feasts. Roast suckling pig, trays of crystal champagne glasses, silver cutlery. I feel depressed when I get home and see our chipped casapupo plates, our simple meals. I remember my mother's definition of a good cook,

'Anyone can go out and buy ingredients but a good cook is one who can go into someone else's kitchen, find very little and make an attractive meal.' Her staple dish in Spain is what she calls 'Poverty Paella'. It is just rice, no mussels or chicken. Sometimes I go to the

North End Road market for fish and meat but mostly it is all bought locally and fresh. We don't have any frozen food. I haven't been brought up with luxury so I don't miss it. My favourite cookbook is *Good French Cooking* by Mapi Toulouse Lautrec. Elizabeth David is the 'guru' but I get put off when before you start on a dish, there's a page about how 'nobody can get this right'. Very daunting! As a working mother I don't have the time but I do love making meringues and cheese soufflés and of course, Mickgough's favourite, rice pudding. The children eat a lot of fish fingers. Our friend Arthur Hacker has Sunday breakfasts, kippers and cognac. All through our pregnancies, Wendy and I are happily smoking our Gauloises, not knowing any better. She has very high standards of appearance. After a couple of hours in the morning, she emerges beautifully dressed and totally made-up with two sets of false eyelashes. She is famous for keeping those on during the birth of her children. Mickgough tells a story about a party at which Kay Kendal is the guest of honour. Everyone is waiting for her arrival, expectantly. She arrives, jeans, t-shirt, pony-tail and scrubbed face – that's my style – Katherine Hepburn was famous for turning up at rehearsals wearing rags.

Jonathan Miller is directing a production of *Alice in Wonderland*. Mickgough will play the March Hare, Peter the Mad Hatter, John Gielgud the Mock Turtle, and Wilfred Lawson the Dormouse. It's a memorable production.

Chapter 27

My Busiest Year

1966 will be the busiest year of my acting life. It begins with Clive Donner wanting me to be in a film called *The Pleasure Girls*. Francesca Annis will play a girl who comes to London, and gets pregnant by Ian McShane's character. Mark Eden, later of *Coronation Street*, also appears. My character never quite gets her man. We are all enjoying working together. When the producers see the rushes, they complain,

'Not enough sex!' so we have to make it raunchier. Scenes that should be in a telephone box are re-filmed, in bed. There is a sort of rebellion. Clive Donner walks out and Gerry O'Hara takes over, and the original film is lost in the cutting. Ian McShane is irresistible … One night, the beautiful blonde Suzanna Leigh gives me a lift home in her sports car. She drives barefooted and keeps her 45s around the gear-stick. She has her own flat off the Edgeware Road. Her independence impresses me. When she steps into our kitchen, I'm cross to see Mickgough and Simon literally drooling!

Next I do a *Thirty-Minute Theatre*, called *Keep on Running*, a 'two-hander'. My boyfriend is a guitarist, who plays *Keep on Running*, by the Spencer Davis Group. We have to part, it's a poignant and tightly written drama.

I AM APPEARING ON JUKE BOX JURY WITH SPIKE MILLIGAN!!! - it's *wonderful* for me to meet him at last. We egg each other on, behave badly, and rubbish all the music they play. We keep saying,

'Bring back The Alberts!'

Mickgough is playing the Celestial Toymaker in *Doctor Who*. He and The Doctor play deadly games. Peter Purves and Jackie Lane are the Doctor's companions. Mick tells me how difficult it is working with William Hartnell. It's a good story, and becomes a classic story, and highly regarded by fans.

Mickgough as The Celestial Toymaker

In *The Saint*, with Roger Moore

I get another *Play of the Week – Toddler on the Run*. This is great, the scripts become more subtle, and the characters three dimensional. We are running on a cold, windy beach, hiding under a boat, I'm playing a working class girl … probably with my 'poshness' peeking through.

It's non-stop. Now I'm in an episode of *The Saint*. Up at Elstree Studios the make-up people are old style movie artists, who want to build up my lips and don't put nearly enough black on my eyes. I go back to my dressing room and do it myself. Roger Moore is another beauty, a very sweet, funny man, the whole set is alive with laughter. I wear my Bloomingdales knickers and earn that nickname, courtesy of the man who will soon be James Bond!

An advantage of being married to well-known Mickgough is that all the people I work with respect him and that rubs off on me. At last, I'm not being preyed upon sexually

I've got a household of seven to eight people to keep running. We now have lovely Mrs A. - her husband is an abusive Irish drunk - she has five kids, and she is a Saint. She comes to clean our house for us. Then we have our lovely Verena and later, Julie Broadbent and her partner Johnny. And Olaf sometimes, and of course Mick and I are busy working. The children's life is regular. Toys away, bath, bed and story, and grown-ups' time after the six o'clock news – at least, that's what we aim for. We've had to let go of Hector. Ever since we had the road up and he had the freedom to run in the road, he kept doing it; he's gone to a good home in the country. We miss him.

We are introduced to a Russian drink - Nikolashka. You take a liqueur glass, fill it with Fundador – the Spanish brandy we like – lay a thin slice of lemon across the top of the glass, a small mound of caster sugar on top, then you wedge the lemon and sugar across your palate and you pour the brandy through, and then you munch and swallow, and your head explodes. So the only thing to do is have another!

I get a part in *The Likely Lads* - the episode is called *The Other Side of the Fence.* James Bolam is such a natural comedian; he can't stop being funny. I play Rodney Bewes's girlfriend. In this story is a young actor called Michael Sheard who will go on to become Doctor Who's most prolific guest actor.

I'm delighted with the amount of work I'm doing, because now I can pay for the stair-carpet, but it's also frustrating because I want to get the house finished before Christmas. So as soon as rehearsals are over I'm back home and out with the paint pot.

'Neke! Your agent's on the 'phone,' -

I'm up for a part in *Doctor Who!* They need a new 'companion'. Verity Lambert is casting, which is good news for me because she has cast me before. Mary Selway, Irene Lamb and Verity are my favourite casting directors. When I meet producer Innes Lloyd we hit it off at once. I read for the part, and I can see that they like me. I go home and I'm busy converting the old coal cupboard under the stairs into a linen cupboard so paint clothes are on when and my agent calls back with the news. *What fun! Doctor Who!* Within hours the whole street knows I've got the part.

In *The Likely Lads*, with Rodney Bewes

Chapter 28

Doctor Who

Over the years I have heard all the tired old clichés about the companions being there to ask questions and scream, and about the sets wobbling. The BBC may not have had a large budget but they managed to produce a magical programme which was hugely popular; breaking scientific ground and opening the minds of the young audience. The writers of *Doctor Who* are so often extremely articulate visionaries. What in those days was science fiction – the War Machines, the robots, the space stations – today, have materialised as fact – computers – satellites in space – and the words 'Tardis' and 'Dalek' are in the dictionary!

We go for publicity shots, I meet my fellow companion Michael Craze, who will become a friend for life (his, sadly). I wear my own clothes – the BBC wardrobe doesn't do designer clothes. For my first story, *The War Machines*, I'm wearing my Marimekko pink and purple dress and lovely little shoes from Deliss. William Hartnell is very short-tempered and unpredictable – just like Mickgough said he would be. He calls me 'My Dear'. We do some exterior shots in Russell Square, and he is recognised by everyone. When you are out filming *Doctor Who*, the response from the public is always extremely positive. *Aaah! Doctor Who!* The nation has taken this programme to its heart.

The producers have decided that the new companion will be a sixties chick, and a bit of a turn-on. I have eye-lashes longer than my skirts, I'm a smart secretary to a scientist, and I'm cheeky with it. I am the first of a long line of sexy *Doctor Who* companions, and my character is called Polly.

There has been much speculation by fans as to Polly's surname. Some have suggested Wright. Some said Lopez – hardly!

She was meant to be upper-middle class – a debutante! Unless of course, her mother went off with a Spanish waiter! Fans have wondered whether Polly and Ben – Mike Craze's character – got together in later years. Michael Craze and I both felt that Polly and Ben simply stayed loving and supporting friends – as indeed did we. Polly is simply Polly, no surname needed.

When we are rehearsing our first story – The War Machines - Mike and I are being polite with William Hartnell. There is a fuss happening in the rehearsal room, Bill is storming out, he doesn't want to work -

'With these black workmen, making a noise in the street below…' None of us know what to make of this. He also keeps forgetting his lines, and tries to make out it's your fault! So all in all, it's not a relaxed rehearsal. John Harvey plays my professor, William Mervyn a politician, and John Cater gets hypnotised by WOTAN – the computer which controls the War Machines. We record as live. On a Saturday night we record the following week's episode. There are very few breaks in the tapes, except where filmed sections are inserted. As the famous title music is played, I have shooting pains of fear in my hands, and I'm wondering why I do this for a living, but as soon as we start – I love it! Prop those sets up, we're off! After each episode is 'in the can', we are off to the pub to celebrate. We start work on Monday mornings at 9:30 and work through till 5:00. On Thursday the technicians come to the rehearsal rooms, and then on Saturday we are in the studio all day. Sunday is our day off, so it's busy, but not punishing.

In the winter at Hammersmith, Bill Hartnell keeps his chauffeur waiting in the cold.

'That's a bit mean!' we say, 'He could have the heater on,' Bill replies,

'Rubbish! What a waste of money!' When we disagree with him, he says,

'Do you know who I am?' And he means it. I have heard that William Hartnell always makes sure he is sitting in the centre of the crowd in the pub so he can't get to the bar to buy a round! I discover that it's true.

On November 23rd 1966, it is Mickgough's 50th birthday and we have a party in our home. Some of my new *Doctor Who* friends come. Once again the candelabra are lit; the house full of flowers, the bath with champagne and we all celebrate 'The Great Man of the Theatre' - Michael Gough Esquire!

Mike Craze and I love our second story – *The Smugglers* – it's about eighteenth century pirates in Cornwall. We film it in a remote and beautiful Cornish bay, and we stay in a lovely old Cornish pub. Bill Hartnell isn't well, so we have a double for the filming. Paul Whitsun-Jones plays an old rogue. Mike and I love our costumes. Unknown to us, William Hartnell has made the decision to leave the series. Sadly *The Smugglers* no longer exists but it is available on audio – a gripping story.

The Tenth Planet is one of eight stories that I do as the only woman in the cast. David Dodimead is a very funny man, a firm favourite of ours. Alan White also appears. This story will become truly historic television, as it introduces the Cybermen and although they have relatively primitive costumes, they are very scary for the kids with their black holes for eyes.

Wendy is in Mallorca, so Peter invites me to the *Bedazzled* premiere. I'm thrilled to bits and I've been telling everybody on *Doctor Who.* I wear a brown velvet trouser suit, Fauntleroy style – crêpe frilled shirt, Bally shoes with big antique buckles. I go in the hired car to pick up Peter. He opens the door, this beautiful man, and he's dressed in a Fauntleroy style, brown velvet suit! So we look like twins and off we go to the premiere. It goes very well, we all enjoy – me, Peter, Eleanor and Dudley. In the early hours, Peter takes me to a gambling club in Piccadilly, with flaming torches at the door. I place a bet on the tables, and I win £10, which is perfect because my suit cost me £10 to have made. Next day, I'm back to *Doctor Who*, and the cast all want to hear how *Bedazzled* was.

I invite the *Tenth Planet* writer, Kit Pedler, to supper. He is a scientist as well as a writer. I've also invited Jonathan Miller because I want to see them spark off each other. Jonathan takes Kit's ideas and runs off the planet with them, comes back to Earth, and Kit's still at the starting post. What a mind Jonathan has.

We have heard rumours of Bill Hartnell's departure. He is not well. We do not know it yet, but he is suffering from atherosclerosis, which is the cause of his lapses of memory and concentration. Rather than cancel such a successful series, the producers come up with the idea that The Doctor – who is an alien after all – can simply regenerate his ageing body. He can just get a new one!

So now, who will replace Bill? There are whispers of Michael Horden, Patrick Wymark, Tommy Steele. On a Monday morning in October, Patrick Troughton walks into the rehearsal room in his little red cardigan, and a huge cheer goes up! He is one of our most esteemed actors.

This regeneration idea is a unique concept - the Doctor will 'morph' into an entirely new body. There is excitement at the idea as well as apprehension. Will the public accept a new actor playing the role? The regeneration is directed by Derek Martinus with class and care.

If it hadn't been for Patrick Troughton, who knows whether the series would even have continued? Would David Tennant be on our screens today, forty years later, thrilling new generations of fans?

It's Christmas 1966, and Pat's first story – *The Power of the Daleks* - directed by Christopher Barry, one of the original BBC TV directors. Pat, Mike and I meet the Daleks for the first time. In the cast we have Pamela-Ann Davy, Bernard Archer, and John Scott Martin playing a Dalek. During rehearsals, he sits in the skirt of his Dalek, and does his knitting during the boring bits. A photographer takes a picture of this because it is so sweet and surreal, but he is not allowed to publish it because the production team is most concerned that the mystery of the Daleks must remain intact.

It's very rewarding working with Pat. He is a consummate professional who we can learn so much from, and he is such a clown, and totally endearing. He asks Mike and me our opinions on ways of playing the role. His son Michael remembers how much he trusted our input which, at the time, we took for granted but now seems an honour. It was Pat's honesty that made him so endearing.

At first he isn't too sure how far to go with his portrayal. We talk about Chaplin and I am thrilled to find that he also loves *Gurney Slade* and *The Goons* – of course!

He is trying out his new costume, which is checked baggy trousers, an old dress coat, a shirt that is too big, and a ghastly curly Harpo Marx wig. We all hate the wig and he looks crestfallen.

'Why not just comb your hair like this?' I say. And I comb it into his trademark Beatles look.

'That's good.' The producers agree. The new Doctor plays a recorder, and Pat needs a haunting tune. I sing him the Irish lullaby that I sing to my children. It becomes his theme tune.

How could we know then that we would become a part of cultural immortality…?

Pat loves playing practical jokes, *Billy Bunter* style. After the first set of stories, I've been to Carnaby Street and had some tee shirts made bearing the slogan 'Come back Bill Hartnell, All is forgiven!' Mike and I step out of the Tardis wearing them and grinning. But our joke is not appreciated. Pat retreats to his dressing room looking crushed, so we ply him with many hugs and whiskies to cheer him up. His immense sensitivity is what made him such a fine actor. Our rehearsal rooms are close enough to the BBC TV Centre in White City for us to have our lunches in the bar. It's a crowded and lively atmosphere, and we are always in the centre of a volatile crowd. Pat loves discussing politics. I meet Brian Blessed who tells me that all the *Z-Cars* boys fancy me rotten! I love the image in the canteen of actors in Tudor costumes eating spaghetti and reading *Time Out.*

Pastel portraits of Ben, Polly and Jamie

One foggy winter night, I'm crossing Putney Bridge on my way home from recording. It's late and there are very few people about so when I hear footsteps behind me I know immediately that I am being followed. I quicken my pace, but so does this man. He's breathing heavily. With my heart pounding, I'm so relieved to dive into the tobacconist at the top of our road. I wait a while to calm myself down, pretending to look at magazines. When I think the stalker has probably given up, I set off again, but to my horror, he's behind me again. Now I'm practically running. When I get to our front door I feel safe and I turn to confront him. I am amazed to see it is a very well known middle aged actor. He's married with many children. Later it transpires that this habit was indeed his dark shadow.

I begin to feel bad because I have so little time to be with Polly and Jasper so I'm compensating by buying them little presents. Now when I get home at night they are more keen on what I've got for them than a kiss. *How quickly that happens.*

We are filming *The Highlanders*. It's about the Jacobite rebellion in Culloden, and it will be the last of *Doctor Who's* great historical stories. We film at Frensham Ponds in Surrey with Hannah Gordon, Donald Bisset and Frazer Hines. Hannah and I plot to outwit a soldier, and we hide in a cave, when Hannah's character says,

'Why are your skirts so short?' and gives me a biscuit. Polly takes a bite and says,

'It's a dog biscuit!'

All that is left of *The Highlanders* is the audio, which is available on CD. And it's another very good story.

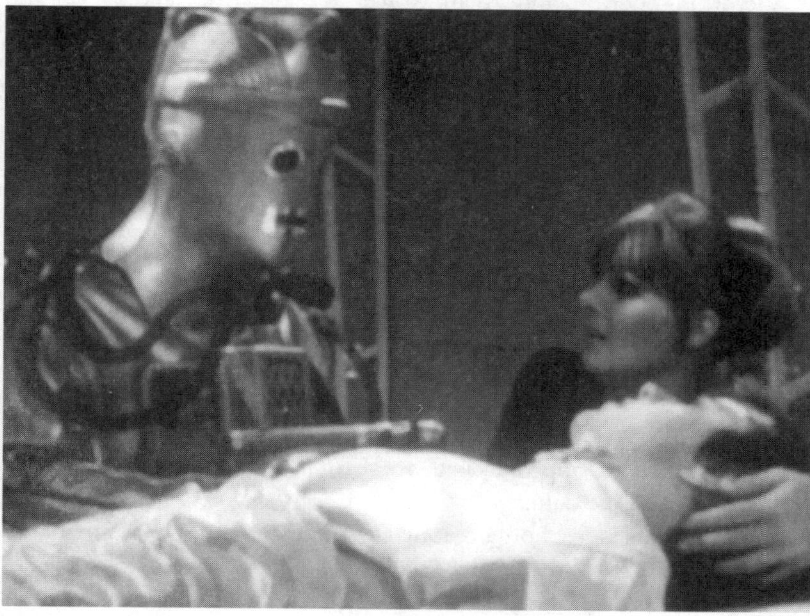

Mike's characterisation of Ben is becoming rather angry and dark, so the production team decide to keep Frazer on as Jamie, because the children can relate to him more, in his wee kilt! He will go on to appear in more *Doctor Who* stories than any other companion in the series' entire history. *The Underwater Menace* is one of our least-favourite stories. Pat and Julia, the director, are at odds, and the wonderful Joseph Furst goes totally over the top with,

'Nussing in ze vorld vill shtop me NOW!' My shell costume hurts me, and the flipping market set is so small that you have to *act* moving. The Fish People are planning to operate on Polly, and she protests,

'No, please stop it!' And then she finds her courage, and her voice drops,

'You're not turning me into a fish!'

Once again, for *The Moonbase*, it's an all-male cast. John Wills plays one of our five Cybermen – a prodigious amount – and they are always played by very tall, hunky actors. We meet the splendid Victor Pemberton and Allan Rowe. We film the landing on the moon, it's two years ahead of real life, although it's not quite as exciting – our moon is in Ealing. Mike and I are really looking forward to flying about 'on the moon', but actually it is torture. We are fitted with Kirby wires, with globes on our heads; they haul us across the studio through thick flurries of polystyrene snow. We are sweating away in the globes, the wires really hurt and poor Michael gets some polystyrene wedged in his nose and later suffers very badly. Because there are now two male companions, Frazer lies unconscious for most of the story, only waking up to call a Cyberman, in his broad Scottish brogue, 'the phantom piper'. Polly mixes a *cocktail* of chemicals and nail varnish to vanquish the Cybermen.

In the studio opposite, is *The 6-5 Special.* Mike and I peek in to listen and see the dancing.

The Tardis arrives on a colony of humans being run by alien crab creatures; this is the story of *The Macra Terror.* An old friend, Anthony Gardner from RADA appears with us. As my daughter Polly watches this scene at home, she sees her mummy's little white boots disappearing inside an enormous crab's mouth, and asks Mickgough,

'Um, is Mummy coming home tonight?'

This scene was cut in some countries as it was considered to be too frightening. Although the story is now lost, ironically, this particular clip has now been unearthed. 40 years later, the Macra - to everyone's surprise - will re-appear in a David Tennant story.

Innes Lloyd calls me into his office,

'You have to choose now, Anneke. Do you want to stay on with Frazer as your companion because we're going to leave Ben in 1966?'

It has been such fun and such hard work. But I think that if I go on, I might become reliant on the £60 a week and I may never get out of it. Also, there is the stigma of being typecast. And I want to be home again with my children. So I decide to leave with Mike.

In *The Faceless Ones* the Tardis lands in the present day – 1966 - at Gatwick Airport and Polly immediately witnesses a murder. Aliens are kidnapping young people. We have Wanda Ventham and Pauline Collins with us for this, our final story. Polly and Ben stay on Earth, we say goodbye to the Doctor and Jamie. There are a lot of tears. It's been such a great time. Mike has met his future wife, Edwina, who has been our floor manager, and I'm enriched beyond words. It's a big night in the pub.

When I leave Doctor Who, I have no idea that so many years later, it will still be such a big part of my life, and that 40 years on, I will stand in the Tardis again, and meet the latest Doctor …

Artwork by Ian Burgess, Cineffigy 2007

Chapter 29

Windmills of Your Mind

Now, of course, I have to change my rhythm, slow down, take the children to the park. It's just what I need, to be quietly at home. Mickgough has been jealous of Pat and Mike, and he's happy that I am now at home with the family, rather than in a studio having fun with a team of young, male actors! Polly is beginning to show signs of musical talent. She plays the piano like a thing possessed. She will go on to play the flute. Jasper is a two year old and into everything.

Mickgough loves reading stories to the children. We have loads of great books for them. I have learned so much from him about parenting. When they get into tantrums,

'That's fine, if you want to have a fit, go ahead, but do it in your room and you can come down when you're finished.' And reverse psychology,

'Listen to me now then, don't close your eyes – keep your eyes open.' They are asleep within minutes. Both Polly and Jasper are very polite children. Somehow or other they know how to respect grown-ups. Perhaps because with all the wonderful people we have living with us, they have always been included. They have lots of little friends and as much regularity as we can manage. Bath, bed and book. When they have birthday parties I love making a birthday table, with a homemade cake as a centrepiece, with all the coloured icing pouring over the sides, and the table scattered with Smarties, loads of streamers dangling over the kitchen lamp, and the darling little faces, lit up with excitement. We play 'pass the parcel', 'musical chairs' and 'sardines'. The parents will come later, and drink sherry, and eat cake, and the children will be tearing around. Annette and Robin Brown, Alice and Nick Pollock, Noel and Sarah Harrison, all enjoying.

Mickgough always has absolute time for the children – these magic little beings. He loves babies too, in fact, he tells me, he wants to have a football team of his own kids! I paint him a painting of a football match – very adventurous – as I am not used to drawing male bodies. He loves it, and has it framed.

Bill Thompson has done a beautiful crayon drawing of Polly, capturing her wistful little expression perfectly. I love this drawing. *I miss it.*

Polly's got little friends from her nursery school. We have big Sunday lunches, it's 'my thing' – cook a huge roast, have friends and wine, a big pudding, and children and babies. Abundance!

Mickgough is doing a play so he is very caught up with that and the garden is becoming very overgrown.

In the holidays, I take the children to see Oma. She now has a flat in an apartment block. The building stands alone in scrubland. Since all the other flats belong to foreigners and are empty, hers is immediately apparent as the balcony is dripping and overflowing in flowers. She is very proud that they are all 'nicked cuttings'.

Later one night, full of wine, she is caught picking flowers in the Paseo. She cheeks the Guardia Seville in Spanish,

'Take your hat off to me; you're talking to a lady!' She has no respect for the Spanish Police. 'They have to sign a contract that says they will kill their mothers for Franco', so whenever she can she will lay into them. She's put into a cell in the old prison for a few days to cool down! From where she writes to me,

'Fascinating building, 11th century I think! Pedro's brought me pillows and wine and I'm peacefully reading uninterrupted.' Our dog, Jacob, is in trouble too. He chased a man on a moped and they put him in the dog pound for three days!

Mickgough and I go to the Academy in Oxford Street to see *Elvira Madigan*, an exquisitely beautiful and sad film. I go to the ladies afterwards to mop up because I'm not just weeping, I'm sobbing loudly.

Jonathan and Rachel Miller come to lunch. We talk of bringing up children. He doesn't feel it is appropriate to inflict our neurotic timetables on our children. He and his wife are busy Doctors. He has installed a nanny – a big, Caribbean lady - to live on a floor of her own with his children. He says that when he arrives they are sucking melons and the clock has stopped a few days before. He brings his son Tom to lunch. Tom has found a saw in the shed and we catch him just in time as he is about to saw through an antique table.

'Ah, the freedom of creativity!' announces Jonathan.

'Yeah – but it's our table!'

We are discussing our children's' education. We really like the radical ideas of A.S. Neil at Summerhill. We go to see the Headmistress at the council school at the end of Hurlingham Road. I feel like she might give me lines, but we like her at once. As we walk down the corridor she waves her hands at some of the children's crazy paintings, black and messy and huge,

'See these? Wonderful – you really can't teach them anything – it all just has to be encouraged'. Heartened by this, we enrol Polly for her first term and put Jasper's name on the books. They will be very happy here.

We are invited to have lunch with Sarah and Robert Bolt who now live in an exquisite old mill house with stables and land beside the river. I am wearing an antique sailor's top. Sarah's beginning to get into horse breeding. They have a Spanish couple cooking and looking after them. At one point the covering of a mare is happening – Sarah is hysterical. The Spaniard is walking this thoroughbred stallion, prancing round and round until he's just ready to leap on the back of the little mare, who's quivering and gushing, the Spaniard cursing under his breath but in the end, he manages. Robert says quietly,

'Not bad, considering he's only used to donkeys!'

For lunch, we sit on a table in the middle of the vast lawn under a very old cedar tree. It's beautifully laid with white cloth and silver. All very elegant. The Spaniard and his wife, proudly approach with a huge salmon on a silver plate, held high. He trips, and the fish shoots several metres across the lawn.

Later we play croquet, which can be a very mean game and can result in very bad feelings. More marriages have broken up on the croquet lawn … So it's Sarah and Mickgough against Robert and I and I must say, Mick is delighting in knocking us into the brambles!

Jasper's Little Hand!

In the park opposite our home we love to watch them play footy. Fulham is full of working-class people. The local shops are the lifeblood of the community. The grocer, chemist, post office – they are all friends. Dear Mr. Gant our grocer, we collect his green shield stamps. Sometimes he waves to us as we whisk by in a chauffeur-driven studio car. We wave happily, but can't pay his bill this month. But over the seven years that we are here, it changes, the old people sell up, the professionals arrive, they tart up the streets, the restaurants move in – 'The Trencherman', 'Carlo's'. Next door a new couple have moved in. She's on horse slimming pills, and he parks his boat which takes up a lot of space in the road.

David Niven buys a house here for a few months; Sarah and I are engaged by him to do the interior. We choose wallpapers and carpets. We have to send samples to Portofino where he lives, and we laugh because we know he will always choose the cheapest, because he is another wealthy old actor, notoriously stingy.

'Did you get a discount on the fridge?' We make his house beautiful. He arrives with his expensive wife in furs. We drink champagne and toast to 'neighbours'. She has had a theft in the hotel room, all her jewels and furs. They never really move in. Yet there is a feeling of community in our little neck of the woods. One day Noel comes into our kitchen with his guitar, and sits on the bench,

'Just written a song. Tell me what you think.' He sings *Windmills of Your Mind*. It will win him an Oscar as the title song in *The Thomas Crown Affair*.

My Aunt Tilly is on the 'phone.

'Can you come? Stanley is dying.' We re-organise, make sure everything can run smoothly without me, pack my Mini Traveller with a few things to cheer my Aunt, and down to Somerset I go.

They have been living in this tiny cottage, with no 'phone and no electricity. It's in the folds of Exmoor, and you have to go down through two fields to reach it. Stanley has been running the Minehead Miniature Railway, very happily tootling around the track in a steam train. They are quiet, country people, walking their dog, Ferry, who they have had since Windsor and the boat days. He has had cancer for some months; as she says, he was keeping his strength up in hospital, drinking his Guinness, but as it got closer they said he could come home to die. Since he's been home he won't eat a thing.

He is in the front room on a camp bed. He's unconscious. He never knows I've come. His breath is painfully loud and heaving and hovers over everything we do. We drink tea and we talk of old times, him in Farnham Common recovering from the war; on the boat fishing. We tidy her little garden, sweep her kitchen, stoke the Rayburn, fill the oil lamps, and all the time, his heaving breath. We pick flowers for Stanley and sit with him. We both weep a lot. This lovely, gentle soul is leaving us, slowly, slowly. The nurse comes to be there at night to give us a break. She's a fussy old bag.

'Where will I sit?' and 'Ooh, I must have a hot water bottle and pillows' One night she wakes us. 'It's very near, you'd better come.' We fly downstairs and just as we enter the room, the loud, rattling breath stops. Tilly is holding his hand and talking to him. I feel deeply and strangely at peace. There is an energy in the room, a sort of…magic, the same magic that was around me when I gave birth to my babies. A presence.

Now the nurse is complaining,

'I'll have to charge you extra, I can't lay him out on my own, he's a big man.'

'Just shut up and make some tea!' I order. Later, Tilly is wrapped in eiderdowns upstairs with a glass of brandy, and the nurse and I do what is needed. This is my first encounter with a dead body, yet curiously, all the time we are removing colostomy bags and washing and dressing it – this is not an easy thing to do, he's a very big man - I have a clear impression this is *merely a body*. Stanley's spirit is upstairs with Tilly.

They come down the steep hills in a hearse and carry the coffin awkwardly down the front steps and away to Minehead. We have to do all the paperwork and organise the funeral. My darling Aunt, heartbroken. Although they have lived together since the war, they never bothered to get married, so she is still Tilly Craxton. Now, these pinched little people with their pinched little rules and laws are saying she has no right to Stanley's possessions – nothing more than a few wild flower books and a fishing rod. Apparently, she has no legal right to sign this and that. I am furious and hurting for her. These ridiculous, antiquated laws (which are only *now* being changed).

After the tiny funeral, I pack her up, put her in my car and drive her home with me. I get her a ticket to Spain so she can be with her sister.

We have a privet hedge at the front of our house. I've never cut it and it's grown huge and unkempt and all out over the street. I've borrowed some clippers from the neighbours and as I'm clipping away, a nasty neighbour passes,

'Huh, about time. That hedge has been lowering the tone of the whole street.'

'Hurray!' I say, 'I'll never cut it again!' *And I don't think I did.*

I've also had my hair cut very short, one inch all over. I want to get away from the Polly in *Doctor Who* image. As I'm relaxing more now, I'm putting on weight too. Damn it!

I keep having strange dreams about Hurlingham Park - I see it all filled with soldiers and trucks and sort of military boxes and people marching about and the sounds of bombing. When I tell our neighbours, the Bryants, about this they say,

'Ah well that's how it was during the war! It was used as a military depot.'

Simon Gough teaches me to play chess. We will spend many evenings in the terracotta kitchen, under the Victorian Lamp, our board spread out on the table. I'm engrossed by the game. I get good enough to beat him and then I lose interest!

Mickgough comes home and I have a big fight with him. I'm carrying our supper tray of kippers into the living room for us to have watching telly when something he says to me is so beastly that I raise the tray up in the air and smash it to the ground. The kippers splatter everywhere among the shattered plates. *What a sight.* Of course, I'm the one who has to wipe it up – I accept that – but I feel somehow satisfied because I have expressed myself totally in the moment.

Simon has fallen for Wendy Cook. They are spending a lot of time together and we are worried that they are becoming lovers.

One night we get an emergency call from Simon. Peter has hit him and he's got to go to hospital. He has a broken jaw. I don't want to know about it. Violence of any kind makes me feel quite ill and afraid. Peter has hit Wendy too, and she's pregnant, so it's very worrying.

I've got a part in another episode of *The Avengers* with Diana Rigg. It's only a small moment but it's great to meet up with Pat Macnee again and in my little scene I'm telling lies to the lovely Diana Rigg in a tie shop. I'm very posh. We used to do a little rhyme for posh vowels,

'*Rind abite a thy-sand pinds for a tine-hice.*' I have the line,

'Cash or account?' but it doesn't come out quite right so I have to go back later and re-record it!

December 10th and Otis Redding, one of the greatest soul legends, dies in a plane crash. We are all listening to his music. He had been playing at the Monterey pop festival with Jimi Hendrix. This is now my music. *Try a Little Tenderness* will be released three months after he dies and become the biggest selling single of all time, up to this point. Mickgough can't keep up. He's defiantly listening to the Beethoven Quartets which he has given *me* for Christmas!

I have been wondering how we can expand the space in the house. I talk it over with Mick.

'If we were to take the ceiling out in the top front room and build a balcony on the ceiling of the back room, we could then have a studio!' He's not convinced, but then he always says *no* to everything, and he's off to Hollywood for six weeks to do *Berserk* with the daunting Joan Crawford, who he later tells me wears special kinds of plasters on either side of her face to hold her face up. At the end of the shoot she will call him to her trailer to give him a token of her thanks, a plastic Coca-Cola biro!

I get Peter Crofton-Sleigh around and together we do the work on the house. We set up a pulley system so all the rubble can be lowered down from the windows into the street below, and not have to be traipsed through the house. We remove the ceiling, and we build the balcony. We make a white marble tiled hearth and a Pithers stove which is a tall metal cylinder which holds anthracite. It's very good for studio spaces. A steep ladder to the space above. With a cold chisel and hammer, I remove all the plaster from the main wall, hanging off a little scaffold. I paint it chocolate brown. It's a great space and a surprise for Mickgough when he comes home. We have our bed up on the balcony. That winter we have cupboards made all along the eaves. It's great having my own money because I can just go ahead and do things.

Robin comes to supper; he tells us a story of how one night, very late, he was driving Joanna Dunham home in his Mini, both of them drunk and laughing; they didn't notice the 'beware' signs, and they drove right into a six-foot deep hole in the middle of Oxford Street. Neither of them were hurt, just a few bruises, but the car had to be taken out by crane!

He needs a story, so he tells his readers about Mickgough and I opening up our roof space. A neighbour reads it and gets on to the council, so now they are hassling us and I'm having nightmares about our roof flying off. But our friend Nathan Silver, American architect, saves the day by tying the roof in with wires.

My agents tell me that Tony Newley wants to see me about a part in his new film – it's got an impossible title – typical Tony - *Can Heironymous Merkin Ever Forget Mercy Hump and Find True Happiness?* I am waiting in the foyer of The Playboy Club with many very pretty girls when the lift door opens and Tony walks across, directly to me, with a big grin.

'Ello Facie!', and he leads me back to the lift. On the way up to the penthouse suite where the producers are, we are shamelessly kissing and ripping each others clothes off. We arrive looking dishevelled. There is some whispering and nods and we are given some time to be with each other. He asks after Polly and then explains that he just wanted to see me but can't use me in the film, because Joan won't stand for it. It sounds like another autobiographical piece. I wish him well,

'Love you Tone.'

'Love you Wills.' and I leave. I don't see him again. Tony and I are spiritually connected forever. If you *really* love someone, you forgive them.

Tony, talking to God in *Mercy Hump*

It's 1968. I've got an audition for the Royal Shakespeare Company. *Yes! Yes!* When the euphoria has worn off, I go into total panic. It will be held at Drury Lane, the biggest theatre in London. I go off to have a refresher course in voice production with Elizabeth Wilmer who works with Iris Warren's method, *The Natural Voice*, lovely and relaxing, on the floor, allowing the breath to fall out with the sound on it, until I'm able to speak, quite loudly, and without forcing, and with lots of resonance. Mick teaches me, *always warm up your voice.* Now he helps me with my two Shakespeare audition pieces and I stand in our new studio in front of the big mirror and practice. The day dawns. I go to the theatre. I'm up on stage and John Barton is directing me and Terry Hands and some other people are out there in the dark stalls.

'Good voice,' he says when I've done my first piece. 'Now, do it as though there's a drunk actor in the wings and he's gonna come on stage, you know, he's coming on now.' Everyone is laughing and smiling. I'm in there for about an hour. I come out as high as a kite. I'm driving myself home down The Mall - *They liked me! They liked me!* – I feel invincible and like I could just push a little button and fly over Buckingham Palace. I go home and I wait for the 'phone to ring. After a week I call my agent.

'Anything from the RSC?'

'No, sorry darling.' After two weeks, the dreaded doubt, like a cancer, has spread. Maybe I wasn't that good. I'm not talented at all, and maybe they could just see that. Much later I heard that Terry Hands' girlfriend was chosen - Helen Mirren.

Martin Luther King has been assassinated. He was standing on his balcony. The world has gone into shock. The entire media is full of nothing else. One of the great men of our time, gone.

Peter invites us to be in the audience of his new BBC series with Dudley - *Not Only, But Also*. This is the first time we see the famous *Pete and Dud* act - their flat caps, their mackintoshes, their baleful expressions. That laughter you can hear in the background … that's us!

That winter we see *Rowan and Martin's Laugh-in*, which becomes an overnight sensation. Goldie Hawn is captivating, and it's wonderfully off the wall and our old friend Roddy Maude-Roxby will appear in it. Roddy went to Eton, then the Royal College of Art, with Peter Blake and David Hockney, and now he is in *Rowan and Martin's Laugh-In* doing a hilarious act with collapsible chairs!

Simon and I play Mozart's Mass in B Minor on the new hi-fi we've got in the studio, we really crank it up and the music rattles around the rafters. Simon suffers from 'black moods'. It's like a black cloud descends on him - and all of us - and he can't help but growl and snarl and frighten us all to bits. He drinks cups of tea all day long sweetened with fifteen lumps of white sugar in each. If he doesn't get these he becomes quite violent. He's never to be seen without a briefcase full of pills and Kleenex. He's now living in a potting shed in the garden of a friend's house in Chelsea. We are always hoping he will get a job. He seems to have so much latent talent - he can act, he can write and he's so passionate. Mick will always feel guilty, and worry about him.

Roddy and Mickgough are working in one of the very first drug addiction centres. It's in the Worlds End, Kings Road, Chelsea, run by the charismatic Dr. Peter Chapple. They will do acting and psychodrama and friendship. Later Patrick Maxwell, a painter, will join them. These four men form a deep bond of friendship and admiration for each other. This is a very special happening for everyone concerned. The lives of the addicts so tragic. It certainly hadn't taken long for the drugs to take hold of the vulnerable and for the pain and destruction to begin.

The centre is next to 'Granny Takes a Trip'. Across the road there's 'Heaven and Hell' which has an amazing pop-art front that Polly and Jasper love. The shops in the Kings Road have gone psychedelic.

Simon gives us a wedding anniversary present, two envelopes that we must open simultaneously. Fold by fold, excited apprehension, *what is it?* Two tickets to Paris for a weekend! *The best present ever!* Although I have been through Paris on our way to Spain, I have never seen the city. Now I'm dreaming of Montmartre and the artist's quarter and the shops in the Champs Elysee. I want to see the Paris of *Les Enfants du Paradis*. Mick has been to Paris often, of course, so he's not keen to 'see the Eiffel Tower'. He made a marvellous film with Peter Sellars in which they both played two crumbling old Parisian teachers.

John Craxton will be in Paris. He has a Princess friend (!) whose flat he has borrowed so we can stay with him. Well, I am so excited I get strep throat. This is an old pattern of mine. We set off in late April, me fairly wobbly and drugged but determined to enjoy these moments. To have the erudite John Craxton as our Parisian guide, sharing with us his favourite works in The Louvre, is one of the honours of my life. And we walk everywhere, so by Saturday night I'm utterly wiped out.

'A lovely little bistro?' I say hopefully.

'No, no, much too expensive. We'll have scrambled eggs at the apartment.'

The students' quarter is full of scuffles - outbreaks of violence which will erupt into full scale riots in a few weeks' time. A major event of the Parisian riots – 8,000 students and teachers are protesting against the French Police. There's a General Strike.

Revolution is in the air … and it is spreading to Britain … there is a move afoot to sweeten the tea trolley at Westminster with LSD.

When the nationwide census happens, we Brits are outraged at the violation of our privacy, so Michael Van Bloeman was tells us all,

'If you rub candle-wax down the answer column on the questionnaire it will melt when it's put through their equipment … '

We go to Cambridge to stay with our friends Caroline and Nathan Silver. He's from New York and has recently published an excellent book on the architecture there. She is a writer of articles about cars and horses. Mickgough fancies her. Roddy Maude-Roxby is with us. It's a large Cambridge Arts and Crafts house in Maddingley Road. It's immaculate in its authenticity. We sit in leather armchairs in the evening drinking whisky. Caroline takes Mickgough - with me the hanger on - to see the early morning rides at the Newmarket stables. What a magical sight, the racehorses galloping in the mist. These stables are run like the military. Caroline will ride in point to points – and straight into Mickgough's fantasies!

We play croquet with a large, American poet of great renown, a scholar on a sabbatical and Germaine Greer, who is an outspoken Australian with a growing reputation as a 'feminist'. I like her very much but she's a bit daunting. After a while these literati are squabbling like 6 year olds!

'You're not playing by the rules!'

'Yes I am!'

'No you're not!' and in a rage Germaine chucks her croquet mallet into the bushes and storms off the lawn.

♫ *We'll drink a drink a drink to Lily the Pink* ♫

- Scaffold

Julie has moved in with her partner, John. He runs 'Minitrek' - which takes people across the Sahara in Land Rovers. They are preparing for an expedition taking scientists into the desert. Julie is a sexy, strong, sweet woman, and can drink all the blokes under the table! I love her. Up in the studio, Barney has made me a vast, twelve-foot-long work-surface on which I have my sewing machine.

Underneath, we have a huge drawer full of all the beautiful photographs we've had taken of us over the years. Huge, thick grainy, sixties-style photos, a truly beautiful collection. Michael Wallis took the one I use on the front of this book. So many will be left to rot … very sad …

I'm cutting out patterns and making Polly dresses and me mini skirts. I get the kids little Oshkosh dungarees from Kids in Gear. I'm making Julie an olive green corduroy cloak with a silk lining and a buckled collar. It is the most adventurous thing I've done so far and I really enjoyed making it. She is delighted and wears it everywhere.

We have great haggis nights. Johnny brings real haggis and we eat them with mashed potatoes and Swedes, and drink Drambuie.

Johnny is a Scottish artist and explorer. He will talk to us endlessly about Pete, his mate who is coming down from Glasgow soon. Eventually Pete comes and they're off to the West End, chuckling with anticipation. I come down in the morning to find Johnny sprawled over the sofa – torn clothes, bloody lips, black eyes, reeking. After a pint or two of coffee,

'Johnny, what happened?'

'Ha ha, 'twas a grand night!' You can't keep a good Celt down!

Mick has got a six-week Art's Council tour of South America with Brenda Bruce coming up. How come he always gets such wonderful places to go and all I get is the south coast in February!

He's packing and I'm feeling abandoned and really envious. He'll be seeing such cities - Rio de Janeiro, where *Orpheo Negro* was filmed. And working with another band of great actors.

'Oh, you lucky thing!'

We all drive to the airport. Polly and Jasper are with me, they want to see him fly off on a plane. We are in the lounge, the other actors are gathering, greeting each other. There's a very pretty assistant Mickgough is eyeing up. He's leaving me, I can feel it.

I drive home feeling empty and flat. It's summer, and life happens in our garden. We eat out all the time. We now have a climbing frame and Polly has her little friends to play with. Jasper is a white-haired three year-old. *The most beautiful children in the world.* I never feel happier than when I have one child's hand in mine and one child on my hip - loving a child is the greatest gift.

My agents call – dear Terry Owen and Bernard Hunter – they are such good people, kind and understanding, and they have got me a lot of work for 1967. They also would like to build me a career. They believe that I have possibilities of going far, they also recognise that I have my needs as a mother - being away in the sticks doing 'worthy' theatre is not for me, I need to be in London doing great telly! They are offering me a choice of a theatre gig up in Sheffield, or an advert in Spain with Peter Yates … *Peter Yates!* He has a great reputation, already one of our best directors. He's done *Summer Holiday*, *One-Way Pendulum* and just recently, *Robbery*.

'I'll go to Spain!' I say. So I make sure that all is running smoothly at home, everyone looking out for the children. Robin and Annette Brown around the corner, our very dear friends, and their two daughters Tiffany and Lisa are Polly's best friends. Robin is a wildlife director and makes wonderful documentaries for Oxford Scientific Films.

Funny how the children hardly notice I've gone.

We are all staying in a modern hotel in Fuengirola. These hotels now seem to be springing up everywhere in Spain. It has a swimming pool, which for me is a great treat. I meet Peter Yates and his wife, Virginia, and they are delightful, and become instant friends. Michael Burkett, who was with me on *Some People*, is also there. The advert is one of the classic *Colgate Ring of Confidence* series. One girl has shining teeth, and the other slopes away sheepishly.

'By the way – which one am I?' I ask Peter.

'Don't you know?'

'No – I just wanted to work with you!'

'Ah,' he says laughing, 'a real actress.' The next day we are driving away from the coast, up through the pine-clad hills, to a tiny hill town, Mijas. It is exquisite, unspoilt, original Spanish. This is what we love about this country. I have to step off an ancient bus in the cobbled square and I turn towards the camera and smile.

BING!! The Ring of Confidence!

That night, a unit supper in a rustic restaurant under the stars. The unit sits around a long table under a vine canopy. Peter and Virginia are extremely classy people and they are used to the best so everything about their shoot is tip-top. So we have the wonderful tapas and the wine and the waiters bring huge vats of gazpacho. Just as we start to enjoy this wonderful peasant soup, the lights go out. *Aaaagghh! Que Pasa!* This is a regular occurrence in Spain so I'm eating my soup in the dark, too good to miss. Candles are bought and I never manage, try as I might, to make gazpacho taste like it did that night.

After work, next day, I have a swim and I'm in my room preparing for yet another great supper when my 'phone goes. It's Michael Burkett.

'Anneke, will you stay there please? I'm coming up.' He sounds very serious. I'm shocked. My mind goes -

I'm in trouble - they're going to give me the sack - what have I done? No. Something's happened. Someone's died. My mother? Nicholas?

In that instant - I know it's you.

Michael enters the room quietly,

'Anneke, news from London – unfortunate accident – your brother has died,'

'Which one?' I say weakly, trying to delay the inevitable.

'Robin.'

Chapter 30

Robin

Full of our favourite *cuba libre*, I'm floating in the pool.

Robin, my brother, my best friend.

Everyone is very kind, but decisions must be made. I talk to my mother, she's been staying with friends in Putney. She is crazed with grief, convinced he has been murdered. She must get out of England. She hates the rain. She must come to me, here in Spain, and we will grieve together under the stars with a flagon of wine.

My agents organise a ticket for her. Friends put her on a plane. The Yates' organise a place for us to stay on the outskirts of Valencia. I send a telegram to Mick in South America.

'After your tour, meet me in Valencia.' One of Robin's journalist friends - Brian – says he will organise the cremation in Golders Green but he is angry that I don't feel the need to go back for the funeral.

He is on the 'phone, shouting and swearing,

'What kind of a bloody sister are you? Not going to be at your brother's funeral!' I'm crying and babbling,

'He's not in a box in Golders Green. You deal with the body; we will mourn his spirit here, in the country he loved.' I'm very clear.

Did it come from you?

I collect my stricken mother from the airport and we are driven to a new house on a building site on the outskirts of town. That first night, we have no electricity so we light a bonfire and under the stars, and with our flagon of wine, we cry together.

And the night puts its arms around us and we feel you so close.

After a week of grieving, my mother's pain is too much to bear. She goes on to Malaga to be with Alex. She will never get over this. Never. I know.

I take a hotel room in Valencia, in preparation for meeting Mick. Now, more than ever, I want to feel his love and support. I go to the airport; he's walking off the plane towards me. I'm stumbling with grief.

'Robin's dead,' After a day, I say, 'I've made money doing this commercial and we're so close to Mallorca, why not let me buy you a ticket and you can go and see Emma? And I'll go back to London and sort things out.' I want him to say,

'No, you need me, I'll stay with you.'

He goes to Mallorca.

I fly home to a world without you. On the plane home I send up a prayer -

'Oh, my Father – how sad you never knew this intelligent, funny, sweet son of yours,'

The children have been told to be kind to me. Their loving cuddles set my tears off again. Polly asks me,

'But Mummy, where's Robin gone?'

'To heaven.'

'Where is that?' Jasper answers, with authority,

'Up ve Kings Woad!'

Now Brian is on the 'phone. He wants to punish me by telling me all about the funeral. I don't want to hear it at this moment, but he's drunk and insistent. Now he's saying that he's going to come over. *Oh god.* I feel unprotected, unable to cope and I'm frightened. I run up the street, with my supper in a frying pan, to get shelter with neighbours.

When Mick returns from his holiday, we talk.

'I somehow can't believe he's dead,'

'Wouldn't go down that road,' he says. 'Next minute, you'll be talking to spiritualists. May as well accept it. When we die, that's the end of it.'

But I know that you come into my dreams. I'm stepping onto a bus, and there you are, jumping off it, laughing, always laughing.

'Robin! But you're dead!'

'Aha, that's what you think!' - as you disappear into the crowd.

I wake up to the emptiness once again, I'm inconsolable. I start making patchworks, sewing is such a saviour. I make up strips of all the remnants of materials, the rich velvety reds and blacks and the ones with all the little flowers on. Pieces of all the clothes I've made the children over the years, these I sew together and then cut as though it is cloth. I make waistcoats for Polly and Jasper, for Christmas, and for Mick, I make a huge magic dressing gown with a lining and a belt and pockets. Later, this will appear on stage in a play but for now, it's a surprise for his birthday.

There is great confusion as to what exactly happened. What we can deduce is that you were on a clandestine story. South American drug barons were touted as one possibility. It transpires that you had changed your name to Richard Grenville a few months before, to protect your family and friends. You were on your way to chase up a lead in Scotland. You were in a bar on Euston station, waiting for a train, when, witnesses say, unprovoked, a man smashed you off your stool. You fell to the ground unconscious. In the ambulance on the way to the hospital, you had an aneurism which burst, and you died. Who was this person? Scotland Yard are involved. We won't pursue it. You are gone and we will miss you forever. It is written in the stars.

Chapter 31

Magical Mystery Tour

Time passes slowly when your heart is broken. Peter and Virginia Yates have taken me under their wing. Virginia is so pretty and has the most exquisite taste in clothes, very smart – beautiful shoes and tailored trousers. She also has the most marvellously glowing skin – I ask her about it.

'It's Countess Scharky, whose regime is *no make-up,* and change your cream every ten days because the skin gets lazy … '

I admire Virginia very much. She is astoundingly bright and has a droll sense of humour. She will go to the Parisian Spring Collection – *to save money!* I feel privileged to count Peter and Virginia as my friends. Our children are the same ages. They have one of those sweet Victorian houses in Notting Hill. I'm envious of the real Spanish tiles in the kitchen - we only have fake ones in lino – and their neat little garden filled with pots of geraniums.

Their favourite restaurant is the San Lorenzo in Beecham Place. It has a tree growing up inside. Many of the 'in crowd' dine there. Peter has just finished directing *The Great Train Robbery* and I go to a celebration meal with Stanley Baker. They are such a kind and generous couple. I give them one of my etchings. I will see this on the wall of their home in Beverley Hills thirty years later.

Simon and I are planning a 'magical mystery tour' for Mick's birthday, a surprise. In October, the censorship laws are revoked. The Lord Chamberlain has got the sack and the very next day, the American musical *Hair* opens. We tell Mick to put on his glad rags and all the way into the West End he's trying to guess where we're taking him. We roll up outside the theatre, with the hottest tickets in town.

♫ *This is the dawning of the 'Age of Aquarius.* ♫

Hair is revelatory. Amazing dancing and they're naked and singing - 'Masturbation can be fun, join the holy order – Kama Sutra – every one!!' And we love it and afterwards, a little supper in our favourite, very simple, family-run French restaurant, Mon Plaisir.

Now it's winter, and the darkest time of the year and there are questions I want answers to.

Questions which until now, I haven't really given any serious thought to. I've been too busy to wonder if there is a God or not, or where we go when we die. Where can I find the answers?

In my anguish the angels rush to hug me and give me sleep and forgetfulness and healing. We are not alone, *only I don't know this then.* And each time it mends a little more. Slowly, slowly, I begin to trust life again.

'There was a door, to which I found no key,
There was a veil past which I could not see'

- The Rubaiyat of Omar Khayam

It's 1969 – a new year and a fresh start. I enrol at the Morley College in Westminster. I want to work in their print-making studio – Adrian runs it. He sees Mickgough dropping me off in our new Renault 4L and later tells me he had us down as 'progressive vegetarians'...

I do lithography, working on stones, like Lautrec. I produce a lovely free drawing of a lunch in the garden. The honeysuckle climbs over the birdcage. Michael Van Bloemen and exotic Sheila are under an umbrella, Mickgough who's talking passionately, the children are playing and I am staring out at you, the viewer. I have to say, it's rather good. I also do one of the Pearly Queens, all their little buttons and their lovely Cockney faces, and hats with feathers. And later still, I move into etching. When I show these to Mickgough, he's rather dismissive, treating it as 'mummy's hobby'. Anyway, I know I love it and I can stand, utterly absorbed for hours, without feeling tired at all.

Sheila wears the American designer Bonnie Cashin, who's philosophy is layers of silk next to the body, then cashmere, loose coats then fur-lined leather all in natural colours – creams and browns. I love it and it's far too expensive for me.

I've taken the children to see my mother. They are asleep after an energetic trip to the beach. My mother and I are sitting on her balcony watching the sunset, we have wine and olives and we are talking about Robin. I'm flicking the olive pips over the edge and in the morning there is a mountain of pips everywhere. On Sunday we walk across the mountains, the pine trees' resin fills the air, wild thyme, myrtles, yellow Spanish broom. In a small town we have Spanish lunch in a huge café with stone floors and filled with Spanish families. Polly and Jasper are being made a fuss of – the Spanish love children, especially blonds. My mother teaches them some Spanish words.

In the little back streets, the people have cane cages in which they keep little exotic birds. One night my mother is a little 'worse for wear' and wants to release the little finches from their prisons. We are protesting.

'That's really stupid! They'll die!' But she's babbling about freedom – and continues with her liberating mission. This woman can be *so* embarrassing!

'One moment of freedom is worth more than a lifetime in a cage!'

Polly is sitting on a bus, on the way to Tossa de Mar. She's wearing a red and white flamenco dress. We take a photo, now sadly lost.

We are stuck at Gerona airport in dreadful heat, not a breath, and the plane is delayed, we are all wilting. My mother says,

'Faint.'

'What?'

'Faint! Go on, trust me.' So using my training, I buckle at the knees.

'Help, help!' (in Catalan), 'My daughter needs help!' Moments later, I'm in a wheelchair and we are going ahead of all the tourists to a cool aeroplane, first class.

Moe, you were the actress.

Chapter 32

Rexy's Toes

In the kitchen, sometimes the 'phone goes and it's Mickgough's 'ex-wife number one' who I have to make horrible lame excuses to but occasionally he will speak to her and the seething, vicious tone of his voice makes me frightened. I vow I'll never get in that position with him. But this time the 'phone goes and it's Rexy!

'Darling, I'm chartering my yacht in Venice and we will go down the coast to Greece. Would you and Mick like to come?'

'Are you kidding?! Yes!' When Mickgough returns from work, I tell him. We are both thrilled to bits. Virginia lends me a lovely, long, silvery dress, because I don't have any evening wear. Mick packs his espadrilles. We have told all our neighbours,

'Off on a yacht with Rex Harrison, yeah!' When we get on the plane, Mick, in his most theatrical voice, says,

'Put the champagne on ice, darling,' to the stewardess. By the time we get to Venice, we are pissed. We get into the water taxi.

'What's the name of the yacht?' Mickgough asks me.

'I don't know, he didn't tell me. You mean you haven't got it?' *Oh God.* Here we are in the Lido surrounded by hundreds of glamorous ships and we don't know which is Rex's. In drunken, made-up Italian, we get our gondolier to start cruising around; Mick is standing up as we approach some vast yacht.

'Rex Harrison, hellooooo, hellooooo, Rexy!'

'No, no,' shaking faces appear at the top. We try another. Now Mick is doing a Rex imitation,

'I've grown accustomed to her face', he sings, all the time wobbling away. Eventually we get an affirmative.

'Si, si, this is his boat, but he's gone to the airport to meet you!' We are shown into our lovely cabin and we unpack. It's all mahogany and white linen and brass taps, very classy. We meet Elizabeth Harris, who is together with Rexy now, and we are all to go to dinner on another yacht. Dirk Bogarde, Trevor Howard, Vladmir Ashkenazi the famous pianist, and his wife. The conversation and the champagne sparkling and everyone gets unbelievably drunk.

I am sitting between Mickgough and Rexy in my silver dress. Waving his fork, Rexy turns to me and whispers in my ear,

'How would you like it if I stuck this fork up your cunt?' I may be drunk, but this completely shocks me. My smile freezes. This bizarre moment passes. The next day our crew is making preparations for our trip, so Mick and I take off to see a bit of Venice. We sit in St. Mark's Square and have a very expensive coffee and he tells me how sad he feels because he and Annie (wife number two) had been such intimate friends with Dirk Bogarde, but now, because of me, he disapproves and Mick misses his friendship. Alec Guinness is also disapproving of me…

We set off. Rex and Elizabeth, her brother and his girlfriend, and Mickgough and me. Trevor Howard will join us later. So six of us and a crew of fifteen! We gather at the back of the yacht. The chilled champagne flows endlessly and the sun loungers are spread about. Elizabeth has her hair wrapped in towels and huge sunglasses and her nose in Agatha Christie for most of the time. Down in their cabin I've seen a whole load of wigs she's bought for the trip. It is our first morning, and we are all relaxing and enjoying.

I'm starting a journal, making notes of the changing coastline, doing little drawings with my pencils, and the sun is gentle. At night we dine in the yacht's dining room, with its oval mahogany table crystal glasses, silver, and the waiters bring us roast beef and Yorkshire pudding and chocolate mousse. The yacht has been stocked up with food from Fortnum's! At one point, I go to help myself to some more veggies,

'Wait!' says Rexy, and presses the button by his side. We wait. I'm protesting,

'I can do it!'

'No, no,' says Rexy, 'that's what I pay them for.' The steward comes, and I get my now cold veggies.

As we travel down the coast, arguments begin to happen. Elizabeth wants to stop in very large ports so that she can go to a hotel, 'phone her children and have her hair done. Rexy and Mick and I want to stop off in all the interesting little fishing ports so we can wander around in the ancient streets and bars. The Captain also only wants to moor in the big ports because it's less hassle. Late one night it's just Rex and me in the salon. I roll him a joint. He gets stoned for the first time. He is sitting on the floor with bare feet. He's happily trying to remember which battery is which for the tape recorder because now he wants music. I do a drawing entitled *Rexy's Toes.*

'Darling,' he says, 'we must get more of that lovely marijuana. I'll tell the crew. Maybe at the next port?'

'Rexy, this is Yugoslavia – they'll get shot!'

We all set off to see some ancient caves. As we are entering deeper and deeper into the dark, dank atmosphere with all the other tourists, Elizabeth has fainted. A terrible fuss, she is carried out, and everyone is most concerned. Rexy says to me dryly,

'It's the fucking slimming pills, darling, they're driving her crazy.'

One night at our Fortnum's dinner, I have a row with Rex. We are talking about theatre – he is of the old school. I'm telling him about Joan Littlewood and her workshop theatre in the East End. No stars, just a team of actors. He hates it.

'That's not theatre!' he storms. 'And what's more, we won't have any more of this. The subject is closed.' Everyone's gone quiet and embarrassed and I'm miserable. We arrive in Dubrovnik. Elizabeth has gone to have her hair done. I'm leaning over the side of our yacht and moored next to us is a beautiful, small family boat. The family are sitting cross-legged on the deck eating huge salads. The father is playing his guitar, the children are laughing. I feel like a spoilt little rich girl and also I feel homesick. I go to Mick.

'I don't like this. They're all so neurotic. Let's leave. I want to go home to the children.' Mickgough can't face Rexy directly so the next morning at the crack of dawn, we leave a note and we tip-toe out of the boat and along the harbour to a taxi and the airport and home to heavenly Fulham and my beautiful children and ordinary life. If that's what it's like being a star, I don't need it. I've learned a very important lesson.

October 20th. The 'phone goes and a strange voice says,

'This is E.L.Wisty of the GPO, happy birthday to you, happy birthday to you ... '

'Peter it's you! I know it's you, isn't it Peter?' He goes right on to the end of the song. Then,

'Thank you very much' and puts the 'phone down. I call him in Hampstead.

'Peter it was you! Thank you for the …'

'I don't know what you are talking about!' I never really am quite sure, though 'E. L. Wisty' should have given it away.

Emma Gough is coming. Lovely Emma is now a young woman and she is a real beauty. Lithe-limbed and long-haired, sparkly-eyed. We celebrate, she and me, by going off and buying her a trendy dress at Biba's. She spends many hours in her dressing gown tinkling on the piano. She's in love … Mickgough is in heaven, he can't do enough for her. He is slightly over the top which is irritating, but it's really good to reconnect with her and she loves her little brother and sister – we never bother with the 'step' word.

Two keen film-makers have come to talk to me about their new project. It will star Peter O'Toole. They are looking for a girl to play opposite him. I have to listen to a lot of bullshit all about interpretation, but the bottom line is that I would be naked and behaving like an animal. They will be testing in a North London studio.

'Will I do the test with Peter?' I ask.

'Er, well, er, no, no, he's busy; we will have a stand in.'

'So you are going to have me crawling around naked, with some strange man, on film. I don't think so thank you!' We never hear from them again, they disappear into thin air.

Barney Broadbent has taken his sister Julie's place in our home and he brings a whole new energy with him. He is a patient of Dr. Sharma, the famous homeopathic doctor, who is nothing short of radical. He will put you on a total clean-out, before he begins to treat you.

'Ten days on boiled onions, then let's see!' I did it.

Mind you – story had it that he was caught out eating sausages, smoking cigars and drinking vodka!

Barney is also into a macrobiotic diet so I'm learning about yin and yang and eating 'what's in season'. His lover is Alice Pollock, the designer, whose shop 'Quorum' she shares with Ossie Clark and Celia Birtwell. Ossie and Celia were at art school together and they design exquisite fabrics made up into flowing shapes. I love going to the shop and watching them in the back room cutting the patterns and gossiping. Celia's designs are now in Top Shop.

Barney has a little black mongrel called Morgan. They have a very touching relationship. He seems to ignore her completely yet she goes with him everywhere and is entirely independent. While he's at work in his offices off Holland Park Road, she's off taking care of her needs. She's got pet butchers and pet old ladies who spoil her with titbits. And when Barney arrives home, she's off around the neighbourhood.

Alice's daughter Cleo is Polly's friend so we are an extended family.

Kensington Market is now a great place for antique clothes but quite expensive. We used to pay sixpence for ours in the jumble sales - now they are charging twelve pounds for a velvet coat. I find the most amazing Erte 1920's coat for five pounds. It's tightly woven silk with a tiny beaded art deco design - I give it to Barney who wears it to parties. He's very flamboyant, old Barney, with his Ossie shirts and snake skin boots, as he goes about his business designing restaurants and clubs.

'Come on, Morgan!' There is a scuttling of little feet – and the two of them are off into the night …

He spends hours reading in the bath with his specs misting up. I want to design specs for him with little wipers. I buy a huge length of very good quality antique pale green velvet and make two pairs of trousers with zips and flies and waistband and flares. I give one pair to Barney (we are the same size) and the other pair I will wear in my next TV series.

Barney and Julie's parents, Dee and Roy Broadbent, met at art school and became farmers in Lincoln when the war broke out. They started a family and eventually bought this lovely old Glebe farmhouse which grew and grew over the years to accommodate their family's need. Roy became a designer but his passion was amateur theatre and they created a thriving amateur theatrical group and eventually a theatre in Lincoln which, when Roy died in the seventies, was named after him. Dee then took up her original love, which was sculpting. They are very dear friends of ours and we share many happy times. One time we go on a barge along the canals of Lincolnshire together, drinking single malt at night. Dee and Roy are the root of a very large and talented family. They suffer huge personal challenges and bear them with such bravery and humour. *I feel proud to have known and loved them.*

It's the start of the summer holidays. From now my life will revolve around school holidays. And *The Daily Mirror* is on the 'phone – they are ready to go to court. After all this time and thousands of my pounds. We have serious discussions, this cannot happen. Polly has just started in school, the last thing we need is a press scandal. And so I drop the case, which is exactly what they wanted. Many years later, in 2005, *The Daily Mirror* prints a kind interview with me. The journalist is an understanding, modern woman.

Chapter 33

Robert Graves

Now there's a family crisis and Mick and Simon must go to Mallorca. I don't want to be left behind this time, so we are all waiting for the taxi to arrive. We've been listening to Albinoni's *Adagio* and watching a programme on the telly about Venice sinking. Jasper is completely glued and won't come away when the taxi comes. He is watching people in Wellington boots – how high will the water rise? Poor Venice may be lost. We fly to Palma and on to Deya and stay in a lovely old hotel in the hills. In the morning we get up and there's a huge storm rattling the old wooden buildings and water and floods everywhere.

'Is this Venice?' asks Jasper.

We've been abandoned. The Gough clan must have talks. So the people in the hotel are kind and give Polly, Jasper and me a picnic and towels and the storm flies away, as they do in the south, and we are picking our way down through the olive groves towards the rugged beach. It's very stony when we get there and not many people. So we wedge ourselves into some large stones and eat our picnic and happiness is ours. As the sun begins to sink, more people come to the beach. Mallorcan families, sunset time, out with the wine, some olives, light a little fire. Onto the rocks on the right steps a tall, naked man with flowing silver hair. He treads carefully but surely, he's done this every day for years. And after some contemplation, when the moment is just right for him, he dives into the turquoise sea. It's Robert Graves, of course. We all go to his house which is called 'Canellun' - Mallorcan for *The Far Away House* - it stands at the bottom of a mountain. We have tea with his wife and Tomas on the large terrace full of figs and orange trees. Simon has lived with them often in his life; this is one of his homes. He has made, and he proudly shows us, the most wonderful huge stone amphitheatre in the limestone rocks in the olive groves overlooking the sea. It is a total labour of love, an enchanted spot amongst the trees with excellent acoustics, which we all try out!

Wendy has bought an old farmhouse near Pollensa, she has had it painted pink, and done it up in her grand style. The Harrods packing cases are still standing beside it. She is now looking curiously like Jackie Onassis, a headscarf over highly piled hairpieces and *huuuge* dark glasses. She's drinking excessively; such is her unhappiness, and trawling around the port in her white open top Triumph, picking up young men. We leave her to it, and head off inland to find some lovely Mallorcan pottery to take home.

I'm standing in an almond orchard, at sunset with Robert Graves. He is telling me why the Greek myths are so confusing,

'They were all on ambrosia - *juice of the gods* - which was made with mushrooms - psychedelic – they were tripping!'

♫ *Lay lady lay….lay across my big brass bed,* ♫
- Bob Dylan

It's summer 1969, long warm days and nights. We have everything out in the garden and I'm living in a bikini. Michael Wallis comes to supper on July 20th and we are watching the men landing on the moon for the first time. I'm standing in our garden and I'm looking up at the moon feeling curiously sad - perhaps we have penetrated a mystery that was not ours to do so.

Peter leaves a message on our new-fangled answer machine,

'I don't want to talk to Anneke – I want to talk to you, you sexy machine – ah, how I long to play with your spools … '

Guy Playfair comes for supper. He sits at our piano and plays blues. He's closed off and I can't reach him, which makes me sad. He's on his way to South America where he will live for many years and write brilliant books on parapsychology.

I've been working with Roddy and the wonderful Drama Teacher Keith Johnstone, upstairs at the Royal Court. Keith runs Theatre Machine and he's a master improviser. I find it very 'alive' to work in this way, no scripts, just in the moment, and you keep saying *YES!* which is very *Zen.* We do exercises called 'Top Dog', 'Master and Servant', and 'Pecking Orders'. We take our improvisation show around to schools, somehow the men always get the laughs – we girls are really only appendages. But I have one successful sketch – I get some young fella out of the audience and I have less than a minute to make a story which ends with 'I love you' – and – it has to be *real!* And it always opens everyone's hearts. The mask-work is very interesting. Keith has an absolute rule,

'When I say *stop*, you take off your mask immediately'. Sometimes these masks take you over and become violent. Theatre Machine goes on for years and Roddy with it.

Polly and Cleo are playing outside on a sunny morning. I hear a crash and a scream and rushing out from the kitchen I find Cleo with a terrible great gash in her little head - blood literally pumping out. I grab a towel and wrap her head tightly, pick her up and whisk them both into the car. In a few minutes we are in Putney hospital and they are stitching her up. It is not till I get us all home that I collapse and shake and sob. As a mother I have this immediate sense of total protection, I don't think about it I just become the 'she bear'.

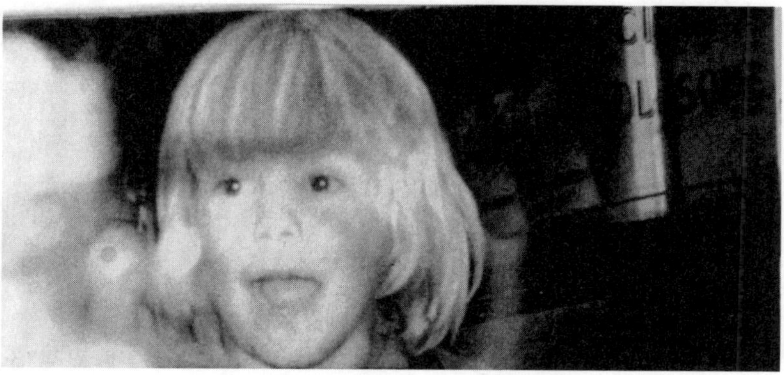

One of the few childhood pictures of Jasper that I have.

Another time I come home to find Mrs A. very worried. While she's been working cleaning our house, Jasper and her two children have been playing upstairs - and she's found an empty Junior Aspirin bottle. They all three look hot and flushed and giggly.

'Jasper, can you remember how many you have taken?'

'Fwee … no, firty fwee!' So off we go to Putney hospital but luckily the doctors don't pump out their little tummies but decide just to keep an eye on them. The Doctor does an x-ray of Jasper's stomach and he shows us the negatives and we see this dark mass.

'What's that?'

'Ribena.' says Jasper. In the end they are all fine.

Julie's boyfriend Johnny is an artist. This morning at breakfast he's been doing a drawing in felt tips on Jasper's bare little chest and tummy, but now it's time for school so we hurriedly pull a tee-shirt over his head and off he goes with Polly. At playtime he's been showing off his new tattoo. We get a call from the head teacher, they're sending him home. He arrives looking utterly crestfallen. At the bottom of the flowery psychedelic artwork are the words 'Fuck the Pope'.

Mick is doing a film of *Women in Love* with Ken Russell, Alan Bates, Oliver Reed, Glenda Jackson and Jennie Linden. They are on location up in Derbyshire. I go up for a few privileged days – Mickgough doesn't like me being around while he's working. The set is a huge beautiful mansion in vast gardens with a lake. Alan remembers me from *Three on a Gas Ring* days. I watch some filming. The large party scene, filled with summer laughter, the ladies in white organdie and large hats, the gentlemen in boaters. There is a stunning young beauty rowing in a boat on the lake with Eric Newby. Tragedy – in the story, they drown. It's Sharon Gurney, who will become Simon's wife. Jennie is anxious because she will have to run in a field, naked. And apparently Alan and Oliver are worried about their naked fight scene because they don't want people to see the size of their willies! The film will become a massive hit. Mick is playing yet another fuddy-duddy Victorian gent. I wouldn't mind but he spends all his time preparing for these roles and becoming these men and so then, that's who I get to share my life and my bed with. Van Gogh, Dr Livingstone – I've slept with them all!

Jasper watching telly

Chapter 34

Strange Report

I'm off to Pinewood to see someone called Buzz Burger. He's an American producer and he's casting for a new series. I'm nervous as usual. Auditions are such extraordinary experiences. All the anxiety, and so much energy is put into looking right – your hair, your eyes, your clothes. You enter the room, the stage, the office, all of you wishing to please. You are in a heightened state; every cell of your being is lit up. Maybe they'll ask you to read. You're smiling, you're doing your best and your heart hasn't stopped thumping since you entered the room. And then it's over. You're shaking hands; you're stepping back into the street. Then comes the wait. You pretend that it's fine and that you've got a few things to do anyway but all the time you're hoping. Eventually you get a *yes* or a *no, I'm sorry*. An actor's life is full of ups and downs and when you've finished a show you need time to come down from that very special place you've been in. So you drink. Peter Sellers tells us that when he was doing *Bruhaha*, before he went on he used to throw up every night because of the fear. But after the show, the world is yours.

We have COLOUR TELEVISION!! We watch *The Virginian* … *Wimbledon* … and … *The Black and White Minstrel Show!*

My audition has been successful and I have a leading role in a major TV series - *Strange Report* - playing opposite Anthony Quayle. They immediately need publicity stills so I go to my friend, John Cole, who does a really beautiful series of photos of me. I'm wearing an Ossie Clark crepe shirt with ruffles. I go down to Pinewood for costume fittings. What is this rubbish they want me to wear?! They've done a deal with an owner of a shop in Carnaby Street so they're getting all these trashy clothes.

'I'm not wearing any of this. I shall wear all my own clothes. You wanted a stylish chick and I am one!' Now they are discussing my teeth and my boobs!

'You must be joking! You employed an actress, not a Barbie doll!' When they show me my studio on the set, I help the set decorators with that too, and add some of my own things. The only thing I can't manage to influence is the abstract paintings my character is supposed to have painted. I think that is such a cliché but I do what I can to make my character real and interesting. I meet Tony, ah, what treasure. I want him for my Dad! Kaz Garas is a sweet-faced young American. We all do photos together. We will film sixteen episodes, ten days an episode, with Sundays off. Now my agent's on the 'phone, with the usual old story,

'Now, because of the budget … blah … blah … blah … you don't get a car. Tony and Kaz do, but you'll have to drive yourself.'

I need to lose some weight fast. The lady next door (the one on the horse slimming pills) tells me of an infamous doctor in Harley Street. He prescribes speed to anyone who will pay, mostly models who are so skinny already that you can hear their bones clattering in the waiting room. After *Strange Report* I stop. I get much too thin.

It's my first morning's filming, and I've had very little sleep, of course, because I'm so anxious. I get up at 4am and drive down to Pinewood. I'm in the make-up chair at 6, and into the arms of my little Jewish angel, Sylvia, who will be my ally and my friend for the entire 32 weeks. I also have a stand-in, Lisa Quinne. Lisa is a beautiful Swedish blonde. I also have my own suite of dressing rooms where, in a while, I will have my paints and music and sewing machine – my studio away from home. In fact, my dressing room has given me a taste, for the first time, of what it would be like to be a free and independent woman.

There is a joke on the set that they have to ask Anneke if she has got *time* to come to the set. I am a creative - it's what I do - and rehearsals can involve a lot of hanging around - so we actors like to do something to pass the time - study form, knit, gossip, and sleep. I like to be creating something. On *Doctor Who* I was into crocheting. I crocheted ties. Innes Lloyd, Patrick Troughton and Mickgough of course all had Anneke ties. Mickgough's socks, I darned in different colours, and he used to show them off at his rehearsals,

'Devoted patchwork socks darling.'

Meanwhile, we are back on the set. I love this work, I've been doing it for eighteen years now and I'm good at it. I am never late, ever. I'm still so punctual that I arrive in the *middle* of the *minute*. My attention is total; my commitment is total, with just perhaps a tiny tendency to crack up with hopeless giggles - *but no!* - I am also a professional and proud to be one.

I will now be working with another great team of people. One of the regulars on *Strange Report* is Charles Lloyd Pack, who I have worked with before in a play of the week, with Pamela Brown. I love him. He's a real old 'actor chappie' - one of the originals, and sweetly eccentric. Always singing funny little ditties,

'Hippity hop, they're over the top and they're all after me'
And Charlie Crichton an 'old-school' director, and Tony and my favourite.

We are doing some night shooting. I have bought, and am wearing, a full length tweed coat from Biba's. A bystander cackles.

'Oo does she fink she looks like? Does she fink that it'll come back into fashion? Ha, ha!' Within a month, everyone is wearing full length coats. *Ha, ha to you!*

Peter Medac is directing, and when we break for lunch, Lisa and I go up to my dressing room for our little 'slimming lunch' – hard boiled eggs, tuna fish and coffee while listening to David Bowie.

♫ *Ground control to Major Tom, take your protein pills and put your helmet on.* ♫

I now have my own chair on set. I have written, in bold felt-tip underneath my name,

'And anyone else who feels like a bit of a sit-down'

When Lisa has finished a long stint standing in for me, I will bring her some tea or juice. We look after each other. Finally, at 6.30, I'm heading out of the gates home. By 7.30, the children are already in bed (usually) and in a few hours I'm up again at 4am. Sundays are my days off to be with my family, make lunch for Mickgough and friends – burning the candle all the way round.

One day, I am filming with the second unit, and Mickgough, who is now jealous of Kaz, checks up on me. He calls the office at Pinewood and asks if I am working that day. One of the secretaries looks at the nearest list, which happens to be the list for the first unit, and informs Mick that I'm not on it. I get a home to an inquisition. I'm offering to call the office in the morning to get them to set the record straight. So he 'lets me off' – this time - he doesn't say sorry.

And now they insist I wear a padded bra, my little breasts are not enough for American viewers.

'I hate wearing bras! I'm into free range titties!' Sometimes Buzz will come on the set and casually run his hand down my back to check … no bra strap!

'Anneke go to wardrobe!' I also hate having to do publicity. I always have. One time a press man is coming down especially from London for a photo shoot. Sylvia has wrapped my head in towels, and covered me in a thick face mask,

'Oh so sorry I forgot!'

'How long to have her ready?' Sylvia says,

'At least 2 hours. I'm so sorry why don't you get Kaz instead?'

One or two of the scripts were certainly less than they should have been, Tony Quayle and I would often rewrite our scenes so they worked better, but if you see the series now - digitally enhanced for DVD - it stands up well. It captures the look and feel of the sixties perfectly.

Four o'clock one morning in late autumn and I'm on my way to work. Quite often I would have my hair in rollers, wearing an antique Bedouin jellaba, driving my Morris Traveller with its extended gear stick. I change down to go into a round-about, and the gear stick comes off in my hand. So the early morning workers see this mad woman in a jellaba and rollers trying to hitch a lift. Eventually, it's a studio worker who's brave enough to stop!

I have a long weekend off which is a relief as things mount up. So on Saturday morning, I'm off up the Fulham Road to the cleaners, pick up a new Ossie shirt to be worn in next weeks episode, get stuck in a traffic jam, the usual Saturday morning stuff. When I return my mother's help is white-faced at the door.

'Mickgough is up in the studio and he's furious.'

'Furious? What about?' I go upstairs to the studio. I hear the sounds of violence and I feel sick. Mick is up on the balcony where we sleep, tearing at the chest of drawers, searching through my underwear. He's growling.

'Grr! where is it? WHERE IS IT?!' He thinks I've been out with a lover, and he is searching for evidence. He wants a reason to be angry with me, so he is hoping that my Dutch cap is in my handbag.

'My Dutch cap? I've been to the cleaners!' I exclaim, with the righteousness of innocence, but my heart is pounding. I've seen this temper before. I climb the steep ladder up to our bed-space to try and calm him down.

'I got stuck in a traffic jam,' He turns and he has his horror movie face on. Now he's hitting and punching me - I'm backing away - trying to protect myself. I stumble backwards over the edge of the bed and there is nowhere else to retreat. So he kicks and shoves me off the balcony.

Ten feet.

I am momentarily floating and then - *crack* - blinding pain – nothing. My eyes open I'm crumpled up on my side. I can see the white ceramic tiles of the fire place. My brow seems to be stuck to them. I pull myself up and feel like I've been run over by a tractor. There is blood all on the tiles, and stuck to me. I just sit there for a while. I don't know what's happened. Then I hear sounds out in the street. The laughter of children - happy sounds. I crawl over to the window and pulling myself up I look down into the street. Polly, Jasper and a little friend. Mickgough holding the boot of the car open and tricycles being loaded in.

'Come along dear heart darlings get into the car! Off we go! Ha, ha!'

Laughter and light.

When I can manage it, I call a friend who comes at once and we go to Putney Hospital and I have two stitches on my brow. I go home with her and rest until it's time to go back to work on Monday. We have a lot of women's talk. When Sylvia sees me she nods, but she doesn't believe my story of bumping into a car door, but I persist with it.

I hate the fact that I have disrupted the days shooting. We have to reverse everything so that we could avoid my injured eye. That night when I get home around half past seven, it's dark. The house is ablaze with light, no curtains or blinds are drawn, I put my key in the lock, but it's locked from inside. I ring the bell and bang. No-one answers. I can hear Mickgough's booming voice, children laughing, music playing, the television on. But no-one is coming.

I'm standing in the street outside my home, locked out. It is the loneliest place in the world. I go around to a neighbour's and call Simon for help. He comes and talks to Mickgough and eventually I am 'allowed' into my home. I am the baddy. I have done wrong. My work continues; we never speak of it. And he never apologises. Ever.

Nowadays, we have the laws, and the psychological understanding about abuse but this was 1969, so I never told anyone. I was too ashamed … for him. I think my friends at Pinewood knew, and Sylvia and Tony were very kind and loving. Later I would discover that he did the same to his previous wives.

Now I will have to learn to trust him again if we were going to carry on. I don't want to face the fact that our marriage is coming apart at the seams. I just think I'll get a huge needle and stitch it back up again. I have to, because I so badly want stability for Polly and Jasper. I want to give them the childhood I never had.

At the end of *Strange Report*, Tony and I are called in to talk to the producers. Since the series has been so popular in the USA they propose to do another 23 episodes and make them in LA. *What did Tony and I think about that?* Tony is brilliant, in his special way, he says,

'I think we need a little time to think about it and we'll let you know soon.' We go away to his dressing-room and talk it through. He is of the opinion that he has had enough. It had been fun but actually, he just wants to take his canal boat slowly down through France with his wife. I say,

'I don't like Hollywood, it's not a place for children, I couldn't be away from them for that long, my marriage would be on the rocks ..'

So that is that, and we go down and tell them. It is hard because they have been so keen and excited, and so sure that we would say yes. It makes our end of series party all the more poignant.

I'm travelling down for the wrap party. I've got an Ossie Clark long black knitted cardigan, black knitted flared trousers, a floaty Celia Birtwell scarf, 30s design, my hair just so. I am driving along in the pissing rain when the windscreen shatters with an almighty crack. I pull over, blindly, and tap a little hole in the windscreen. *Shit! I must keep going, or I'll be late and all the big wigs are there, it's VIP day*! So I drive along with pouring rain coming in through the little hole, makeup, clothes everything ruined. But everyone is so delightful to be with, I've forgotten about the ghastly journey and I'm enjoying the hugs and the friendship. Dear Tony, how I shall miss him, and Sylvia and even old Buzz Burger. You always take cards at the end of a show, and really mean to see each other again, but you rarely do. In the time you've spent working together you've become such friends with whole bunch of people. Parting is always tinged with sadness.

Barney and I have come up with a super design for a bunk bed for Polly and Jasper's room. One bed under the window and the other at right-angles above, with holes cut into the block board for steps. The whole thing painted different jolly colours. When it's finished they love it. Polly is the eldest, so of course, she's on the top. This makes much more room for their clothes and toys.

Polly's going to ballet classes. We take a photo of her. It's very dear. She's wearing black culottes. She has her little hand on the barre, she's doing *Pliés*. Her tongue is out in deep concentration.

Jasper, meanwhile, has asked me politely if I would kindly not pick him up from school wearing my bedouin jellaba.

We see a program called *Candid Camera*. Jonathan Routh walking down the Portobello Road with a top hat which is on fire. People studiously ignore it. Hilarious and new. Barry Humphries tells us stories of how he goes on the underground with a friend who's wearing dark glasses and a stick. Barry abuses him, and asks the other passengers,

'What would you do if you had a blind brother?' as he kicks him. 'He's such a drag!' Finally he gets off the train, and leaves his friend behind. He just loves the reaction of the angry passengers.

A Dutch reporter has come to interview me. It seems the Dutch have reclaimed me! I have been invited to go to Amsterdam to appear on a Dutch TV show. I am on the cover of the Dutch TV paper.

'LOOK WHO'S COME HOME!'

Mickgough comes with me and we are met at Schipol Airport by a dishy young Dutchman who will be our guide. We stay in a hotel in the very heart of the city. I'm so happy to be eating the Dutch breakfast I know and love – cheese and *spekulaas* and clear tea - they don't put milk in tea in Holland. I ask to see Anne Frank's house and the 'pot' plants growing on the decks of the houseboats. I'm rather shy when I do the chat show interview because my Dutch is rusty. But it's quickly over and we are taken on a sailing boat by our guide, who is talking Dutch to me, and Mickgough is sulking.

When Mickgough is away in America, a young and beautiful painter enters my life. He is building cupboards upstairs for us. As the days go by, we surrender to our desires. It's my turn.

BAR

It is so good to be with someone my age, but I break the rules. I fall in love.

When Jillybeans tells Mick, I'm severely punished. *Slag! Whore!* I can't believe his hypocrisy. He hasn't ever been faithful to me. So, miserable and confused, I promise not to see the painter again, and although it's painful to turn my back on all that lovely love, I end it. It is made clear to me that I am the one in the wrong. I am told,

'You can go anytime you like but you don't get any money and you don't get the children'.

When I talk to Jillybeans today she remembers

'The way he was treating you – I felt sorry for you – I just thought he ought to know what it was doing to you. Of course you took a lover – you needed one!'

Mai Zetterling and her husband David Hughes come to dinner with us. They want to talk to Mickgough about playing Van Gogh in a film that CBC and BBC have put up the money for. They are a bright and attractive couple. She is a Swedish film star, an attractive green-eyed blonde, and has recently starred opposite Peter Sellars in *Only Two Can Play*. She is wearing a velvet kaftan. David has a deep sexy voice and intelligent eyes, and is one of our most respected critics, and an award winning writer. Mickgough is very keen. They have a year to make it. Filming in the Borinage and Provence. It all sounds so exciting and I'm envious.

'Oh I'll be left behind again!'

'No! No!' say Mai and David, 'You must come out to France too!' I am thrilled. My mother has instilled a love of Van Gogh in me. They will start as soon as Mickgough is free. Later, one of our friends sends Mick a New Year card - a picture of Mickgough with a bandage on his ear. *Happy New Ear!* Mick will have to have his hair dyed red. It's going grey now so when the dye is applied it turns it *pink!*

We go to have supper with Mai and David. They live in an old dispensary in Southwark. We all cook and prepare the meal together, talking, drinking, chopping herbs on a vast table. David plays rambling Bach on the organ. They have bought a farmhouse in Provence, very near where our friend Elizabeth Frink and her husband Ted live. We will all be there soon.

I have bought Mickgough a lovely antique wing chair in terracotta leather. I got it up the Kings Road. I have great fun secretly storing it with neighbours, wrapping it in Christmas paper and getting it under the tree late in the night. It was jolly expensive. Mick gives Emma and I long white Afghan coats.

Over the years we see quite a lot of Edward Fox. He is coming for comfort. His father has cancer and is dying. Poor Ed - it's very hard on him.

I haven't seen Nicholas for a while, and now he's standing in our studio – he has become a good looking young man. He talks just like Roy, which I find unnerving – he calls us 'you artistic types'. We live in different worlds now. I don't know then that I won't see him again.

Björn has gone off with a young girl and my heartbroken mother is back in England and not very well physically – she really hasn't been able to pick herself up after Robin. But she's putting a brave face on it. She's here to earn some money so she's got a job in the sweater department of Harrods. One of the rules is that if a customer wishes to smoke, you may smoke with them. So she's encouraging all her customers,

'Let's have a lovely smoke and then we can think about it. Now, the blue or the black?' while sniggering. 'Pah, who cares? Rich old bags, more money than sense. I usually get them to leave me the packet. Mmm, Du Maurier, better than Woodbines.'

She proudly gives us each a beautiful cashmere sweater from Harrods. Cashmere is very expensive. Mine is a soft pink cable knit and I'm mad about it. Mickgough is grudging with his thanks, but delightedly she tells us she's nicked them all so she doesn't care, she's off back to Spain.

She's managed to get Robin's ashes but has had terrible trouble with the authorities because they don't want to let her take them out of the country. She's figuring ways of concealing him, that would make him laugh. She manages it in the end and scatters him under his favourite mimosa tree in Formentera.

Chapter 35

Lion in Winter

January 1st 1970. The 'phone goes. It's 'Plunkers' - Mick's agent Plunket Green. Mick comes up to me in the studio.

'I've got three plays to do in Nova Scotia; I shall be away for three months. I'm just checking it's alright with you?'

'Well, actually it isn't! You've been away so much! Can't we come with you?'

'Oh alright, I'll tell Plunkers I won't do it!' I hear him on the 'phone.

'Sorry old dear. Anneke says I can't.' After a bit he comes back up. 'Well they say you can come, and they'll pay for you and the children.'

Alright! An adventure!

I start making fur coats for Polly and Jasper, Mick has gone ahead to start rehearsing. We will follow. It's huge long flight. But Polly and Jasper get to sit up front with the captain. They are in heaven. When we arrive in Halifax Mick's not there to meet us, a PA drives us to the house they have found for us. It's in a residential area on the outskirts of the city, and snow is up to the ground floor windows. We are tired but excited, the children snuggle up. Downtown is 45 minutes drive away, Mick now tells me he will be rehearsing all day and playing at night so I'm not going to see much of him. Punishing me for being there? No, he's having an affair with one of the actresses, of course.

When we arrive in the house it is very cluttered, with curtains and drapes and carpets and doilies. I have packed it all up very carefully and now we have a lovely polished wooden floor and big cushions. Virginia Yates has sent me some fabulous Indian silk saris, so I am busy making some first night dresses for the ladies of the company. I make a dress out of table cloth material - with very pretty little flowers with some antique lace which later Sharon Gurney borrows to wear at a garden party at Buckingham Palace. *My little homemade dress!*

Here I am in this strange place, in deep, deep snow. The theatre company is helping me to find my feet. I get the children into the local school, I don't have a car, the shops are a few blocks away and we don't know have any Canadian winter gear. I only have my Chelsea leather boots which are hopeless. There are huge supermarkets, the like of which I have never seen. One day I'm sitting in the Laundromat, so gripped by the book I'm reading - all about 'karma' - that I'm not keeping an eye on the washing, and I have shrunk all our lovely cashmere sweaters from Harrods. *Instant Karma!*

Polly and Jasper are not happy in this vast Canadian school. And I don't like the way they lock the kids in during school hours. One of the members of the theatre company has a friend who works with children and we decide to run a free school up in the attic of the house. One or two of the other actors also have floating children so within a few weeks of arriving we are running a free school. Kurt is an inspirational teacher. They are making music and creating art and reading about nature and the stars.

Meanwhile I have met an extraordinary couple. My next teachers. Linda is teaching me yoga, and they meditate. Richard gives me some important books to read – Aldous Huxley, Ouspensky, I read a story about Gurdjieff - how the elite of New York invite this spiritual master to give them a talk. They arrange a party with lots of brandy and cigars and they all get wildly drunk. Then they have it away with each others spouses. The evening ends in bouts of drunken violence. Gurdjieff has left. His silence eloquent. I also read *Be Here Now* by Ram Dass – my mind is opening …

The first night of *Lion in Winter* and the stage crew come to mine for tea and a 'smoke' and then we are all off to the theatre.

Linda and Richard and I get stoned giggles, the performance takes twice as long because the stage crew are carrying the props on and off very meditatively. Mickgough is beside himself with rage when he finds out!

Mick's director invites us to his home on the coast. It's right on the very edge of the sea. Underneath the wooden balcony there are huge lobster pots which are immersed in the water. They're full of lobsters and we will have a lobster feast. We each eat at least *three* washed down with rum, and milk and butter.

Chapter 36

A Trip to Reality

Now Richard and Linda are saying,

'What you need is to take some LSD. You have been studying enough, now it is time for the actual experience of blowing your mind'. They will administer a massive dose and care for me while I'm on it. Mickgough is interested and encouraging. I go with them to their cabin on the coast, which sits on the edge of a cliff, looking out over the wild Atlantic seas. It's an A-frame with a woodstove and a balcony and full of shells and flowers and books and a spinning wheel and an old iron cooking range. I stay with them for a few days preparing. The day dawns and I'm actually quite frightened but they are reassuring. Linda keeps telling me to pee -

'Because once it comes on you'll forget.' This, I find more worrying than anything, so I'm sitting on the loo when I realise it's too late. I'm laughing and laughing and I'm on a trip. I have been given a massive dose and I am transported beyond myself out into the nether regions. I lay upstairs looking at the knots in the wood. Robin is with me. He's holding my hand and describing this world to me. Many hours later I peer over the balcony, and I am a child with no mind. There is a lovely lady baking bread and a man playing guitar.

'Can I come down?'

'Of course!' I'm not sure who I am - I can't feel my edges …

In the early hours of the morning I am crawling around the woods sobbing in gratitude, watching the stones breathe. All separation has gone. I belong. I will never be the same again. After a few days I go back to Mickgough, Polly and Jasper and hug them. I am so grateful to have them to love. I've woken up out of the dream I was living.

Things look different to me now.

We are to go back to London ahead of Mickgough. Our Canadian neighbours are having something called a 'barbecue' as a farewell party for us. This is great! Cooking and eating outside! They roast marshmallows. *Super!* (our new word!)

When the taxi draws up to our front door, we discover that it's been smashed in. Barney has been lovers with Andrew Oldham's wife, and Andrew had come round with the 'heavies', and smashed our door and window. Barney and Sheila had ran out of the back door and across the garden fences and away. Barney's very embarrassed and promises he'll get it replaced. The neighbours are all of a twitter. Andrew Oldham, the manager of the Rolling Stones, was very flamboyantly dressed –

'In yellow leather trousers, gold boots and Mongolian furs!'

'Never mind that – what about our front door?!'

Chapter 37

A Year in Provence

Mickgough is off to work on *Vincent.* I talk to Barney about taking LSD and all the things that I've seen. I can feel that I want to take a new direction, but I'm not sure …

Mai and David have sent me a ticket to come down to Provence. On the train, I have a sleeper, which I share with a very garlicky Frenchman. I don't like sleeping with strangers … you know what I mean! I am wearing my white Afghan coat, a rainbow sweater, and my lovely Red Indian moccasins from California. When I arrive at the station very early in the morning it is deserted. I worry. Did I get the place right? Did they know it was this train? After what seems a long while a jeep comes down the road towards me tooting. It's them! And piling me in the back we're off to a local market to shop. Ah! The fabulous French way of life. We wander around the market in Uzes, the cheeses, the vegetables and the heavenly bread. We sit in a café in the sun for a little Pastis. We drive to the northern outskirts of Nimes, and at the end of a ravishing valley, forgotten by the 20th century, under the gentian blue sky, is their silk farm, built in 1641. They are in the process of renovating it. The main room has a huge armoire which is full of Mai's preserves and an immense open fireplace, a stone-tiled floor, great oak beams, a table and an oil lamp and everywhere there are volumes of books about Van Gogh, we all read his wonderful letters to his brother. We have bedrooms with windows covered in vines and jasmine, but no panes, because for the rest, it's a ruin, and pooping has to be done with a spade, a loo roll and a trip into the olive groves.

John Bulmer, who was at Cambridge with Peter, takes beautiful photographs and comes from the Bulmer Cider family. He is the cameraman and they have been filming some initial bits and pieces. The film is going to be not only about Van Gogh, but also the creative process of how Michael Gough the actor becomes the character. Mick spends a week not eating, or washing, and drinking only pastis - which is absinthe without the hallucinogenic wormwood – to gain insights into Van Gogh's mind. Our bedroom wall is full of self-portraits of Vincent – he's absorbing him – it's an alchemical process. Once again we are all preparing the food together. Mai and David are real 'bon viveurs' and great cooks. The *Cote du Rhone* flows and flows. After supper we sit out under the stars and the Cyprus trees and talk about Vincent. After the first week we are off to see the novelist and poet Lawrence Durrell. I wish Robin could see me now, because we love *Bitter Lemons* and *The Alexandra Quartet*. We will have much needed baths in his house. When we arrive they all disappear to bathe and I am left alone in the salon with 'Larry'. The fire is blazing and he is stretched luxuriously out on a chaise-longue. There is another, on which I perch, nervously. I don't know what to say in case it all comes out wrong so I stay in agonised silence. He carries on as if I'm not there. We don't speak, for a torturous amount of time. Eventually, I think.

'Well, fuck you!' The others come back and we all go into dinner which is served by his French housekeeper. We talk of the film, and Larry's brother Gerald, who lives nearby, and of Mai and David's plans to make wine and cheese on their farm.

We go to see Liz Frink, the sculptor, and Ted, in another old French farmhouse in the Provencal hills. Her sculptures – huge, helmeted, heads - are on the pillars of the gateway to the drive. We are drinking pastis in her stone living room. I do a little sketch of her leaning against the marble fireplace in a blue sweater with a large pink flower knitted into it. She is a very strong and handsome woman. We ask her how her work is coming along. She goes pale and becomes introverted.

'I'm stuck!' she says crossly. 'I'm forcing myself to sweep the studio every day just to get myself in there.' I am very interested in the creative process.

David is putting off getting down to writing the script so he's fixing light-bulbs.

Mai has a cold. She's sitting at the table; she has retreated into a blanket. and we have to politely knock on the sides of it.

'Would you like some tissane?' Grunts. A little hand will shoot out and take the tea inside her cave. She's incommunicado.

I take a mat, and I'm doing yoga in the olive groves.

One day we are filming in the almond orchards in the Carmargue. We are there for the blossom. John will only film in the early morning and the late afternoon because the light is softer. I see my first Hoopoe, large and terracotta coloured with black and white stripy wings. It's very distinctive and has a lovely crest on its head - once seen never forgotten. Mai lays out a tablecloth and we have a picnic under the trees – French terracotta plates, silver cutlery, napkins and crystal wine glasses - very stylish. As we are eating, the owner of the orchard arrives; he is riding a Carmargue stallion with a Spanish saddle and bridle. Wearing a black Spanish hat and leather chaps he looks like he's come straight from the world of *Zorro!* He invites us to drinks, so after work we go to his ranch and see his amazing white horses. This is very special for Mickgough and me. We go to Carcassonne and walking around the ancient ramparts, I have déjà vu, *I know* this place, and I feel Robin with me ... Now my two weeks are up and I must leave. It's been one of the best times in my life.

Mai Zetterling will go on to become the most respected woman film-maker of the decade. She and David have an old cleaning van which they use as a caravan and a cutting room. They take it all over the United States, going to film festivals. At one big festival, with big names from all over, there is a huge board in the lobby of the hotel, with the names of the guests and how they were arriving - private jet, helicopter, limousine. At the bottom it says *Mai Zetterling - Cleaning Van.*

Now, Mickgough has got the part of Doctor Livingstone in a TV Drama called *The Search for the Nile.* He is off to Africa to film, and will continue with *Vincent* in Belgium in the winter. I will never see this beautiful film they made.

I take the children to see Oma in Spain. Pedro is over the moon to see Jasper again and throws him up on his shoulders and takes him off to the Port to see the boats. Oma and Polly and I shop for the white lacy socks and little white slip-on shoes that Polly loves. One evening, sitting with our toes in the sand in a beach bar, we are drinking carajillios and we watch Polly doing an ecstatic dance on the water's edge. My mother and I are both entranced by her wild, unselfconscious beauty.

Sitting on my mother's balcony, we talk of Robin as we always do. We've made a pact to think about him at sunset time. She tells me that she is upset because the blocks of flats are sprouting up all around her. She says she was watching the Spanish builders climbing around the bamboo scaffolding, when suddenly there was a shout,

'Oiga! Cuidado!' They all jumped off and the building duly collapsed.

'Hopeless!' she says 'They are trying to do it so cheaply.' She's fed up because she's lost her sea-view and all the fish and chippers are coming. She's going to sell-up and set off to California to see Uncle Hans, and then she wants to go around Mexico on a bus.

Back in London, I'm sitting on a bench in Hampstead with Peter, watching our children playing by the pond. We talk of real things, beyond the dreaded lust and desire, fame and ego. We speak of jealousy that leads to violence – the shame and remorse. He waves his hand towards his children,

'In the end, that's what's real, they are what matters.' He worships his two daughters. A lot has been written about how difficult it was to really get to know Peter Cook; his humour would be a barrier. I was lucky to have many real moments with him.

In Mexico in the nineties, I'm with a bunch of friends and I'm suddenly telling stories about The Establishment days. The next day, I get a call from England.

Peter is dead.

To Peter's Spirit – thank you for the flowers.

Jasper, with Lucy and Daisy Cook

Peter Cook. The Father of sixties satire. My Dear Friend.

Chapter 38

The Go-Between

Mick has a film to do - *The Go-Between.* It will be filmed in Norfolk during the summer holidays. So we rent a lovely old house in Cley-next-the-Sea and it's holiday time. The actors on the film are all old friends. Alan Bates, Edward Fox, Julie Christie, Margaret Leighton, and Joe Losey, Gavrik's father is directing. They are working in this truly beautiful eighteenth century mansion – Melton Constable Hall – which is falling into decay on the edge of farmland. Polly and Jasper and I spend our days on Cley beach. It's hot and we take picnics, and we start to make some local friends. Cley is a tiny little village with a huge windmill and we tootle about in the Renault 4L exploring. We go to Blakeney and see the harbour and boats. After filming, Mickgough joins us and we go to the Dun Cow pub looking out over the marshes.

'This is very beautiful place!' Filming progresses and they are doing a cricket match. All the old local boys are given period costumes and they sit around commenting on the match, in their wonderful Norfolk accents. One of them, George, is asked,

'Have you ever been to London?'

'Nope, but I been to Peterborough!'

Edward looks really handsome playing cricket. Mickgough is playing yet another crusty Victorian gent. The assistant to Joe Losey calls out across the green,

'Okay, quiet please, we are shooting now!' Jasper says, very worried,

'Who are they shooting?'

Alan Bates takes us out to supper, to the 'Madhatters' in Weybourne. He is with his beautiful highly-strung wife. She thinks she couldn't survive in the countryside,

'What do people do in the country? And can you get your clothes cleaned?' I can always be myself in Alan's company.

I love the image of Margaret Leighton as this Edwardian Lady, entering the wardrobe department in the house - her delicate beauty, her white Organdie dress, and frantically tugging at her wig.

'These fuckin' fruit flies are getting in my soddin' wig and driving me INSANE!'

They have terrible trouble with the deadly nightshade in the film. By the time they get around to shooting that scene it has very nearly died. It's so obvious, when you see it that it's a dead plant.

The designer of the film, Carmen Dillon, transforms the crumbling mansion into a full-scale Edwardian home – working kitchens, dreamy libraries, schoolboys rattling up and down on the stairs, the lawns are cut for croquet …

When the filming is over, the film crew pack up and leave, and the house falls back into loneliness and dilapidation, and the crack across its façade gets bigger.

Polly and Jasper and I are driving around exploring. We come through a tiny village. There is a Georgian faced farmhouse peeping out over a hedge with a huge bay tree and a FOR SALE sign. My heart leaps, we back up fast and we sit there looking at it.

'Wouldn't it be fun to live there?'

'Yes, Yes! Let's go and look at it.' So we explore. We park the car and walk down the drive.

It doesn't look as though anyone has lived in it for quite a while – peering through the windows we can see thirties tiled fireplaces, concrete floors – so it needs a lot of work – the barn at the side has 1643 carved into its lintel and there are signs of an old cobbled yard. There are more barns filled with the usual rubbish. There is a concrete grain-dryer building, half an acre of field with nettles and docks. There are some tiny cottages opposite, a lovely old church and a pub and at the end of the street is a village shop.

We just love it! This was a sign, the seed which had been germinating since Canada, was an idea to chuck it all in and come and live in the countryside, and now here is this house. We go back to Cley and call Savilles – they tell me it's on the market for £3,000. We can't wait to take Mickgough to see it. He is as excited as we are, so now we must ask Peggy Thomson if we can do it. She says we can. Our offer is accepted. We now have a new home in Norfolk. The whole process flows in a couple of weeks to conclusion (Mind you, I am on Valium for most of that time!). In a while we will put Hurlingham Road on the market.

One day, we are in the local town of Holt, when we bump into Roddy Maude-Roxby of all people.

'What are *you* doing here?' Turns out he and his family have bought a house in the very next village to ours.

One of the actors on *The Go-Between* is Roger Lloyd Pack, whose father I had worked with on *Strange Report*. He finds and rents a sweet little rural cottage nearby …

Mickgough learning his lines

Chapter 39

Norfolk

♫ *You may say I'm a dreamer, but I'm not the only one* ♫
- John Lennon

Now I have to convince everyone of the wisdom of this move. It's hard when you're following your intuition to explain it to others. My mother says,

'It seems a terrible waste to give up everything you've been working so hard to achieve, but you do what you want - you always do!' Wallis is very sad – he won't come to see us – he hates the country.

My agents are very clear,

'Anneke, what a waste. You are just at the place to command good work and higher fees. You'll give up your independence if you have to rely on Mick for money.' In the end they get it. My children are more important to me. I have to save the marriage. They have been so good to me and seen me through some tough and busy times. They are good agents, and good people. This is the end of my 18-year long professional acting career … for the moment …

Simon and Sharon are getting married. We all love this they are so passionate about each other. And she seems to be able to stand up to him which bodes well. It's going to be a massive wedding. Her family are connected to royalty, and with Simon's Robert Graves connection it's quite an event. Old actors, lots of friends, huge crowd, all at Brompton Oratory. Polly and Jasper are going to be Bridesmaid and Page and Rachel Gurney has chosen some fabulous olive green velvet which costs a fortune. It's all going to be green and white and very tasty. I am to make Jasper's trousers and Polly's white organdie dress. I'm very nervous when I come to cut the velvet - one snip in the wrong direction and – *disaster!* But they look great and fit him well.

Polly is precious in her little white dress with a green belt and

Jim Broadbent, Ken Slavin , Mickgough, Me and Jasper.
Polly is hidden behind me. Mickgough is wearing his costume from *The Go-Between*, and I've borrowed Sheila's hat …

flowers in her hair. She loves Sharon to bits and this is fulfilling all her little girl fantasies. There is a big rehearsal. Mickgough is protesting about walking down the aisle with Diana Graves again.

'Last time I walked down the aisle with the bitch it was a disaster'. I am seated right at the back of the church with the public, so I can't really see how sweet it all looks. There is a lavish party in a hotel. Simon certainly knows how to do things. There are mountains of wedding presents. Soon they will be off for their honeymoon in the sun. Some very wealthy godparents are signed up.

After the photos and the speeches, the children have eaten so much sugar they are becoming very overexcited.

'I think it's time to take Polly and Jasper home now Mick,'

'Why don't you do that dear?' He's schmoozing with Alec Guinness and friends.

Some young ladies and gentlemen are throwing up in the shrubs outside the hotel. Polly and Jasper and I are off home.

We've got a couple of Barney's friends staying with us in London. Jonathan and Linda. Jonathan is an artist and is mad about geodesic domes, and he makes models that sit on our kitchen table. He reads the *Whole Earth Catalog*. Linda is very sexy and pretty and makes wonderful bread. Her father is Max Aitken who owns a lot of newspapers. Linda is The Honourable Linda Aitken. She has curly blonde hair, wears weird clothes, and smokes dope. They are listening to *The Grateful Dead* and *Jefferson Starship*.

'Jonathan plays guitar all the time,' says Linda. They talk of going back to the land, becoming self-sufficient, using methane for the car. They've got lots of ideas about a healthy, more tuned-in lifestyle. They will follow us up to Norfolk and buy the cottage opposite our house, so we will be an extended family again.

'Mick says he doesn't mind if I get fat, eat chocolate and have more babies.' Wallis replies,

'I'm sure he doesn't!' I'm hoping that if I stop acting, Mick will stop being so angry with me all the time. Also, we can give our children a healthy, country life. I enrol them in the local school next to the church and the beech woods.

We can't wait to start work in the farmhouse so we spend a weekend at the pub across the road – The Jolly Farmer – the publican Charlie Cox and his wife are welcoming. We take sledgehammers and are busy bashing out the modern fireplace in the huge old kitchen – we are hoping to get back to the medieval bread ovens. It's extremely dusty – we wear masks – we're doing well and have created a huge hole – Jasper is helping us with his hammer. *Tap, tap.* Suddenly a rumbling, and a crashing of rubble, and Jasper emerges totally covered in soot and coughing. We take him back to the pub to get washed.

'Blast!' Says Charlie. 'Ee looks like a blackamoor!'

I feel quite sad to leave Hurlingham Road, the first real home of my own. When we first arrived I planted a peach pip in the garden - it's grown into a tree and this last summer has produced 35 peaches. Mickgough says he likes his homes to be like railway stations - lots of people coming and going. There have been lots of people living with us in the last few years and it's all been very eventful.

The most colourful decade we have ever known is over. So many of our friends have either split up or moved on now. Peter and Wendy have separated, Noel and Sarah are off to California, Virginia and Peter Yates are going to live in New York, and they all pack up their homes, where we have enjoyed so many lovely gatherings.

I make an etching of our country home. We must open the windows up (they got bricked-in when the window taxes came in). We'll be able to afford central heating! After all the changes we've made, and the work we've put into Hurlingham Road, it will sell for £27,000. We are absolutely amazed at this, and it will fund the building works in Norfolk. Mick is off to do another film with Joan Crawford in America. It's called *Trog.* Polly, Jasper and I have rented a very old thatched cottage where we will spend Christmas. It overlooks the marshes on the north Norfolk Coast. It's absolutely freezing. The winds are ferocious and the locals tell us,

'If you can survive a Norfolk winter you can survive anything, the winds come straight from Russia.' They also tell us that this cottage is haunted. The children overhear this and are worried -

'Will we see ghosts?' I become very calm and brave.

'No no, no need to worry.'

But alone in my bed that night I am scared. So one night I decide to 'face the fear', and talk myself through it.

What are you afraid of?
It's a man.
What's he doing?
He's coming in through the window.
*What does he look lik*e?
He looks like … Roy.

As soon as I've identified it, my angst evaporates. Yet there is still a presence in the kitchen of this house so Polly and Jasper and I light a candle and we say to 'the spirit',

'Will you please leave us alone so we can enjoy our Christmas?'

During the Profumo scandal, people on the street thought I was Mandy Rice Davies.

'Oi, Mandy!' I would ignore these jibes and walk haughtily on with my nose in the air. Men in the street, men on the buses, in the tubes, men at my work, women's envious glances. All this had led me to feel very self-conscious. Being pretty can be a lonely place. The men do numbers around you and so do the women. So now I read the Zen Masters who tell us to go in search of who we are. This resonates within. Enough of the external it's time to search for something more real, honest, true.

I have seen how the rich and privileged live, and how much we can hurt each other, all in the name of love. I have known and loved and worked with some of the most talented people of the decade, *and* I have been abused, betrayed and deeply scarred. Surely we human beings are more than this? So now I'm looking for happiness with my two beautiful children – and I do, in spite of everything, love Mickgough.

I'm 28. Of course, there's a part of me that longs to go dancing, or lie in haystacks and make abandoned love to lovely young men instead of making rice pudding for this old man while he finishes his jigsaw puzzles! But I love my children so I will try to be what Mickgough wants me to be. And, I've bought Germaine's sensational new book, *The Female Eunuch,* just in case …

Chapter 40

A Brand New Day

It's early spring; I've dropped the children off at their new school and I'm off to the farmhouse to start work. I'm listening to Van Morrison on the record player as I start stripping off the old wallpaper.

♫ *When all the dark clouds roll away*
And the sun begins to shine
I see my freedom from across the way
And it comes right in on time ♫

Our new life begins……

Epilogue

Those first thirty years were 'grist for the mill' – the journey towards empowerment begins. I embrace 'the good life' with enthusiasm and hang on to the marriage as long as I can … then I'm off, travelling to the east in search of Buddhism. I find opium in the mountains of Laos. Jasper and I join the first westerners to be in the Ashram of Bhagwan Shree Rajneesh in India, and we live and love and dance and work in this astounding community for some years.

When the biggest tragedy of all hits me, I retreat to an artists' colony on a small island in British Columbia, where among the whales and the eagles, I heal. I live in Gypsy Wagons, tree-houses and yurts. I live naked and alone in a jungle, and in a commune of thousands in Oregon. I meet and love such beautiful human beings – pioneers of new thought and alternative living. I become a painter, interior decorator and gardener. I have so many adventures and so many heartbreaks.

I'm amazed when the *Doctor Who* world catches up with me 30 years later, and I get to work with four more Doctors!

I move back in the folds of the English countryside, not far from Sir Richard Grenville's home, and the mystery surrounding Robin's death deepens.

It's been my own authentic journey. It's a long road, learning about love and trust. I'm grateful to existence for every breath of it.

Anneke
2007

Thank you to the following people, for pre-ordering this book.

Barnaby Eaton-Jones
Ali Pearce
Steve Gibson
Stephen Griffiths
Mark Cooper
Jackie Thompson
Cary Woodward
Jon Bond
Alexander Bond
Rebekah Bond
Geoff Leonard
Richard Leong
James C McFetridge
Johnathan Molyneux
Anthony Robertson
Paul Clulow
Ann Morris-Hobley
Neill Morris-Hobley
Ben Melberg
David Dickinson
Richard Parker
Malcolm Bowdler
Al Samujh
Diane Blackwell
Lee Filipek
Stephen Young
Alex Cafetzogklov
David Simon
John Douglas Huggins
Alister Pearson
Robert J.E. Simpson
Paul Howes
Robert Lannigan
Robert Cutting
Josslyn Bond
Richard Downs
Paul Garbutt
Robert Day
Neil Whiteley
David J Hamblin
James Mason
David Wood
Kevin Green
Russell Cook
Chris MacAllister
Graeme Pritchard
Jonathan Melville
Stephen Eramo
Chris Westbrook
Rodger Dillon
Robert Taylor
Arthur J Forbes
Mike Davey
David Clifford Taylor
Matt Evendon
Robert Dick
Mikael Barnard
Paul Goodhead
Nigel Nicholls
Kate Taylor
John Taylor
James Bland
A. John Main
David Chandler
Lee Rose
Martin Wiggins
Bryan Simcott
Ceri Laing
Neil Short
Steven Evans
Andrew Meadows
Ken Clark
Steven Hill
Hayden Harris
David Bickerstaff
Charlie Ross
Louise Norris
Stephen Broome
Graham Baird
Jason Thomas
Maureen Neathway
Garron Martin
Nicola Morton
Stephen Pasqua
Roddy McDougall
Edward Wilson
Rory Fairbairn
James McGauley
Jimmy McPaul
Alan Miscandlon
Bruce McNair
Derek P Hartley
Robert G Brogan
Brian Flynn
Julie Holdsworth
Sean Holdsworth
Steve & Ann Hodge
Nigel Anderson
Gary Heron
Martin Wakefield
Graham Groom
Hazel Schultz
Colin Dalglish
Robert Mitchell
David McCallum
Carl Akers
Lisa & Carole Higgins
Colin Kilgour
Sarah Walker
Georgia Millet-Clark
Richard Freeman
Karyn & Andy Spencer
Miles Northcott
Lee Rawlings
Colin Handscomb
Paul Davey
Christopher Winwood
Ian McLachlan
Ian Wilson
Mark Williams
Michael Vernon
Jeffrey Miller
Martin Thomas
Darren Chandler
David Simons
Mary McLean-Farmer
Holger Wacker
Karl Scarisbrick
Leslie Bray

Graham Symms
Simon & Sasha Hewitt
Chris Moore
Sean McGauley
Trevor Kirby
Tracy Gill
Mike Rymill
Ben Eastap
Ruth Mellor
Jonathan Miles
Debbie Langton
Peter Boyle
Mark Attwood
Diana Sholl
Richard Black
Darren Allen
Andrew Clarke
John G Hughes
Michael N Flint
David P May
Carl T Davies
Alec Hepburn
Mike Brumpton
David Martin
Chris Parks
Richard Walters
Russell Buer
Tony Eccles
Richard Harris
Dylan Parry
Colin Smith
Shaun Ashton
Eleanor Maddocks
Daren Pye
Michael McManus
Rob Dunlop
Alan Fawcus
Mark English
Stuart Cann
Aaron Gregson
Francis Price
Ben Brown
Paul Hughes
Brian King
Lizbeth Myles
Nigel Messenger
Larry Dyde
Andrew Smith
Allen Dace
Margaret Deutsch
Andrew & Carolyn Barrett
Thomas Lyles
Patrick Bellis
Gary Knowles
Julian Knott
Brandon Tempany
Liz Large
Britt Dawes
Gavin French
Paul Norman
Stephen Stratford
Jonathan Wood
Simon Guerrier
Michael 'Todd' Willoughby
David Hirst
Richard Paterson
Barbara Stevenson
Chris Dale
Sulamite Tepfers
James Guthrie
Andy Keast-Marriott
Neil Christie
Christian Cawley
Tim Neal
Philip Brennan
Nicholas Hayward
Richard Hewison
Ken, Sarah & Charlotte Logan
James Barton
Stephen James Walker
Adrian Petford
Richard Adams
Simon Wright
Sean Marsh
Meredith Adams
Joe Lidster